D1595851

# Transcendent Reason

# Transcendent Reason

*James Marsh*
*and the Forms of*
*Romantic Thought*

## Peter Carafiol

A Florida State University Book

UNIVERSITY PRESSES OF FLORIDA

Tallahassee

Library of Congress Cataloging in Publication Data

Carafiol, Peter.
  Transcendent reason.

  "A Florida State University book."
  Bibliography: p.
  Includes index.
  1. Marsh, James, 1794–1842.  I. Title.
B931.M3C37  1982    191    82–13617
ISBN 0–8130–0732–1

University Presses of Florida is the central agency for scholarly publishing of the State of Florida's university system. Its offices are located
at 15 NW 15th Street, Gainesville, FL 32603. Works published by University Presses of Florida are evaluated and selected for publication by a
faculty editorial committee of any one of Florida's nine public universities: Florida A&M University (Tallahassee), Florida Atlantic University
(Boca Raton), Florida International University (Miami), Florida State
University (Tallahassee), University of Central Florida (Orlando), University of Florida (Gainesville), University of North Florida (Jacksonville),
University of South Florida (Tampa), University of West Florida
(Pensacola).

To
William C. Spengemann,
Explorer and Guide

# CONTENTS

vii

# Contents

## 5
## From Edwards to Emerson: The Romantic Mind and Social Forms
*115*

# ACKNOWLEDGMENTS

To BEGIN WITH, my wife Eileen, though she has never felt a part of this book. I might have written this or some other without her, but I couldn't take any pleasure in it.

I am very grateful to the editorial and production staff of Florida State University Press and University Presses of Florida for the care and energy they have devoted to the preparation of this book. Others have a place in this work because they had taken their place in my mind when I began to write it. For earliest encouragement, training, and the assurance that this sort of thing is worth doing, I'm grateful to David Sofield, William Pritchard, and Leo Marx, to Fred Fisher, and to Amherst College. We all need great teachers, but I feel particularly blessed. French Fogle taught me that a passion for literature can last a lifetime and yield the soundest judgment. Albert Friedman saw no contradiction between learning and a lively mind. Marshall Waingrow offered an economy and style that made the most of a nice distinction. There are no better models.

From the very earliest stages of this project, Emily Peterson,

James Marsh's great-granddaughter, has maintained an enthusiasm that laughed at delay and disappointment. She has been its presiding angel.

Dan Peck and Geoffrey Harpham willingly read early drafts of the book by their own exacting standards, and told me the truth. From Barbara Harman I first heard the word, "theory," and from Steve Mailloux I heard it over and over. Each initiated me into a discourse that I now cannot do without. In its last stages, the book benefited incalculably from the rigorous standards of an unidentified reviewer. This public thanks is the most direct I can give him.

In a sense, both this project and my professional life began more than 11 years ago when I first ventured into the English Department at Claremont Graduate School and met its chairman. He introduced me to this work, and while I wrote and rewrote it, he was always my audience.

# PREFACE

WITH A characteristic distance that disguised autobiography as social criticism, Henry James once observed that America suffers from the "naive need of young societies to get themselves explained." Whether or not this need is "naive," it is plain that American writers have been doggedly self-reflective, searching the flux of our past for clues to the unified national identity at the heart of the democratic state. Thus the appeal for such writers—from Mather's Nehemias Americanus on—of the archetypal figure whose identity is one with that of the nation he represents. Such fictive figures (the Franklin of *The Autobiography*, "Walt" Whitman, an American) are valuable insofar as they help us to discover ourselves in our past and hence to construe that past as more substantially our own. Yet this same democratic impulse in American scholarship to unite the many in the individual, to subsume difference within the national identity, produces at least two evils. First, it necessarily distorts the "representative" figures who are both its subject and its method, forgetting that their fame depends, after all, not on their "American-ness" but precisely on their individuality, on the unusual, even unique, contributions they made to their culture. And second, the leveling quest for unity and coherence tends to blur the distinctions that differentiate Puritan from Federalist from Romantic, Mather from Franklin from Emerson. The search for essence threatens to reduce complexity to sameness.

In this book, I have tried an alternate way of "explaining" America, one that may look, superficially, like a rather unlikely version of the usual way, and therefore may itself need some explaining. This book started out, more than ten years ago, as a conventional critical biography of James Marsh, a study of a "transitional" figure in American intellectual history. But Marsh led no literary or political movement. He cannot be identified with a formative system of philosophical principles. He embodies no single period in American culture. Clearly, he will not do as a mythic emblem of the national character. Insofar as he informs us, he must do so in some other way. Accordingly, somewhere along the line in the development of this volume, the ways in which Marsh's story seemed to frustrate traditional models of cultural inheritance and historical coherence suggested some untraditional ones, and the book in its present form is no longer "about" Marsh in the usual sense. Marsh and his life have been displaced from the center of the work, which now uses him as a frame for the issues that filtered through him and as a focus for the historical and theoretical questions raised in my earlier attempt to write traditional intellectual history.

This intellectual process, rather than Marsh's personal experience, is my true subject. I have focused on the *strategies* Marsh brought to his task and have tried to clarify their adequacy and their consequences, social and intellectual. My interest and aims have been literary rather than biographical. I have not chronicled Marsh's acts in the world, nor have I drawn a detailed portrait of religious factionalism in New England or of Marsh's life and thought for its own sake. Instead, I have examined the acts of Marsh's mind as he contended with the spiritual dilemma of his day in order to portray the ideological and aesthetic consequences of the cultural debate in which his work participated.

My reasons for adopting this strategy have been partly theoretical and partly simply a matter of personal interest. As I suggested above, one of the directions in which this work has led me is an inquiry into the assumptions and methodologies of traditional historiography (however much this work is still inextricably engaged with them). Marsh's work and the intellectual developments surrounding it simply refused to fit within traditional forms and the sorts of explanations they imply. Untraditional forms of explanation were called for, ones less biographical and less dependent on direct historical connections. From the first, I have been convinced that Marsh's interest resides not in the shape or circumstances of his life, nor in the direct historical influence or theological importance of his systematic thought, but in the perspective he provides on the spiritual and intellectual debates of his time. Marsh is a medium of inquiry, a lens that gives clearer focus to questions that have always been central to American literary scholarship.

First among these is the relation of the cultural outburst of the nineteenth century to its intellectual "origins" in American Puritanism. At once more Puritan than Emerson's works and more Romantic than Jonathan Edwards's, Marsh's writings identify the gap *between*, a gap which the myth of national identity had been designed to cover over. Attempts to make connections between Puritan and Transcendentalist, to identify their shared essence, have generally been tenuous, depending for their coherence on impressionistic appeals to temperamental affinities or at best on thematic or stylistic similarities between texts written by different authors at different times and places. In his Janus-faced embodiment of Puritan and Romantic, expressing both, yet blind to the divisions within himself, Marsh dramatizes the distinctions and hence the relationships between them. His works represent their respective positions rather than any assumed but hidden identity, and they do so in the work of one author and thus with an elegant economy and clarity.

The coherence of this view of American thought depends on no imposed fictive identity. It is the necessarily provisional and fragile coherence of a mind engaged in sorting out the issues that fathered the American Renaissance, and its conflicts or contradictions reveal the hidden stress points, the fault lines where Puritan and Transcendentalist meet. Marsh's writings clarify the transformations that produce *difference*, that distinguish Romantic from Puritan. Viewed so, the whole of Marsh's work incarnates the intellectual flux that gave rise to Transcendentalism and figures forth the profound consequences of Transcendental thought.

Not surprisingly, Marsh viewed himself very differently. He was a philosophical idealist, a believer in God and in an essential oneness that grounded all things, and he worked to promote that oneness in religion and society. In order to unify divergent theological factions, Marsh called on forces of modern philosophy that were bound to dismantle the very forms and traditional assumptions he wished to preserve. Like Jonathan Edwards nearly a hundred years before, Marsh stood on the ground of Orthodox dogma squarely between diverging lines of cultural development and tried to hold them together. But his task was much more difficult than Edwards's, for he was separated by nearly two hundred years from the seventeenth-century Puritan sources of his piety, living in the midst of a society devoted to common sense. In effect, one hundred years after Edwards, Marsh still strove to harmonize America's secular present with its Puritan past, and his efforts could only dramatize their incongruity and usher in a vision alien to both. By the nineteenth century, piety and reason had spread so far apart that Marsh was able to imagine their harmonious union only symbolically. When he tried to bind them in social institutions, he stepped back into authoritarian Orthodoxy, and when he tried to reconcile them in art, he stepped forward into Romanticism.

The existing scholarly view of Marsh does no justice to the complexity of this position. Marsh is generally known simply for the historical influence of his American edition (1829) of Coleridge's *Aids to Reflection*, one of the works that prompted the formation of the Transcendental Club in 1836. This edition made Coleridge's thought accessible for the first time to Americans who had previously either scorned Coleridge as one of those murky "Transcendental" philosophers with whom no reasonable man need bother or, like Emerson, viewed his works without particular interest. But the existing view does not discover the problematic nature of Marsh's influence—that in his

"Preliminary Essay" to *Aids*, Marsh presented Coleridge in American dress and in the process made him a new man, one who could speak the language of inspiration to the shapers of American literary culture. When we read Marsh's essay, as we must, back through our familiarity with Transcendentalism, its ambiguous idealism makes it sound at first like any number of Transcendentalist tracts. This impression and the impact of the essay on Emerson, Ripley, Alcott, and others, have led modern scholars to label Marsh a provincial northern cousin of the Boston Transcendentalists and an importer of European Romanticism.[1] This is the role that Odell Shepard had in mind when he called Marsh's *Aids* the Old Testament of Transcendentalism and Emerson's *Nature* the New.

Shepard's figure is apt, however, only insofar as Emerson and his associates mined Marsh's text for metaphors that would express and validate beliefs which the prophet himself did not envision and would never have approved. It overlooks Marsh's Orthodox motives and ignores the transforming potential of his strategies for enacting them. For all his influence in Concord, Marsh was no Transcendentalist, and he deplored the unorthodox opinions his scholarship had helped to foster. By heritage, training, and temperament, Marsh was tied to Orthodox tradition, and he abhorred Emerson's utterances, complaining that they "contain with scarcely a decent disguise nothing less than an Epicurean atheism dressed up in a style seducing and to many perhaps, deceptive." Marsh hoped to restore to American Congregationalism the spiritual flame that had been snuffed out by deism, secularism, doctrinal debate, and skepticism.

But Marsh's thought consistently carries implications that work against his Orthodox intent. When, for example, he removed *Aids* from the context of Coleridge's complete works, from the circumstances that led to its composition, and from the audience for whom it was intended; modified it by his introduction, notes, and appendices; and then dropped it down into New England amidst theological debates and cultural circumstances quite foreign in many respects to those Coleridge knew, he inevitably changed its meaning in ways he could only partially control. It became Marsh's book in the same sense that the passages from Dante in the "Wasteland" became Eliot's or that Duchamps appropriated the Mona Lisa by painting a moustache on her. Marsh transformed Coleridge in the same way that Coleridge transformed Kant, or that Emerson in turn, transformed Marsh to answer his own particular needs. In the process, he unwittingly prepared the ground for radical steps into both Transcendentalism and Romantic aesthetics. In fact, the problems that Marsh encountered in his attempts to establish a new foundation for American faith prefigured those with which Emerson and Melville would struggle a decade or two later, and which came to define and dominate nineteenth-century thought.

FOR THE most part this study has, over a long period, persisted in organizing itself. Starting out in the theological predicament of nineteenth-century New England, it has discovered its own way and evolved its own interests as issues raised in one section generated the questions that motivated the next. Thus, chapter 1 can be read as a schema of the alternatives open to a New Englander in quest of spiritual authority, a quest that drove most theological debate in the early nineteenth century. Marsh's conviction that the available alternatives all depended on the same dangerously false premises prompted the inquiries that led him, finally, to Coleridge (and Romanticism). This chapter also investigates the potentials and limitations of interpretive authorities in Marsh's New England and examines his conclusion that only an internal authority could preserve both humane values and divine faith.

Chapter 2 traces Marsh's intellectual affinities to St. Paul, the Cambridge Platonists, the German Faith Philosophers, Kant, and the English Romantic poets. Each reveals an element of the solution that Marsh believed he found complete in *Aids to Reflection*. Chapter 3 then details Marsh's translation of *Aids* from an English into an American book. This transformation is both cultural and intellectual. It suggests the alterations required to make English Romanticism American, and it traces the process by which absolute authority, once reserved to the divine Word, comes to be lodged finally and absolutely in the mind. It also suggests the ways in which the act of articulation (Marsh's attempt to "describe" Coleridge's thought in the "Preliminary Essay") not only falls short of but positively reconstructs intention. It dramatizes the shadow that Eliot discerned between the conception and the creation. This chapter and chapter 2 do not document literary inheritance; they elaborate the creative process by which thinkers appropriate the work of others to dress their own existing motives. Thus I do not stress continuity (what is handed down and conserved) so much as what is changed, misunderstood, or ignored.

Chapter 4 describes the varied reception of *Aids* by its American audience. It examines the ways in which readers usurp authority from the text. The assumptions of each reader shaped his reading of *Aids* and allowed more or less scope for the unfolding implications of Marsh's thought. I argue that the readers of *Aids* not only *mis*read it, they actually *recreated* its meaning (actually assigned the work its meaning) out of their own habits and preconceptions. This process dramatizes the contradictions between Marsh's Orthodox intentions and his radical effects; even in the reading of his own work, the traditional authorities Marsh was trying to preserve gave way before the authority of the individual mind that *Aids* helped to establish in America.

Chapter 5 focuses on the interplay in Marsh's thought between preestablished, universal authority and an internal, personal, developing one as Marsh tries in the nineteenth century to fulfill the Puritan errand by enacting God's will in social institutions. It follows the alterations in Marsh's thought from one social context to another, tracing his movement from vigorous adherence to doctrinal truth and clerical authority in church polity, to a radical view of art as an authority superior to nature and Scripture. Each change in context corresponds to a step in an intellectual (rather than an historical) journey from Orthodoxy to Transcendentalism, and maps out the changing perspectives of a traveler along the way.

Marsh was an historical catalyst, precipitating a reaction in which he did not himself participate and through which he remained unchanged while American culture, by following his lead, left him behind. Even he was willfully blind to the wider import of his work. He viewed his radical method through Orthodox eyes, overlooking its subversive effects and his part in them just as historians have largely overlooked him in favor of those who more boldly took up his method to support a new intellectual movement. True conservatives of Marsh's sort make by design too small, too prudent a splash to attract the historian's attention and are therefore generally ignored in accounts of the intellectual currents of their time. Yet, in their genuinely double vision, they are the very models of cultural change.

# Transcendent Reason

# 1

## A Ground Unconditioned:
## Spiritual Authority in New England

> The problem of Philosophy . . . is, for all
> that exists conditionally, to find a ground
> unconditioned and absolute.
> —Emerson, *Nature*

In the early nineteenth century, as for two hundred years before, New England's ministers ritually decried a falling off of faith. Orthodox *and* Unitarian piously recalled the legendary fervor of their Puritan grandfathers and longed to taste the richer religious brew of past generations. The discourse in which they pursued these aims, however, belied this spiritual impulse. By neglecting fervent religious feeling and concentrating instead on the more familiar, definable, and conventionally debatable issue of religious authority, it invoked the mind rather than the heart, made analytical distinctions where it might have urged essential sympathy, and thus generated the theological conflicts that increasingly fragmented New England faith. In the early stages of this conflict, Orthodoxy maintained Scripture against Unitarian moral conscience and common sense. But by 1840, these antagonists both faced a new threat that forced them together into a joint defense of objective and verifiable authority, whether Scriptural or communal, against an internal and individual authority that promised immediate personal access to divine truth.

3

At the height of this new debate, Andrews Norton set aside his habitual antipathy for the old Orthodoxy to enlist it in his attack on Transcendentalist philosophy. To sharpen his arguments against George Ripley and Theodore Parker, Norton republished two articles in which Charles Hodge, J. W. Alexander, and Albert Dod, the foremost professors at Princeton Theological Seminary, condemned the influence of obscure foreign philosophies on the "New School" and pronounced that a sound American religious philosophy could come only from a native American pen. "It might have been better for us," the Princeton professors wrote, "if the proposal for change had come *ab intra*, if one of our own productive minds had been led to forsake the beaten track and point out a higher path. But such has not been the case. It has so happened, that no great native philosophical leader has yet arisen to draw away one scholar from the common routine."[1]

The essayists' insistence that the savior of American faith must come from within refers superficially to a geographical and cultural boundary, but in fact their words carry heavier freight. They assumed that the answers to America's religious woes could only come from within that set of familiar preconceptions, dogmas, and values that already ruled American theology. Princeton looked for no surprises, so it was inevitable that, although it acknowledged the need for theological reform in New England, like Norton it detested the radical recommendations of the Transcendentalists. Hodge, Alexander, and Dod were looking for a second Jonathan Edwards, an Orthodox prophet to revitalize their faith without altering its essential form. The provisional alliance between Princeton and Harvard reveals their suppressed kinship, a shared stake in the theological *status quo*. Both opposed philosophical or religious innovation of anything more than a cosmetic kind, and both rested their faith on philosophical principles that partook more of the solid and substantial than of the spiritual.

This opposition explains the Princeton professors' disinclination to consider James Marsh as their Orthodox prophet, though he arose virtually in their midst. When Marsh did appear among New England theological controversialists, it was in the very German and English philosophical garb they most feared. So despite the Orthodoxy of his motives and of his back-

4

ground and training at Andover Theological Seminary, he was a sheep in wolf's clothing, and Princeton, unwilling and unable to look beneath the frightening exterior, was not about to admit him into the fold, much less to acknowledge him as spiritual shepherd. Nor were they brought around by Marsh's expressed aims, which were much like those in the Princeton essays: he, too, hoped to inject a new spirit into Orthodoxy without disturbing its doctrine.[2] In this, however, Princeton was not entirely undiscerning, for Marsh's thought was far more radical than he himself supposed and would bear strange fruit despite the Orthodox soil in which it had been nurtured, signaling a crucial shift of authority in New England faith.

Disagreements over the "source of religious authority" have been identified by William Hutchison as the crux of the conflict between Unitarianism and the Transcendentalists.[3] But it might be more accurate to say that the search for religious authority has always generated Protestant theological debate, particularly in America, where it dominated the religious scene from the time Anne Hutchinson began to meet privately with friends to elaborate on the minister's last sermon. Marsh surveyed the theological scene while a student at Andover at a crucial time in the history of New England theological controversy. In 1819, Unitarianism had finally declared its separate identity after years of half-heartedly protesting its Orthodoxy. Orthodoxy itself had become so internally split by its multiple defenses against Unitarian criticism that the very term defied definition.[4] The controversialists were becoming ever more polarized and rigid. There could be no constructive exchange of ideas since each side saw the very existence of the other as a violation of its integrity and a threat to its future.

As Marsh looked around him he saw that no faction embodied his own practical faith. He became convinced that New England theologians, whether at Andover, Yale, Princeton, or Harvard, evaded the most pressing questions of the time. In letters written during his final summer at Andover to his fiancée, Lucia Wheelock, Marsh declared his distaste for the tepid intellectual waters of America in the early nineteenth century.

Few, indeed, let me assure you even of those who undertake, as professional men, to examine and establish

5

the principles of their faith, know anything of the doubts and questions arising from serious metaphysical inquiry. Their principles are, in fact, fully established in their own minds, before they begin to examine them. They will boast, perhaps, of having dived into the very quagmire of skepticism, and fathomed its hidden depths; when, if the truth were known, they have probably floated along the surface or coasted the shores of this mighty deep, in the cock-boat of their own opinionated self-confidence. They see that all below is dark and dreamy; and fancy . . . they can hear the groans of Sodom and Gomorrah beneath them. No wonder they choose the upper air, and leave unruffled the abyss below.[5]

American theology, grounded resolutely on materialist philosophies, suffered from its own unwillingness to press beyond well-worn and comfortable preconceptions in search of a foundation for faith that accounted both for personal religious experience and Christian doctrine.

Marsh, on the other hand, like his Puritan forbears, envisioned Orthodoxy as a personal commitment to an *absolute* authority. But like his nineteenth-century colleagues at Harvard or Yale, he subscribed to an optimistic faith in the powers and rights of individuals. Puritan theology had managed to make room for individual interpretation within a system of absolute authority only by acknowledging that God's will can never be known with certainty. This willful uncertainty informs the history of Puritan intolerance—the trials of Hutchinson and Williams, the expulsion of Quakers—and is dramatized by the constant disagreement and compromise among the Puritan judges, many of whom discovered in themselves or their colleagues an uncomfortable measure of agreement with the accused.

The Puritans compensated for this uncertainty when, diverging from the strictest Calvinism, they tried to rationalize doctrine, making it more palatable to minds that were increasingly reluctant to admit their total helplessness and dependence.[6] The mission to the New World itself enacted Puritan optimism and respect for human initiative as did New England's federal theology by which God voluntarily conformed to human notions of justice. For this first generation of American

Puritans, English persecution and a sense of cosmic purpose enforced a strained and necessarily illogical balance between the authorities of individual piety and doctrine. Once human standards became a measure of the divine will, however, that will lost its absolute authority and became subject to individual interpretation. Once religious truth came to depend to some extent on human interpretation, each generation had to set its own balance between human and divine authority, one which preserved divinity without sacrificing independence. The world of nature expanded to meet the world of spirit. Human authority and that of revelation met on more equal terms;[7] they were no longer simply two aspects of one harmonious system. Instead, they expressed essentially different and mutually exclusive interpretations of the universe with God at the center of one and man at the center of the other. By 1800, man was in the ascendent, revelation was clearly on the defensive even among its supporters, and piety had been driven underground or banished to the realm of the rude rural evangelist.

As Americans found it more and more difficult to justify God's ways to men, many ministers, liberal and conservative, gave up the attempt and tried to ignore difficulties they could not untangle, resolving to make Christianity as simple and acceptable as possible.[8] For all their collective scholarship, none of the combatants was eager to delve too deeply into questions that might upset his preconceived system. The public tone is represented by Rufus Choate, a brilliant but unabashedly pragmatic lawyer and politician, who espoused tangible rather than eternal verities. Choate was Marsh's roommate for a year during their tutorships at Dartmouth, and no one was more aware of the intellectual gulf between them than Choate himself. He viewed Marsh's studies with the discomfort and insecurity typical of many New Englanders in the face of speculative metaphysics. "That ocean of German theology and metaphysics (not to mention criticism)," he exclaimed, "—Ah, Marsh, you may swim alone in that if you will, and much good may it do you! I never could swim in it myself at any rate . . . and have long since made up my mind that any smaller fry than a leviathan stand no sort of chance in its disturbed muddy and unfathomable waters."[9]

Choate's untroubled confession of ignorance suggests that

the nineteenth century feared the consequences of speculation more than it desired spiritual assurance. Metaphysical certainty came, if it came at all, with such labor and difficulty that it seemed hardly worth the pursuit. The precepts that had made individuality possible for the Puritans—faith in absolute divine authority and its correlative admission that man cannot comprehend many of the most fundamental issues of life—seemed impractical, even downright dangerous, in an age of triumphant science and progress.

In the conflict between personal and communal authorities, key terms, particularly "reason," which bore the burden of human power and potential, proved fluid, themselves subject to differing interpretations and definitions as they became vehicles for one or another set of assumptions or motives. Such terms never own one consistent definition. As each generation redefined the rational and gave the mind more competence to comprehend experience, the balance between human and divine authority shifted and had to be established anew in order to preserve the metaphysical assurance that was fundamental to faith.

UNITARIANS were desperately uncomfortable with metaphysical uncertainty and eager to secure truth, even if it were only the most limited sort. For them, the problem of religious authority had become particularly acute. In their dispute with Congregationalism, they had repudiated the Orthodox claim that Scripture was the infallible word of God, and their insistence that the individual must have the right to free inquiry denied them the alternative of locating spiritual authority in the institutional church. Moreover, the Scottish Common Sense philosophy with which they justified their secular mercantile interests effectually ruled out a personal spiritual vision. As an unexpected by-product of so defining their faith they found themselves cut off from the three traditional sources of theological certainty: Scripture, the church, and direct revelation. Yet they were no more anxious than John Winthrop had been to open the doors to anarchy. The real question, as A. P. Peabody recognized, was not "whether truth is to be received on the authority of God or on that of Jesus. It is whether truth is to be taken on any authority higher or other than our own."[10]

New England Unitarians feared anarchy more than anything else, and they tried to ignore metaphysical doubts at least
partly in reaction to social upheaval both in the Old World and
the New. The stability of the new nation was still uncertain, and
those uncertainties had not been soothed by the excesses of the
French Revolution or domestic disturbances like Shays's Rebellion. In this atmosphere, Unitarians felt comfortable with intellectual inquiry itself only as it carried them directly from a
body of commonly held assumptions or observations to an affir-
mation of their common preconceptions.[11] About technical theological or spiritual questions most Unitarians affected the
smug complacency that had so bemused Henry Adams. "That
the most intelligent clergy, in the most moral conditions he ever
knew," Adams recalled, "should have solved all the problems of
the universe so thoroughly as to have quite ceased making itself
anxious about past or future, and should have persuaded itself
that all the problems which have convulsed human thought
from earliest recorded time, were not worth discussing, seemed
to him the most curious social phenomenon he had to account
for in a long life. . . . Difficulties might be ignored; doubts were
a waste of thought, nothing exacted solution. Boston had solved
the universe. . . . The problem was worked out."[12]

Unitarianism had been inspired by a growing confidence in
the authority of everyday life. Cherishing a heartfelt desire for
piety and faith, it lived on an intellectual foundation that encouraged a sense of human power and exuded confidence in
man's ability to compel the world to meet his needs. Insofar as
the drama of man's existence was to be acted out and his success or failure determined in this world, his interest in the next
naturally declined. The social ambition and desperate circumstances that had moved the Puritans to establish a city on a hill
as an example to the world—God's will expressed in social
forms—had abated somewhat and been transformed, and the
equal energies of their Unitarian descendants found expression
in community improvements and urged them to advance an
American challenge to English cultural supremacy. Reading
from an early draft of the Gospel of Wealth, they began to con-
fuse material and moral success, generating a preference for
cultural attainments over personal piety, for social grace over
divine.

9

In order to avert skepticism and reinforce the metaphysical assurance on which they believed the civil peace depended, New England Unitarians relied on the Scottish Common Sense philosophy of Dugald Stewart, Thomas Reid, and Thomas Brown. They viewed "Scottish metaphysics" not as a refutation of Locke's notion that all knowledge comes through the senses, but as a way of avoiding the logical consequences of his principles as they were developed into skepticism by Hume and as a necessary clarification of Locke's true import.[13] The Unitarian faith erected on Scottish philosophy was dogmatically simple.[14] It asserted that Scripture was revealed but was subject to logical analysis; that Christ was the cornerstone of faith but not a member of the Godhead; and that man was morally perfectible. It supported these propositions with a vague but heartfelt religious sentiment rather than with argumentation: the controversial pamphlets of Norton or Ware are characterized by allegedly self-evident assertions rather than by attempts at logical demonstration.[15] The Scots endowed each man with an innate and infallible faculty for perceiving the most fundamental philosophical and theological truths. They assured Unitarians that all important truths were self-evident, their demonstration both unnecessary and impossible.

Unitarians could reassure themselves of the accessibility of truth only by confining it within the narrow compass of the senses and of cultural tradition. Abstract speculation could only lead *out* of the light readily available to all, creating confusion and fostering error. Scottish Common Sense, like Ramist logic before it, provided middle-class academicians and theologians with a practical philosophy free from unsettling complications, pedantry, or jargon.[16] American educators used the Scots against extremism in any form, idealistic or materialistic. The innate moral sense offered a metaphysical panacea for the frustration and uncertainty that made exploring abstruse spiritual questions unhealthy for the individual and the state. Like Franklin before them, the Unitarian leadership believed that society improved only as the eventual consequence of beneficent influences exerted by those virtuous men—themselves—who held social responsibility in their own capable hands.[17] They relied on the metaphysical conservatism of the Common Sense philosophy to preserve the *status quo* that worked so much to their advantage.

They viewed even Common Sense philosophy selectively, however. While they embraced those elements of it that rationalized their moral preconceptions and supported their social preeminence, they failed to recognize that it was subject to another interpretation, that the common moral sense could be viewed by less cautious inquirers like Emerson as a sort of spiritual inner light leading to radical theological innovation. In dealing with heretics such as the Transcendentalists, Unitarianism was caught in a logical dilemma created by its own desires to invoke divine sanction for the existing social order and for the individual moral sense. If laws reflect the will of God, then disagreement with those laws must be both criminal and heretical. But such heresy is difficult to account for if the divine plan is supposed to be imprinted, at least in its broad outlines, on the minds of each citizen. When George Ripley questioned Unitarian principles in his review of James Martineau, Andrews Norton was forced into the same dubious argument that John Cotton had used against Roger Williams's doctrines of the primacy of conscience.[18] It was not possible that the true dictates of Ripley's conscience could be in error, so the only alternative must be that he had failed properly to consult his conscience in the first place. In short, Norton claimed, Ripley did not know his own mind—a view that Ripley understandably resented.

Unitarianism was ill-equipped to cope with Transcendentalist claims to subjective authority. In his famous essay on "The Latest Form of Infidelity," Norton espouses uncertainty itself as a Unitarian creed, not to allow for the idiosyncrasies of individual faith as the Puritans had, but to support objective authorities. In the process, he espouses all the dogmatic rationalism of seventeenth-century Puritanism but none of its spiritual zeal.

To the demand for certainty, let it come from whom it may, I answer that I know of no absolute certainty, beyond the limit of momentary consciousness, a certainty that vanishes the instant it exists, and is lost in the region of metaphysical doubt. . . . We proceed throughout upon probabilities. . . . There can be no intuition, no direct perception of the truth of Christianity, no metaphysical certainty. . . . Our belief in those truths the evidence of which we cannot examine for ourselves, is founded in greater or less degree on the testimony of others who have examined their evidence, and whom we regard as intelligent and trustworthy.[19]

While in theory the Scots comforted Unitarians with immediate intuitive access to absolute moral truth, in practice as Norton suggests, individual moral insight was severely restricted. It could confirm his own existence, the reality of the objects he perceived, and the principle of causality, but it could not illuminate the daily issues of behavior and belief that constitute theology and morals. Truth for the Unitarians depended on facts, not on faith. It had to be derived directly from empirical evidence, the testimony of tradition and of social leaders like Norton. If the evidence was trustworthy, it demanded rational assent, but without such evidence belief was merely superstitious enthusiasm.[20] These views cast Norton in a typically conservative role. To those who questioned prevailing dogmas, he responded by stating his own beliefs more unequivocally, more extremely, more dogmatically, drowning out both the arguments of his critics and his own whispering doubts.

Of course, Norton's statements represent the extreme of Unitarian rhetoric rather than the majority sentiment.* In fact, many Unitarians criticized Norton for his violent overreaction and accused him of doing more harm than good to the Unitarian cause. Norton's dogmatic elitism distanced preachers still further from the unlearned masses than had the complex Technologia upon which Thomas Shepard and Thomas Hooker rested their faith. Norton's arguments depended on the sort of awesome Biblical scholarship that very few in New England could even attempt. When he surveyed Biblical criticism in his monumental *Evidences of the Genuineness of the Gospels*, he actually undermined the relatively simple faith of less scholarly Christians by eroding their confidence in the uniform truth and divine source of Scripture.[21] Yet, if many moderate Unitarians disapproved of Norton's opinions, more than one pragmatic cit-

---

* In fact, the portraits of Unitarianism and of Orthodoxy presented here are not designed to represent the majority opinion of either camp. Instead, I am interested here in exploring the logical consequences of the Unitarian and Orthodox metaphysics, especially since it was these consequences that motivated Marsh.

izen of Boston found reassurance in his tone and agreed with the moderate Rufus Johnson, editor of the *Christian Register*, that "it is really refreshing in the midst of these flitting phantasms, shadows and clouds which are lowering on the regions of theology, to hear a certain, decided, penetrating calmly confident voice."[22] The universal order that had once been entrusted to the unknowable will of God had to be proved by objective evidence and enforced by human agents, a strategy which effectively cut Unitarians off from internal spiritual sources of faith. In the absence of any direct access to spiritual truth, which Unitarians denied to fend off dogmatism, they turned to the authority of the past to guide the present. But by doing so, they repressed the very individualist impulses that had given rise to Unitarianism in the first place and brought on the spiritual rebellion they hoped to avert.

THE SAME reliance on objective spiritual authority that directed Unitarian theology was, somewhat surprisingly, no less dominant within Orthodoxy, and led, Marsh believed, to equally grave consequences there. In a letter to Coleridge, Marsh identified the essential similarity of the ostensibly opposed Unitarian and Congregationalist systems and underscored their mutual opposition to pietist principles. "In theology," Marsh explained, "the works of Edwards have had, and still have . . . a very great influence. . . . You will readily see the near affinity which exists between these philosophical views and those of Brown; and yet it happens that the Unitarians, while they reject Edwards for his Calvinism, as it is here called, give currency to Brown for views that would seem to lead to what is most objectionable in the work on the Freedom of the Will."[23] Behind both the Scottish philosophy of the Unitarians and the Edwardsean philosophy of the Congregationalists, Marsh perceived the common principle that moral and spiritual knowledge depended ultimately on empirical authorities, that neither offered a method by which individuals could have direct access to spiritual truth. Marsh blamed Edwards, who dominated New England theology into the nineteenth century, for leading Congregationalism far from its origins in personal religious experience. Many nineteenth-century Orthodox ministers had, Marsh believed, contracted the spiritual malady of their time and looked like Unitarians in Orthodox robes.[24] Even those who still preached the rigorous letter of the divine law and staunchly defended innate depravity and predestination against Unitarian attacks had been forced down from a lofty spiritual defense of their faith to the low plain of common sense and logic, the native ground of their Unitarian opponents. In their defense of faith, conservatives adopted strategies that ranged from complacent authoritarian fundamentalism to accommodation with sensationalist philosophy to pious moralism, positions that Marsh could also find, slightly altered, in Unitarianism.

Blind obedience to Scripture was centered at Princeton, but it resided at Andover as well, where Marsh got his first lessons in the narrow-mindedness of New England Orthodoxy and the drawbacks of unquestioning obedience to Scriptural law. The Andover faculty remembered too well the Unitarian takeover at Harvard and distrusted any wandering from the path they had so carefully laid out to strictly Orthodox conclusions.[25] So great, in fact, was the fear of heresy at Andover that not even its own respected professors were above suspicion. Moses Stuart brought German literature to Andover to offer students like Marsh the most advanced theological scholarship of the day. Marsh was Stuart's prize student, and he found German scholarship indispensable to any advanced work in Biblical studies. But most of the Andover faculty were less sanguine about Germanic influence. Stuart remarked, "it was whispered that I was not only secretly gone over to the Germans, but was leading the Seminary over with me, and . . . encouraging our young men to the study of the deistical 'Rationalism,' and besides this . . . that it was as much as the other professors could do to keep the Seminary from going over to Unitarianism."[26]

Ironically Stuart himself had always been one of the most stalwart defenders of the strict Calvinism that turned on him on this occasion. Although he sampled German scholarship, he did so because, like many Americans after 1812, he was attracted to non-British sources of culture, not because he was eager for new perspectives on religious truth.[27] In fact, his theology came straight out of the English tradition, and for all his pioneering work in German criticism, Stuart never saw to the logical ends of those inquiries. He distrusted the Germans as much as his colleagues did, warning that liberals would eventually adopt the heresies of German Romanticism and "at last go full length with the most liberal of them all."[28] Stuart's was the simplest and the most inflexible line of Orthodox defense. He was unmatched in his mastery of theological history and exegetical scholarship, and his arguments against Unitarian "heresies" combined his remarkable learning with subtle analyses of complex verbal distinctions and presented the whole in a commonsensical style designed to demolish the sophistication of his urbane adversaries. Ultimately, however, Stuart grounded everything firmly on the testimony of Scripture. To the Unitarians' moral argument against Calvinism, Stuart returned the "rationality" of believing Scriptural doctrine even if it appears to violate natural law or social morality. He argued that God's ways transcend human understanding and that Scripture offers the only and infallible guide.[29] Such convictions need no profound philosophical justification. It was enough for Stuart that a doctrine had Scripture behind it. Once he had assured himself of that authority, the truth was beyond dispute.

Princeton defended Biblical authority with only slightly more recourse to metaphysical justification, and the metaphysic it used was oddly Lockean. Archibald Alexander and Charles Hodge waged the defense of Scripture from Princeton for fifty years. Yet even these conservative defenders of the old faith felt that it must at least *seem* rational, and they appealed, just as Channing or Norton had, to Locke, though in a halfhearted and ambiguous way. Along with conservative churchmen from Ames to Edwards, Hodge argued the strict imputation of original sin from Adam and the absolutely free and irresistible grace of God. In order to reconcile this view with modern philosophy, he simply pointed out that since we receive no sensory impressions in spiritual matters, the only "facts" on which judgments can be based must come from Scripture. Thus, Scripture is the only and absolute authority on all religious questions. Its pronouncements must be accepted uncritically on faith, no matter how absurd or offensive they may seem, since religious truth is otherwise entirely inaccessible to human understanding.[30] This caricature of Locke suggests the unspoken alliance of Hodge (and Orthodoxy) with Unitarianism, for like Norton's reliance on tradition, it denied individual insight into spiritual truths.

15

Although the unyielding legalism of Hodge and Stuart may seem, as it did to many in their own day, out of keeping with growing confidence in man's rational powers, it is worth remembering that they were trying, despite all the difficulties of a hostile cultural environment, to preserve the vision of divine omnipotence that had sustained and empowered Puritan faith. Seventeenth-century Puritans gratefully acknowledged that God's ways need not conform to man's. John Robinson, one of the guiding lights of the congregation at Scrooby and an influential apologist for Calvinist doctrines among the New England congregations, might have been speaking directly to Norton as he made his inability to understand God's working on the crucial issue of original sin an article of faith, quoting chapter and verse of Scripture as sufficient authority: "I answer . . . that the manner of God's working herein is to me, and to all men, inconceivable; and withal avouch, that he, who will not confess, that God can, and could in Adam's sin, by his infinite wisdom and power . . . order and dispose of things, without violation to his holiness, or violence to the creature's will, as no mortal man is able to conceive the manner thereof, is himself in a high degree guilty of that pride which was Adam's ruin, by which he desired to be as God in knowledge (Gen. chap. 3)."[31] Robinson, like Stuart and Hodge, portrayed man as a helpless creature incapable of comprehending the objects of an infinitely superior being. He still saw the world as the scene of a divine drama in which man played a rather uncomprehending part, and he gloried in the enlightening revelation of Scripture. In the nineteenth century, however, religion was isolated in a predominantly secular world—one among many contestants for metaphysical supremacy. Hodge and Stuart were specialists assigned to care for spiritual needs as lawyers looked after the laws or doctors the sick, and they were reduced to an acceptance of Scriptural authority for its own sake, haggling over its meaning and import as their one area of competence.

Nathaniel Taylor, president of Yale, stands out as the man who, more than any other, tried to adapt Orthodoxy to these modern conditions.[32] In this respect, Taylor's motives were very much like Marsh's. Both were, fundamentally, defenders of Orthodoxy, but they did not get the credit they might have expected from the Orthodox community because they employed innovative arguments from modern philosophy that their Orthodox brethren distrusted. Taylor's thought grew out of the New Divinity wing of New England theology. His system combined the arguments of Bellamy, Hopkins, and Emmons with Common Sense philosophy to produce a practical and, more importantly, palatable Orthodoxy in which New Englanders could live more comfortably than they could in the stricter confines of Andover or Princeton. While Hodge piously strove to preserve the authority of Scripture, Taylor tackled the practical problem of making Orthodoxy acceptable to the average nineteenth-century citizen who could not match Hodge for piety and did not care to try.

Taylor always insisted that his thought had not strayed from the doctrine of the Westminster Confession, and he believed that his efforts were all intended to express Edwards's true meaning, but an examination of his rationale for original sin or for the existence of sin itself, for freedom of the will or for conversion reveals that his Scottish philosophy altered fundamentally the Orthodox system it was intended to preserve, and that Taylor shared an implicit intellectual kinship with Unitarianism of which he himself was unaware. Original sin, for example, is, according to Taylor, actually *learned* during selfish infancy and is thus "original" in name only. In conversion, this principle of selfishness is lifted by Grace, leaving the repentant sinner free to follow God's will—not because of his detached love of Being itself as Edwards would have it, but because he sees divine will as the ultimate source of his *own personal happiness*.

Taylor's views reveal both the bankruptcy of conventional Orthodox apologetics and, more importantly, the folly of using Scottish philosophy to squeeze new life from the old church forms. The strategies Orthodox theologians used to justify their faith had lost their potency, and Unitarian alternatives created as many problems as they solved. Scripture alone was no longer adequate, empirical facts could be interpreted to suit any number of conclusions, and "Common Sense" seemed to undermine rather than support Calvinist principles that remained crucial to the coherence of Orthodox faith. Orthodox doctrines simply could not be defended by a philosophy of sensation. The need was for an entirely new source of authority, but none of the dis-

17

putants was inclined to seek it or equipped to recognize it when it appeared.

Two CENTURIES of philosophical and theological change had made Marsh's own piety intellectually unfashionable in his society, breeding a frustration that generated much of his dissatisfaction with New England religious thought. Existing New England theologies offered no models for a truly *spiritual** authority, one that would once again offer unmediated access to God. While his Orthodox professors defended doctrine from which the spirit had fled, Marsh felt a strong personal faith but had difficulty expressing it in a culture that was no longer so hospitable to piety as it had been two hundred years earlier.

The Orthodoxy of Marsh's temperament was closely related to his rural Vermont origins. He was born in July 1794 in Hartford, Vermont and raised in a staunchly Orthodox rural atmosphere at a time when Unitarianism was entrenching itself in liberal Boston.[33] He spent most of his early life on the family farm, isolated from the intellectual and social energies emanating from Boston and pervading much of New England, which shook and often transformed the faith of his urban contemporaries. His later contact at Dartmouth and Harvard with the most advanced culture available to New Englanders, his friendship with many of America's most sophisticated thinkers, could not erase the influences of his first eighteen years. Marsh grew up in a family characterized by an atmosphere of solid respectability, devoted to the practical concerns of farming, and possessing some prominence in Vermont affairs. His grandfather had been Lieutenant Governor, and his father had spent his life managing the large family farm. Marsh was intended to follow his father on the farm and was happy with the prospect. It was James's older brother, Roswell, who had been elected to go to

---

* As I use it here and throughout the book, the word "spiritual" in phrases like "spiritual truth" or "spiritual religion" or "spiritual philosophy" can be taken as shorthand for the presence of the absolute directly to the mind without mediation. The term "spiritual" is used this way by Marsh to distinguish religious truth and philosophical truth so generated from their empirical counterparts, which were dominant in the discourse of the time.

college. But Roswell was not a dutiful son. He balked at the indignity of carrying a leg of mutton off to Dartmouth in partial payment of his board and ran away from home, leaving the way to Dartmouth open for James. So it was James who went off to Dartmouth in the fall of 1813, presumably with a leg of mutton perched on one frail shoulder, to meet the controversies of New England intellectual life.*

Dartmouth's most important impact on Marsh, however, was not intellectual but religious. In 1815, the college was still awash in the eddies of the Second Great Awakening. The numerous conversions both in the college and elsewhere monopolized the thoughts of the students and the community, and the most important question for each student and teacher was whether he "had hopes." Marsh was ripe for the religious harvest, and in 1815 he was converted and committed himself to God's service. Marsh's description of his conversion could as easily have come from the pen of a seventeenth-century Puritan saint. In the course of his soul-searching, he went through each of the obligatory stages of Puritan conversion, passing from the temptations of a "rebellious heart" to near despair over his own sin and worthlessness in God's sight—the first sign of hope—until finally, he says, "the things of another world completely filled my mind and God appeared to me to be all in all. . . . I saw not particular application of his mercy to myself; but he appeared infinitely glorious, and I felt that if I had ten thousand souls, I could with confidence commit them to his mercy and care." [34]

Marsh dutifully recorded every twist and turn of his soul and examined himself unflinchingly, not so much to determine the state of his own feelings or to discover evidences of his own sincerity as to find evidence of God's will working in him. But Calvinist theology warned against a certainty too easily obtainable or untroubled by doubts, and Marsh had his measure of the latter.

> At times, I have feared that my peace arose rather from the decay of religious affections, than from true evangelical faith. Yet I thought, from self-examination, that I dis-

---

* The details of Marsh's life are given in a chronology in the Appendix.

covered some marks of a growing principle of Christian life. I thought my desires after holiness and an increase of the Christian graces, together with a sense of my own sinfulness and the imperfections of my best performances, were becoming more strong and furnished some evidence of a state of grace.[35]

Like Michael Wigglesworth, Thomas Hooker, the Mathers, or Jonathan Edwards, Marsh questioned every motive, trembled over each fluctuation in his devotion, and found the best "evidence of a state of grace" in his conviction of his own "sinfulness" and "imperfection." He became increasingly certain of his election, not because he felt holy, or because he shared the divine spirit, but because he saw himself more and more as God must see him, full of sin and weakness. Marsh's conversion experience was a vestige of a tradition rapidly dying out in the early nineteenth century to be replaced by the convictions of Joseph Buckminster and Henry Ware, Jr., who found man free of original sin and therefore in no need of salvation. For God's grace, Ware substituted lessons in *The Formation of A Christian Character* to instruct readers who wanted to increase their "likeness to God." Marsh would have been appalled by the very idea of a man's "likeness to God," and he would have admonished Ware that salvation comes only to those who cultivate a spiritually healthy sense of their infinite unlikeness.[36]

Like his Puritan forebears, Marsh thought of himself as God's servant and subordinated human wishes to the divine will. For example, when he received word of his father's fatal illness he reacted with characteristic resignation, complaining not of the impending death itself but only that the dying man "expresses less clear and animated views of the great objects of our faith and hope and love than I could wish to see him,"[37] and devoutly hoping that he would see his father's "thoughts wholly fixed and intent on heaven and his heart there before he is called to possess his inheritance."[38] In Marsh's day, a certain resignation in such moments was not fatalism, it was simply an acquiescence to the grim facts of life. In his letters, Marsh reveals an appalling work-a-day familiarity with personal tragedy—disease, death, madness. His own family was riddled with consumption. It killed both of his wives and it would kill him too. They lived intimately with it for years with nothing to do but await the end God had chosen for them.

When each of his wives died, Marsh sincerely invoked the obligatory moral of the vanity of all human action and the utter dependence of helpless mankind on its omnipotent creator in terms nearly identical to those of Samuel Danforth, who met the death of his three children in an epidemic by saying, "I trust the Lord hath done what he hath done in wisdom, and faithfulness, and dear love; and that in taking these pleasant things from me, he exerciseth as tender affection unto me, as I now express towards them in mourning for the loss of them."[39] This struggle for victory over human nature has been described as "an epitome of the Puritan psyche," and although modern readers may think it deficient in human sympathy and affection, it "proceeds not from heartlessness but from disciplining the heart."[40] It is based on the conviction (losing popularity by Marsh's time) that the world works in ways beyond human understanding—God's ways, not man's—and that the two need not coincide.

This faith in divine authority aligns Marsh with his Puritan ancestors and distinguishes him from nineteenth-century liberals, Unitarian and Transcendentalist alike. Unlike a young Emerson or Ripley raised in the moral optimism of liberal Boston, Marsh breathed the air of piety from birth. He habitually found truth in revelation and in the established principles of Congregationalism. Although, like Orthodox divines of all times, he questioned the theoretical justifications and interpretations of doctrine, he never doubted doctrine itself. His personal faith reveals an Orthodox rigor and fervor indistinguishable from that of Thomas Hooker or John Cotton. It is the very fervor that Emerson missed in the "pale negations" of Unitarianism, and it points to the centrality of Orthodox values in Marsh's life. Although he generally avoided the Puritans' inflexible dogmatism and their predilection for a strictly logical system of demonstration, he imitated their other-worldly submission to the divine will, their habit of unflinching spiritual self-examination, and their devotion to the active service of God in the world, enacting a truly Puritan fidelity to a demanding and unyield-

21

ing faith.[41] Marsh's early letters burst with the enthusiasm of new-found belief, and the state of his soul and of the souls of his friends provides the greatest if not the only subject of discussion.[42]

These deep religious convictions made a career in the ministry the obvious, really the only choice for Marsh, even when it burdened him with duties for which he was ill-suited. He was by temperament a "man of letters" in a culture wary of any learning not turned to some more practical end. The option of putting off a career to pursue a life of self-culture was simply not available to him, as it was to Emerson, Thoreau, and Alcott. He shared too many of the earnest Christian values of his culture to rebel so openly against its expectations. Education was as near as he could come to the contemplative life. It ratified his bookish inclinations and satisfied his real, though tender, impulses to spiritual leadership. Like many of his contemporaries, Marsh felt that his occupation failed to *enact* his true spirit. His yearning for a true vocation was a living example of the Romantic urge to give the private self an outward formal expression, without which it could not be known at all. The effort was to be a complete man at rest in his proper place in society. But each particular form seemed incomplete, a disturbing fragment of broken promise.[43] Unable to imagine a life that would adequately express his spirit, he muted and confined that spirit within the boundaries of an available life.

Marsh's mixed feelings about his ministerial calling dramatize his inability to imitate the Puritan union of internal spirit and external form, of the private man with the public function.[44] For English Puritans, the friction between the inner and outer callings had been less acute. The very existence of a gathered church, one produced by the natural congregation of saints in a largely sinful society, expressed publicly the private faith of its members. The Puritan world was plastic, capable of shaping itself to fit the demands faith made upon it. The worldly actions of saints did not tie them to the world. On the contrary, the saints imparted their own spiritual elevation to their vocations, lifting them out of worldly corruption. In effect, they created a second world of God within the larger, damned world of men. Form gave way to faith, superficial appearances to spiritual reality.[45]

When the Puritans came to America, they naturally carried with them the antiformal attitudes that had served them so well in England and tried to apply them to new conditions that made new and often conflicting demands upon them. Sacvan Bercovitch has pointed out the potency of the Puritan conviction that America would realize Scriptural prophecy. With the migration from England, the spiritual nation of Israel became one with the political "nation" of Massachusetts Bay; the ideal was made real. This self-imposed mission required a more dramatic manifestation of personal sainthood than had life in England. In a society of saints, one in which the divine will was to assume social form, mere assertion of sainthood was no longer sufficient to distinguish the saint from his less spiritual fellows. Acts were no longer sanctified by the spiritual status of the actor. Public activities had to reflect the state of the soul. They had to be evidently holy acts.

These expectations lived on into the nineteenth century despite the passing of the cultural setting which had given them their function. In a society that respected the practical and banished the spiritual, men of spirit had no regular institutional outlet for their faith, no true worldly vocation. The ministry, which had served this purpose for an earlier age, was often viewed by nineteenth-century New Englanders as just one among many trades. Ministers were paid, often grudgingly, a rather inadequate salary by their congregations to perform their prescribed tasks—ministering to the sick, comforting the dying, listening to the secular troubles of parishioners, and mediating their disputes. Such activities left little time even for writing Sunday's sermon, much less for the study and thought that had once been considered essential to a minister's work. Marsh's earliest anticipations of the course of his career are free from such worries and suggest the high pitch of his calling to enact his faith in the world. Before his ordination, Marsh admitted no conflict between pastoral duties and inner faith. "I could not die in peace," he said, "without the consciousness of having at least attempted something, as a coworker with the holy men, who are honored as the instruments of God in doing his own glorious work. . . . I am beginning to prepare myself for the active duties of a minister, and am ready to believe I shall find more pleasure in it than I have ever done in my studies."[46]

23

This early zeal was grounded, however, in youthful idealism and a rather unrealistic impression of a minister's life. Marsh preferred to view the activities of a minister as a sort of friendly, casual, domestic intercourse rather than as an often tedious routine of attendance upon the everyday spiritual needs of a New England community. He revealed the naive idealism of his eagerness to take up pastoral duties in this description of an afternoon's conversation with a cousin and childhood playmate:

> She is all heart and soul—loves her husband loves her children, and what is more prays for them all with a very ardent love for the religion which she would have them also enjoy. Such a sight is to me extremely interesting and I have never had higher notions of the happiness which a minister of the gospel *might* enjoy with his parishioners than from conversing with her. I felt I am sure for once that I would prefer it to any other which the world might afford.[47]

Even in this pleasant idyll, however, Marsh could not entirely suppress the doubts that clouded his view of his chosen career. His relieved "for once" reveals that he was not always so sanguine about his vocation and implies that the anticipation he expressed here might be short-lived.

Indeed, as the time came to leave his scholarly pursuits at Andover for practical responsibilities, his certainty began to waver. After leaving Andover in 1822, Marsh underwent "a long and painful season of suspense" in trying to determine "the field which Providence [had] allotted" him.[48] In this difficulty, he retired to his father's farm hoping that study and meditation would ease stubborn doubts about his fitness for public life. This retreat, however, taught him only that isolation could not resolve his conflicts between Christian duty and privatist impulses. He could not be a Thoreau. The old Puritan demand to do God's work in the world was too strong in him and, after a few months, Joseph Torrey records, Marsh "at last resolved to throw himself into the scenes of life, where exertion would be called for, and struggle to perform what the providence of God should seem to point out as his duty in the world."[49]

The precipitous plunge into the teaching and ministerial duties that followed at Hampden-Sydney, Virginia, beginning in 1823, did little to quiet Marsh's inner uncertainty. On the contrary, it only deepened his fear of public action. Like both Emerson and Hawthorne, Marsh complained all his life of his "constitutional coldness and reserve." He alternately desired and dreaded society. "I was never made for society," he said;

> the feelings that might flow spontaneously in solitude with my friends, are chilled, and all powers of sympathy destroyed, by the intercourse of the world. I have not learned and never can learn, to throw myself into the bustle of society and enjoy the unrestrained intercourse of feelings. Either my heart is not sufficiently susceptible by nature, or I have loaded it too much with the lumber of learning, and kept it mewed too long in the cell of the student.[50]

At a time when scholars sometimes spent eighteen hours a day in their studies, the venerable antagonism between thought and life took on more literal significance. Some, like Theodore Parker, worked themselves into an early grave. When they did not, the abstruse issues that took up most of their waking time effectively alienated them from their less studious fellows. This was Marsh's fear. Early in his life Marsh seems to have been eager for social intercourse. He was strongly attracted by the images of social life he found in the letters of Shenstone, Gay, Cowper, and others. "Such a state of society" he wrote, "seems to me to promise much more exercise of social feelings and sympathies, than our constrained, cautious and freezing reserve."[51] Yet what sounds here like eagerness for society was more likely nostalgia for the relaxed, unselfconscious (because so artfully constructed) relationships portrayed in literature, that is, for an imagined rather than a real state. Literature gave Marsh the emotional satisfaction of society while he sat secure and alone in his own room. When he faced the real prospect of social duties rather than the literary ideal, his eagerness cooled into the "freezing reserve" he so deplored.

Unable to avoid either the sense of guilty isolation or the unrelenting discomfort of public employment, Marsh began early in his adult life to seek peace through meek submission to divine providence. In effect, Marsh was trading one traditional Christian outlook on life for another, writing himself out of the drama of personal redemption and into providential history. Instead of assuming responsibility for the shape of his own life and pursuing in the process his independent spiritual progress toward God, he submitted his life to the influence of time and worldly events and implicitly abdicated responsibility for it, satisfying himself with social rather than personal advancement. In 1820, though Marsh dutifully embraced his providential duty, he did so in terms that suggest the high price of such submission. "It is easier," he wrote, "and I am aware, it is much better suited to my inclination—to feel one's self *free* from responsibility, and at liberty to be governed by the impulse of the moment than to be a man among men, to form and maintain a character on elevated, uniform and consistent principles. . . . To form and support such a character in this way should and will assure a more enviable reputation than all the accomplishments and acquirements of mere intellectual greatness."[52]

This passage is full of irony in light of Marsh's longing for scholarly attainment and for the capacity to be spontaneous rather than self-consciously deliberate. Here, in a stiff caricature of the uncompromising Puritan manner, he portrays Christian responsibility as the art of the unpleasant, the conquest of the artificial over the natural. In the process, he formulates two conflicting notions of character that have their analogues in all of his thought. The character more suited to Marsh's inclinations encourages freedom and action in reponse to "the impulse of the moment." Its spontaneity and natural individualism suggest distaste for institutional authority. The other character, that of a "man among men," is mechanically "formed and maintained" and acts inflexibly but predictably according to preconceived and consistent principles. Society and his sense of Christian duty led Marsh to suppress his most natural self in favor of an artificial character that would facilitate social intercourse and support social values. While society rewarded conformity with reputation, presumably the spontaneous life of "mere intellectual greatness" threatened ostracism from society, but offered private satisfaction.

As Marsh's life stubbornly continued to shape itself along uncongenial lines, his outlook became increasingly deterministic. In 1830, he had counseled self-forgetfulness and hard work as the best tonic for personal doubts and disappointment. Unable to express his true self in the outside world, he took up "active duties which infer and induce oblivion of self."[53] Edwards had recommended such self-abandonment as an essential step in the progress of the soul toward God. But by selflessness he had intended unselfishness, the pursuit of divine rather than individual ends, generally quieting the demands of the self. In Marsh, however, the self spoke too loudly to be ignored and too persistently to be quieted. It had to be drowned out in a flood of frenetic activity. One had to keep too busy to notice.

By 1837, Marsh's personal encounter with the demands of duty and the expectations of society immobilized reflection and paralyzed the inner powers. "For a great part of my life," he mused, "I have felt myself chained to situations in which I felt myself paralyzed in the exertion of my powers and vainly longed for freedom. But I now feel that had I yielded less to such feelings, and gone out to do my utmost more or less in the sphere of duty in which I found myself placed, I should have saved myself vast trouble and done the world more good."[54] This description of the man of affairs longing for the chance to retire into spiritual contemplation but compliant to duty was the mainstay of Puritan rhetoric. But the Puritans adopted it largely as a literary convention, a strategy that would enable a biographer to treat his subject as the perfect Christian figure, at once removed from the world and active in it.[55] Marsh, in contrast, seems to have felt it as a real conflict, and he also seems to gain a peculiar satisfaction from contemplating his own misery.

In fact, Marsh's complaints may have had strategic benefits of their own. In describing his misplaced life, Marsh is creating a conservative American analogue of the English Romantic hero he both admired and feared. While the Byronic type revels in the genius that raises him above his fellows as a sort of compensation for his unavoidable alienation, Marsh, in the American style, lamented his inability to lead a private scholarly life while all the while pursuing a public one with a success that ought to have been embarrassingly evident. To compensate for life's restrictions, Marsh bowed meekly to duty in a way that implied his chosen status and the indispensability of his work. Thus he could both celebrate the value of his life as he had lived it and suggest still greater things for himself in the life that might have been.

After several years as president of the University of Vermont, Marsh brooded more and more on his longing for the freedom to pursue the answers to America's spiritual difficulties. His continuing inability to ease the financial burdens under which the university had suffered even before he became president hardened his conviction that he was unfit for the life in which providence had placed him. Repeatedly after 1832, Marsh complained of his discomfort at Vermont. He was invariably pessimistic about the present and future state of the university and condemned the effectiveness of his own leadership. Between 1833 and 1835, he contemplated a number of moves to other universities—Dartmouth, Yale, New York University—where, he convinced himself, he would be able to study and teach in peace. At Vermont, he felt debilitated by the financial duties of his office and longed for a life less in the public eye. Ignoring all objections to the contrary, he insisted that he had lost community support, that neither the university nor the public wanted him to stay on as president.[56]

While it is true that Marsh's administration had come under some criticism from those concerned about the financial stability of the university, Marsh's own assertion that he had been "dishonored" there, that "I am doing nothing and have done hoping to do anything while I remain here,"[57] seems plainly exaggerated. The unusual strength of his feelings on this matter in the absence of any real occasion for them suggests that Marsh viewed his own life in a highly symbolic light and that in his frustration with the distinctions of his administrative chores he cast himself in a classic American drama as a sort of latter-day Jonathan Edwards, America's lonely philosophical hero, scorned at home but appreciated abroad, hounded out of his official position and banished but freed thereby to complete his great work, to build a new American religious philosophy. Even in this respect, however, Marsh's life refused to fit his wishes. The Vermont Corporation reluctantly accepted his resignation from the presidency and allowed him to remain on strictly as a member of the faculty, free to teach and study without the distractions of fund-raising or the necessity of justifying the University's educational program to its critics. Even this change did not satisfy him, however, any more than the life of isolated study he pined for would have. The life he truly desired was an unattainable ideal, blending the best elements of the active and contemplative. He was trapped between irreconcilable philosophies, a victim of the American demand that he give his protean spirit a coherent and consistent social form.

Unable to discover this ideal form in life, Marsh turned more and more to his writing as a way to reconcile Christian duty and private study. "I am sometimes almost resolved to give up this vain attempt to act in public, and devote myself to study, till an opportunity to be useful as a literary man shall present itself. I am satisfied that I shall never do anything valuable in any other way; and the attempt only leaves such a feeling of discouragement and dissatisfaction with myself, as makes me unhappy and in the end unfits me for doing anything."[58] Marsh hoped to combine his natural inclinations and talents with the public requirements of his faith by using his pen as an instrument of broad social change. "Every man who can wield a pen," he wrote with unusually strong feeling born of his relief at having discovered a direction,

> and who sees the state and prospects of this country, ought to feel himself called on to use it in the promotion of moral principles and right views of religious and moral improvement. . . . I would aim . . . to influence the views of men, and rouse all who have the capacity to something of enthusiasm in promoting the solid and permanent moral interests and the highest happiness of this free and happy country. . . .[59]

Marsh envisioned his own writing as an analogue of faith, a mediating force capable of reunifying the country and mending the division between South and North, a division that simply expressed geographically the split in his own mind between faith and reason, freedom and duty, inclination and authority. Although Marsh lauded the South as the last refuge of spiritual fervor in the modern age and preferred its warmth and evangelical spirit to New England's rigid manners and unfeeling logic, his stay at Hampden-Sydney convinced him that slavery was burying Southern intellectuals in moral and intellectual lassitude. With his pen, Marsh planned to unify the nation and his own sensibility under a rational spiritualism that would blend Southern feeling and religious vitality with Northern moral fortitude and energy.

Unfortunately, Marsh's views of his writing were divided along lines identical to those dividing the nation and his own mind. On one hand, Marsh depended on his writing to bridge the gap between himself and the public of which he would have liked to feel himself a part. His writing provided the only intercourse possible between his innermost self and the outside world. At the same time, he recognized that his scholarship irrevocably separated him from those around him, both by removing him physically from public activity and by endowing him with knowledge and interests that distinguished him intellectually and spiritually from the common citizen. Marsh's instrument of mediation guaranteed his exclusion because it was itself a creature of the private world more than of the public. Living first in the mind, it owed its final allegiance there, and in its ultimate influence had to betray Marsh's intent.[60] Marsh could write about the world at any length, but with each word he removed himself one step farther from being a man in it.

ALTHOUGH MARSH desperately wished to feel a part of his society, his feeling of separation from it and his discomfort in socially prescribed roles reflect the degree to which New England religious institutions cramped his faith. In this sense, Marsh's plans to revise New England theology represent an attempt to reunite himself with his culture by displacing the theological assumptions that excluded him. Marsh had, at one time or another, lived through all the doubts that led to conflict among Orthodox and liberal factions. In his early years, he had hesitated between the opposed solutions offered by Unitarian moralism and Congregationalist legalism. Each had its appeal. Suspended over the "abyss" of "metaphysical depths," not even Marsh was utterly deaf to the call of Scottish Common Sense. "I find myself," he said in 1821, "too strongly inclined to admit Brown's theory, independently of the reasoning by which it is supported, from the simplicity which it introduces into all our speculations on the phenomena and powers of nature."[61] But at the same time, Marsh showed the influence of his Andover mentor, Moses Stuart, in his early retreat into the refuge of Scripture. In 1821, Marsh admitted, "I may question the origin and the authority of the Scriptures: but when I have admitted their divine original, I have only to ask what they teach."[62]

Ultimately, however, he found both positions untenable. Both seemed soulless to him; both were authoritarian and doctrinaire; both denied personal justification; both had lost to a degree the spirituality of earlier Protestantism that was being revived in the evangelical movements among the lower classes. In sharp contrast to most of his contemporaries in and out of Boston, Marsh was bent on getting at spiritual truth no matter how rough the road. Torrey notes that Marsh sought a more comprehensive system that "could meet more completely all the facts of his own consciousness and explain the deeper mysteries of his spiritual being."[63] As a young man still at Andover, he outlined his ambitions to his future wife:

> The man . . . who at this day undertakes to settle for himself the various systems of theology, must not only unravel the mysteries of 'fate, freewill, foreknowledge absolute, &c., without getting lost in their mazes, but while floundering in an everlasting 'hubbub wild' of ancient learning crazed, and made to dance, . . . to the 'harmonious discord' of some German Metaphysical bagpipe, he . . . must meet the theories of the philologist and the theories of the philosopher. He must silence, says one, every whisper of emotion, and let reason teach him. Listen to the heart, says another; it is the very sanctuary and the oracle of truth. . . . Truly, a man in such a course, if like Dante he has his Beatrice, or divine love for a guide, may arrive at heaven at last; but, like Dante, he must do it by first going through hell and purgatory.[64]

This passage is unusually metaphorical for Marsh, and it figures clearly his ambiguous posture—half Puritan, half Romantic. Marsh's appeal to Dante ties him to tradition in Christianity and in literature, and his determination to oppose the intellectual current and plunge into the "murky depth," to "settle for himself the various systems of theology," catches the tone of his pietistic Puritan mentality.

But his ambitions to unite intellect and emotion and the route of his intellectual pilgrimage to truth recapitulate a typically Romantic version of the Christian progress. By rejecting the easy solutions of the Common Sense philosophy, Marsh acted in what Perry Miller characterized as the true New England antinomian tradition, accepting "no helps from tradition or legend," ignoring "the props of conventions and the pillows of custom," and testing "all things by the touchstone of absolute truth."[65] His assertion that metaphysical salvation comes only by passing through painful experience might as easily have come from Wordsworth or Hawthorne.[66] Marsh could not set off on his exploration of the "deeper mysteries of his spiritual being" with the confidence of a Norton or a Taylor. Even with the guidance of divine love he could be only conditionally sure of reaching "heaven at last."

Yet Marsh scorned the limited truths of Unitarian philosophy. He would not swallow his faith secondhand from tradition. His dispute with the established theologies sprang from his conviction that God's "being has no relation to time. The absolute ground must be self grounded."[67] Defections from Orthodoxy and the obvious superficiality and secularism of Unitarianism convinced Marsh that, as Sydney Ahlstrom says, "Mid-eighteenth-century Edinburgh could not solve the problems of mid-nineteenth-century New England."[68] A new system was essential.

Marsh's search for this new route to theological and metaphysical certainty thrust him into the center of a peculiarly American intellectual debate. At odds were apparently polar values—tradition and originality, society and the individual, rationality and faith, the natural and the supernatural—conflicts that had been implicit in American culture from the start. They were posed by the very notion of democracy, but they had never achieved the pitch of interest they reached in the early nineteenth century when the need to define America coincided with threats to the social order and the growth of a new philosophy and science that cast doubts on the stability of any form. Marsh's position among the issues in this debate—or more accurately, his several positions—represent alternative strategies for resolving conflicts about individual power that had troubled

Americans for two hundred years. His very inability to formulate one fixed and authoritative stance, even for himself, reflects the unbridgeable distance that separated him from the official dogmatic assurance of the Puritans and located him on the borders of the problematic territory that we call Romanticism.

# 2

## Avatars of Coleridge:
## From Pauline Faith to Romantic Poetics

To reflect is to receive truth immediately
from God without any medium.
—Emerson, *Journals*

T HE TERMS in which Unitarians and Congregationalists endowed their oracles with absolute authority failed to recognize that all merely human truth is subject to change
in time. It is the product of human action and can therefore be
interpreted and altered by man. In short, its authority is conditional rather than absolute. For Norton or Taylor, the mind held
no mysteries. Its laws were known. They imitated the laws of
the universe. Even when Norton placed absolute truth beyond
man's reach, he did so with the deeper conviction that there
was no real need to bother about such metaphysical niceties
anyway, that all *important* truth was readily accessible. Orthodox scholars enforced revelation and applied modern tech-
niques of Biblical scholarship selectively, ignoring them when
they shook Scriptural integrity and citing them when they supported "timeless" doctrine. Both Orthodoxy and Unitarianism
rested their theologies on the conditional authority of tradition
and then tried to treat the truths they discovered there as if
they were "unconditioned and absolute."

In the New England of Norton or Stuart, God seemed still more aloof than he had two hundred years earlier, and neither Unitarianism nor Congregationalism provided a clear path to His door. Neither provided a "Way" to replace the abandoned "New England Way" of their grandfathers. Both substituted abstract knowledge for the spiritual journey that had constituted a Christian life. They had no way of linking the forms of religion, its philosophical structure, its doctrines, with the spiritual feelings that could give their religion life. Both the dominant sects failed to introduce the believer to God.

Marsh condemned Unitarianism and Congregationalism for their inability to accommodate expressions of personal faith. Yet despite his wish to return religious authority to the spiritual world, Marsh could not entirely abandon natural facts nor deny the changes that one hundred years of Lockean influence had made in America's religious attitudes; those changes were also a part of his own mind. In the nineteenth century, educated New Englanders demanded rationality even of their religion. To accommodate spiritualism to nineteenth-century intellectual demands, Marsh had to reshape it to accommodate the very rationalist standards that had stripped Puritanism of its spirituality. He had to make the supernatural rational.

Marsh wanted both to preserve traditional Christian doctrine with its vision of spiritual ascent or pilgrimage toward a supernatural goal and to strengthen an assurance that he imagined Christians had enjoyed before modern Biblical scholarship undermined Scriptural authority and empirical philosophy limited knowledge to the senses. He projected one comprehensive system of belief which would harmonize the physical and the spiritual. Torrey testifies to Marsh's quest for a self-validating system of inquiry that "would vindicate the results to which it led, by being one and identical with the constitution of the human intellect itself."[1] Marsh sought a new philosophy of the mind, one that would complement nineteenth-century optimism. Meyer Abrams characterizes such attempts to accommodate the traditional Christian progress to modern psychology and social realities as the essence of Romanticism,[2] and Marsh's engagement in it reveals how deeply the roots of American Romanticism are planted in nineteenth-century American theological controversy.

Marsh's dissatisfaction with authoritarian Orthodox and Unitarian theologies led him to the edge of American Romanticism. The whole journey was an attempt to define reason and the rational, to assess what man can expect to *know* in his world, to discover whether in fact it is actually *his* at all. He was convinced that Scripture alone could not speak to the problems of contemporary life, and he was equally unable to ignore Lockean skepticism or bask in the waters of Common Sense. So Marsh began an inquiry that gave him a unique perspective on American religion. In his reading, Marsh touched down at crucial points in the venerable Christian conflict between individual belief and institutional authority, incorporating into his thought as he went along elements left out of account by Orthodox and Unitarian thinkers. Collectively, these elements produced a new understanding of the mind, one that challenged the power of all authority, religious and social alike.

Marsh was trapped in what Perry Miller has called "the dilemma of a rational New England mind caught in shifting connotations of the word reason."[3] And his reformulation of reason to meet nineteenth-century spiritual needs provides a case study in the reflexivity of intellectual influence. Marsh's reason was no inherited or borrowed concept received passively from prior "sources." It was created in an intimate and complex negotiation among his own intentions, the current social and intellectual context, and the raw material of past thought. In this negotiation, Marsh's unspoken preconceptions and assumptions repeatedly overwhelmed the texts he examined. In his wide reading, Marsh was naturally attracted to writers who addressed issues (the relation between mind and faith) that spoke to his needs. But the ideas of these writers had been fitted for their original contexts, and when Marsh lifted them out of those contexts, blended them, and applied them to his own, they were subtly but profoundly altered. As a result, his own writings carry embedded implications of which Marsh himself was never aware, but which, to other eyes, proved infinitely suggestive.

The relations among these texts, and among the features that each produced out of the cultural contexts that originally gave them force, also produced a new language to describe the balance between human, institutional, and divine authorities. Each text added its own associations to this language, while the contradictions between them, the features that identify them as local to a particular time and place, disappeared for Marsh as he read them with an eye for his own personal and intellectual motives. The product is not a system of thought displaying formal philosophical coherence but an amalgam of elements taken from texts that had been themselves on the fringe of formal philosophy and that were tinged with what philosophers have, for their own reasons, branded as mysticism.

This amalgam subverts and evades those philosophical standards and even challenges their most fundamental assumptions. Specifying the relations among these texts helps us to distinguish the English Romantic view of the mind from Marsh's and Marsh's, in turn, from Emerson's, clarifying at the same time the motives that accompany the variant formulations. It helps us to isolate those components of Coleridge's thought that met Marsh's (and America's) needs. Finally, it enables us to place the American texts in their proper perspective as a part of a debate that had occupied western thought for two thousand years—as Coleridge would say, distinct, but not divided from alternate versions.

Marsh's reading took him in two apparently conflicting directions. For lessons in spiritual faith he read fervent, sometimes mystical writers whose works presented their personal experience in all its original revelatory power. But he also read more deliberate and systematic thinkers who avoided personal expression in order to give their work the intellectual force of analytical precision. The differences between these two literary preferences were also the differences dividing American theology—spirit v. form, piety v. system. Coleridge's thought, the final amalgam of Marsh's reading, seemed such a powerful model for a vital *public* faith perhaps because it resolved this split within his *private* spiritual and intellectual education.

St. Paul, the German Faith philosophers, and the English Romantic poets appealed to Marsh less for their systematic thought than for their personal enactment of spiritual experience. Marsh had already learned the sterility of a religious system apart from a truly Godly life. St. Paul was the heart and wellspring of Protestant spirituality, and Marsh turned to him repeatedly to replenish his faith in the inner spiritual voice. It was the Pauline spirit more than any formal philosophy that Marsh wanted to conjure up in the American heart and mind.

"We want men," he asserted, "who comprehending the philosophy and spirit of the age, have at the same time the spirit, the active zeal, and the eloquence of Paul."[4] The *Epistle to the Romans* gave Marsh, as it did all evangelically inclined Protestants, ammunition against orthodoxy in any form. To oppose the Hebrew orthodoxy, Paul had insisted on divine grace over law, spirituality over carnality, and personal participation in the mysteries of faith and in Christ's death and resurrection. Luther had used these convictions against the Church of Rome, the Puritans had used them against the Anglicans, and Anne Hutchinson and Roger Williams had used them against the Puritans. By using them against empirical religion in New England, therefore, Marsh extended a line of Christian pietism which in its appeal to individual faith rather than to institutional authority had been a defining characteristic of Protestant dissent. This tradition coincided neatly with American individualism and was in direct opposition to the Lockean model of a passive mechanical mind. The antinomian spirit of Protestantism is implicitly progressive in its call for a continual spiritual war against the secularizing forces of institutions. Yet, this progressive spirit most often expressed itself, as it did with Marsh, in reactionary language—the return to primitive Christianity. Thus the language of Paul could mobilize religious tradition in support of theological reform and redirected Orthodox nostalgia for the spiritual golden age into a sense of Christian mission.

Pauline pietism spoke to the most glaring deficiencies in Lockean experience. Paul offered a faith that was confirmed in spirit itself rather than in external authorities, one that naturally expressed the soul rather than imposing an artificial form from without. The authority of externals fell before the Pauline doctrine that this world, appealing as it might be, is a prelude to life, not life itself. The visible world, Paul confirms, exists only to be remade, transcended. Spiritual rebirth opens up the invisible spiritual world that offers the only true satisfaction, the only certain peace.

Above all, Paul gave Marsh an authoritative sanction for the transfer of the Christian drama from the external world to the internal. The story of Paul struck blind on the road to Damascus but freed by his affliction to turn inward, to develop his inner sight, took on special resonance when Marsh read it in the context of Locke's contention that there is nothing in the mind that was not first in the senses. For Scripture or tradition, Paul substituted conscience, the indwelling will of God immutable and absolute, as a guide to moral action. The place of the natural order within the divine is revealed. The partial is made whole, and, instead of seeing experience from the limited human perspective, the regenerate man views it through God's eyes as a perfect expression of His will. New England readers from John Winthrop on had expressed such "enthusiasm" to preserve the stability of the state. Paul's message did not encourage Marsh to tolerate the readiness in Boston or in New Haven to cultivate natural appearances rather than spiritual reality. Only the truth, the authority of the spirit could satisfy Marsh's need for a more direct relationship with God than either Unitarian moral admonitions or Orthodox doctrinal pronouncements could offer.

Thus, Paul shaped Marsh's opposition to the prevailing theologies as Marsh shaped Paul into an anti-Lockean polemicist for his new nineteenth-century Orthodoxy, making it supernatural, antiempirical, and individual. Although Paul spoke eloquently against rigid orthodoxies, however, he could not heal wounds that had been inflicted by modern science and philosophy. In the modern world, confidence in man's spiritual powers had to be reconciled to the authority of the external world that science had made an ineradicable part of the modern mind.

THIS responsiveness to nineteenth-century conditions was the distinguishing mark of the German faith philosophers[5] whom Marsh first discovered when he was studying under Moses Stuart at Andover. He found there a kindred pietist spirit dissenting, as he was, from Lockean materialism.[6] German theologians had adopted this spirit in response to religious needs very similar to Marsh's. Walzel asserts that the Platonism common to Marsh and the Germans appeared most strongly in thinkers who, like Hamaan, "were in particularly close touch with the religious, pietistic side of German thought and feeling rather than with the rationalistic side."[7]

Marsh's remarks about German philosophers other than Kant indicate that he shared their piety and their antimaterialist sentiments rather than their theological opinions. The Germans of the *Sturm und Drang* were antirationalists. They repudiated spirit-killing analysis and made a positive value of unreason. Hamaan's philosophy of irrationality supported faith and deflated the pride of intellect and class that dominated German culture at the time by dramatizing the gulf separating the divine mind from feeble human reason. He was outraged by claims to universality made by Germans or Americans in behalf of truths derived by the intellect. Such pride, he believed, led to the absurd conclusion that divine truth must correspond to the tastes of a specific age and place. On the contrary, Hamann suggested, God's ways so far transcend man's comprehension that they must appear irrational.[8]

While Marsh was excited by the freedom and the spirituality implicit in this notion, he could not accept its denial of the mind's powers. Similarly, although Herder influenced Marsh more than any other German thinker, Marsh never gave him his full approval. Marsh was attracted to Herder's religious spirit, his elevation of faith over dogma in religion and of feeling over discursive reason in poetry. But his particular interpretations of Christian doctrine were too radical for Marsh's Orthodox sensibility. "My belief is," Marsh wrote, "that such is the character and spirit of [Herder's *The Spirit of Hebrew Poetry*] taken as a whole, as to give it an influence highly beneficial to the cause of truth and of sound Biblical learning among us, if only it be read in the spirit that dictated it, and to correct in the general result, whatever individual errors of opinion it may contain."[9]

Just as Marsh looked inward rather than outward for spiritual truth, he learned from Herder to prize the *spirit* of a philosophy over its particular doctrines. In a vein that Ripley followed later against Norton, Herder argued that even the teachings of Jesus gain their power not from "tradition or authority" but from their own inward character.[10] In his review of Moses Stuart's *Commentary On Hebrews*, Marsh insists that to understand spiritual texts we must have in our hearts the spiritual realities to which they refer. This appeal to spirit over doctrine is one of the basic strategies by which idealists in all times have accounted for the difficulty of embodying spirit in an adequate form. Marsh used it to defend Stuart, Herder, and Coleridge. Later Frederic Henry Hedge would use it to defend Transcendental philosophy against Unitarian charges of obscurity. While Unitarians needed to understand in order to believe, the motto of the new philosophy (one which was shared, Marsh believed, by the earliest Christians and by the Cambridge Platonists) was the Augustinian injunction to "believe so that you may understand."[11] Hamann and Herder appealed to Marsh because of their pietistic effort to nurture a spiritual relationship between man and his universe in a rational age. They helped him to widen the narrow portals of analytic reason and to make room for an alternative view of experience. They failed, however, to provide a philosophical vindication of faith, and they strayed alarmingly from acceptable dogmatic positions. Their antirationalist limitation of reason to local and relative truths was too extreme for Marsh's tastes and too much like evangelistic rantings for his approval.

In the English Romantic poets, however Marsh found spirit enacted in a Christian life, and moral strength and spiritual vitality expressed in a passionate language that promised to satisfy his need for a practical faith.[12] Romantic poetry reminded Marsh of the spiritual fervor he admired in the sermons of seventeenth-century preachers and missed in the coldly formal, logically structured dogmatic discourses of his contemporaries. At first his preference for vitality in verse led him to Byron. Byron, Marsh wrote musing perhaps on the emotional poverty of his own life, "seems to live more than other men. He has conceived a being in his imagination of stronger powers, or greater capacity for suffering and enjoying than the race of mortals, and he has learned to live in him."[13] For Marsh, to feel and act with fervor was being itself, while mechanical, impersonal action amounted to spiritual nonbeing or death. All around him men professed Christian sentiments without manifesting the active spirit which Marsh felt should accompany their professions.

Marsh envied Byron's capacity for the emotional expression that gave form to his most profound feelings, and he wanted to incorporate it into a Christian life. "Why," he wrote in 1819, "should not the disciple of Christ feel as profoundly, and learn to express as energetically the power of moral sentiment as the poet or infidel?"[14] Marsh's affection for Byron represents the interest of Orthodox as well as liberal theologians in making the moral principle an influence that encourages poetic expression in literature rather than one that censors it, and suggests the essential moralism of the American Romantic movement.[15] Still, Byron revealed a bit too much of the infidel in the poet, and Marsh's affection for him, like his appreciation of the German idealists, was qualified from the first. Even as he confessed his envy for Byron's superhuman passions, he cautioned that his correspondent would "soon be tired of him as an example" and protested that he could never "approve his moral feelings or commend the moral tenor of his works."[16] Like many American readers caught in the conflicts of freedom and democracy, Marsh was put off by Byron's excesses as much as he was attracted to them. Uncontrolled passion, he feared, led too easily to license, and he sought a source of deep feelings united with moral discipline.

He discovered this union of feeling and discipline in the poetry of Wordsworth. William Charvat points out that with the critical discovery of Wordsworth, "American criticism seemed to sigh that there at last was what it had been looking for, spirituality without unintelligibility, vitality without sensuality, edification without didacticism, good workmanship, and finally, a type of romance satisfying to everyone in that it lifted the reader above the common life without taking him out of it."[17] Wordsworth's moral poetry of the common life answered Marsh's need for a poetic expression of practical, spiritual discipline. "There is in them," he said of Wordsworth and the other Romantic poets,

> a power of thought that elevates, enlarges, and strengthens the intellectual powers, while it elevates the whole soul, and fixes it in calmer seats of moral strength. It is the poetry that, of all, I would prefer to make my habitual study. Nor would I study it as I used to study poetry, but with a direct practical purpose to nurse my own faculties, to imbibe its spirit, to breathe its purity, and recurring constantly to the Gospel, the still purer fountain from which it derives its characteristic excellencies, to form that exalted character which should be the aim of every Christian.[18]

In Marsh's view, Wordsworth's poetry elevated the mind and the soul to the height of passionate experience, intellectual and spiritual, without risking the wild and dangerous flights that marred Byron's work. Although it did not answer Marsh's need for a philosophical system, it possessed the spirit of the Gospels, the eloquence of the seventeenth-century divines, and the reason which was so important to post-Enlightenment readers, and it embodied all of these not in a set of abstractions but in a poetics of common human experience. From Paul, the Germans, and the Romantics, Marsh distilled a kindred spirit of piety and spiritual energy. They encouraged him in his own personal faith, yet they did not suggest a way to externalize and systematize that faith. Simply *having* faith was not enough. Marsh shared the Puritan need to make piety available to reason and by that means to public view.

EACH generation of Americans had shared, in its own way, Marsh's belief that the mind could receive spiritual insight and that such insight could and ought to be expressed in systematic forms. What changed between 1620 and 1820 was the willingness of Americans to accept the conclusions of the unaided reason and, more importantly, to control those conclusions and justify them. The Puritans saw reason as an instrument of perception made defective by sin but still useful so long as it was governed by the rules of a formal logic, skirted mere subjectivism, and conformed to dogma. Ramus's logic-guided reason had provided the optimism without which rational activity would have been all but impossible in the stern Puritan world of depravity and human dependence. It promised that conclusions logically reached would be true for the natural world, and that men could grasp the order of the universe because it was essentially one with the order of the mind.[19] This fundamental coincidence between the orders of mind, nature, and Christian doctrine was the essence of the Puritan Technologia, and Puritan reason was responsible for discerning that unity despite differences of appearance. For Ramus, spiritual truth was not discovered or arrived at through a process of deduction. It was simply perceived. Such truth needs no proof. It carries its own validity by its very nature and the nature of Ramus's method for discerning it.

Marsh wished to reproduce this immediate certainty in a form appropriate to the nineteenth century. His aim, that is, was not to renew Puritan doctrine but to revivify the *structure* of Puritan faith, to *imitate* its formal features, supporting and justifying them with arguments that took into account two hundred years of theological and philosophical discourse. Marsh also shared with the Puritans an ambivalence about whether reason acted as an instrument for discerning truth or embodied truth in itself, representing God's image in the mind of man. The Puritans had found precedents for their view in Aristotle; Marsh found precedents for his in Plato. The Puritans were more inclined to describe reason as truth, and *logic* as its instrument, in conformity with their greater distrust of unaided or uncontrolled human action. Marsh's greater confidence in the mind permitted him to see truth as inward rather than external. By abandoning the Puritan reliance on an external instrument with which to unearth an external truth and control subjective wanderings, Marsh freed himself to see truth and the instrument for its discovery as inward and one, and this propelled him headlong into Romanticism.

IN HIS study of systematic philosophy, Marsh sought a balance between two authorities, one individual and subjective and the other social and objective. The former threatened spiritual anarchy, the latter dogmatic tyranny. As a mediator between these opposed forces, Marsh sought out writers who had been mediators for their own day between private and public visions of faith. At about the same time that he was studying Paul, Marsh also read Plato intensively and was particularly impressed by Plato's English Renaissance disciples, the Cambridge Platonists—Benjamin Whichcote, Henry More, and Ralph Cudworth—who *lived* Pauline spiritualism in the philosophical struggles of the seventeenth century.[20] The Cambridge Platonists supported Marsh's confidence in the spiritual correspondence between nature and the mind of man, his belief in the powers of human reason, and his distaste for philosophical materialism. As Marsh perceived them, they had conceived a sophisticated philosophical system to support spiritual religion and applied that speculative philosophy to the practical problems of Christian life.

Because of their role in the theological debates of the seventeenth century, the Cambridge Platonists seemed a nearly perfect model for Marsh's own attempts to rejoin New England's theological factions. They were removed by nearly two hundred years from the religious controversies that caused so much ill feeling in New England, and they were generally respected as mediators between the various English Protestant sects. Caught between a nascent confidence in secular reason and entrenched dogmatic orthodoxy, the Cambridge Platonists tried to correct the deficiencies and combine the advantages of each. On one hand, they disapproved of the flagrant immorality of secular manners and abhorred the spiritual vacuum created by materialist philosophy. But they were optimistic about the potential of a more potent intellectual reason, an optimism which bred impatience with Calvinist insistence on hopeless depravity and irrevocable predestination. In short, they tried to cultivate a hybrid theology, uniting the best of the contending systems and avoiding both spiritual aridity and dogmatic irrationality.[21] In Plato's philosophy the Cambridge Platonists found an authoritative model for the admixture of rationality and spirituality they needed. In early 1829, Marsh planned to publish selected writings of certain seventeenth-century theologians in order to reinject into public life the vitality that had seeped out of American religion during a hundred years of Lockean dominance. "The more intimate my acquaintance with them becomes" he wrote, "the more decidedly do they appear to me every way better fitted to make the religion of Christians 'inward' spiritual and instinct with spiritual life than the corresponding works in most general circulation among us."[22]

The core of English Platonism was Plotinus's notion that the soul cannot see divine beauty until it has first turned within and discovered that beauty there.[23] This insistence on man's indwelling divinity made the Cambridge Platonists seem to Marsh the perfect exemplars of devotion to the spiritual life. "Their minds," Marsh wrote, "were raised above the narrow peculiarities of a speculative system by a more habitual contemplation of the great fundamental truths of reason and revelation. They had formed themselves, and aimed to form others, to the habit of intense and earnest *reflection* upon their own moral and spiritual being, and retired inward in order to ascend upward."[24]

This Christian version of Platonic meditation rested on an emanation theory of creation in which Meyer Abrams discerns the source of the organic metaphor so important to the Romantics. The Cambridge Platonists envisioned the universe as a complete and unified whole, beginning and ending in God, with each part sustained by divine energy. In man, this energy took the form of the "seeds of light" planted in the mind.[25] These were the object of the reflection the Cambridge Platonists recommended, for having discovered them one could ascend with them in their return to their divine source. This Cambridge Platonist philosophy offered an alternative to Lockean knowledge, a model for breaking down the barriers between the cold rationality of Lockeanism and religious feeling. Benjamin Whichcote, the father of Cambridge Platonism, prefigured Marsh's position when he wrote, "I oppose not rational to spiritual, for spiritual is most rational."[26]

The language of human reason in which the Cambridge Platonists had embodied their idealism helped Marsh to articulate an intellectually defensible faith. He adopted their imaginative redefinition of reason as the divine intellect in the human mind to support his view of "intense and earnest *reflection*" as a nonlogical process that requires a leap of faith and leads to personal participation in, rather than intellectual understanding of, the Christian mysteries. Like the Cambridge Platonists, Marsh used "reason" and "rational" to denote a "divine and supernatural light" that suffuses creation and unites it into an organic whole to which man gains access by God's grace. This rhetorical strategy made the spiritualist pill that Marsh wanted to administer more palatable to his audience, which had learned to restrict truth within the straight walls of the intellect.

And yet, the Cambridge Platonists were important to the development of Marsh's thought precisely because he viewed them through the distorting lenses of his own biases and needs. He recognized only that element of their philosophy which worked to keep man's spiritual lamp burning in opposition to the new philosophies of Descartes and Hobbes.[27] In fact, the Cambridge Platonists formulated their system in response to theological problems that were in many respects quite different from Marsh's. By stressing the soul's moral state in the here and now rather than its preparation for divine salvation, and by arguing that God's laws are good independent of his divine authority (that he decrees them because they are good, not that

they are good because he decrees them), the Cambridge Platonists actually prepared the way for the movement into eighteenth-century rationalism. In this sense they were the counterparts of early American Arminians like Colman or Mayhew,
who also found support in Plato for their inclination to give
man more control over his own spiritual fate. Moreover, the
simple fact that the Cambridge Platonists wrote before Locke
prevented them from speaking directly to the needs of nineteenth-century New England. They had aimed primarily to
make a greater place for the intellect in an age which they saw
as excessively enthusiastic. Although they recognized Hobbes
as a threat from the materialist pole, less obviously materialistic systems such as Descartes's strongly attracted them. Marsh,
of course, faced precisely the opposite situation. He was struggling toward a rational statement of spiritual philosophy that
would recognize and respond to the materialist bias of nineteenth-century thought.

In his further reading in German philosophy, Marsh discovered the writings of Immanuel Kant and found an elaborate
speculative philosophy that combined philosophical precision
with a spiritual rebuttal of the Lockean materialism he objected to in Edwards. While Hamann and Herder expressed
spiritual fervor, Kant, as Marsh viewed him through Coleridge's
eyes, outlined the philosophical *system* Marsh needed to return
spirituality to metaphysics in American thought. In his first
reading of Kant, Marsh depended heavily on Coleridge's interpretation to smooth over the difficulties of Kant's language, and
as Marjorie Nicolson has observed, at this early stage Marsh
was not fully aware of the differences between Kant's concept of
the mind's relation to nature and his own.[28] But Marsh's writings soon display a more sophisticated understanding of Kant's
thought, coinciding with a deliberate attempt to fit it to American needs. Marsh did not share Kant's willingness to accept an
irreconcilable tension between man's physical and spiritual
faculties; Kant's separation of nature and reason would only
have frustrated Marsh's union of sensual and spiritual truths,
a motive which was central to his thought since it promised
a spiritual ideal that Kant put beyond man's ken. Kant con-
tented himself with the *likelihood* of divine superintendence,
but Marsh needed certain knowledge of it. Consequently, Marsh

revised the Kantian separation of reason and understanding, making the understanding subordinate to but not separate from reason.

Though we might say with some justice that Marsh's thought is simply Kant's with the addition of God's grace, it is too simple to say, as critics generally have, that Romantic writers ignore, overlook, or misunderstand the distinction between Pure and Practical Reason. Kant's limitations on the Practical Reason rested on his conviction that certainty is impossible in the absence of intuitively given materials for reason to work on. Since supersensible truth cannot, Kant argued, be given in that way, reason has no proper object of study. Marsh argued, on the other hand, that even without grace, reason could turn inward to reflect on its own workings as the best example of divine order available to man. The absolute *proof* that this order is valid comes only, he felt, with *experience*—the experience of grace, which joins human and divine reason. Kant denied that such reflection proves the truths it offers; he denied it because he sought truth in the *scientific* sense, that is, as a proposition that could be demonstrated and objectively verified. Marsh, however, like the Cambridge Platonists, saw reflection as leading to grace and argued that in the inward *experience* of grace lies the *only* certain knowledge of spiritual truth. For Marsh, these truths not only did not need to be proved in Kant's sense, they transcended utterly the very possibility of such proof.

Just as Paul and the Cambridge Platonists helped Marsh shift the scene of the Christian drama to the mind, Kant helped him reconstitute the vast metaphysical gulf separating the internal and the external as a psychological distinction between two complementary mental powers, understanding and reason. With Kant's help, Marsh was able to argue from *a priori* principles of the mind to God, and to argue against mechanism in favor of dynamism. By combining a Platonist view of reason as transcendent truth itself with Kant's notion that reason actively shapes truth rather than passively receiving it, Marsh discovered a Romantic philosophy of the spirit, a philosophy he then rediscovered in the writings of Samuel Taylor Coleridge.

As John Dewey pointed out, "all the circumstances conspired" to bring Marsh and Coleridge together.[29] Coleridge fused the spiritual fervor, practical piety, and moral strength of German idealist philosophy (and English Romantic poetry), with the systematic metaphysics of Edwards, the Cambridge Platonists, and Kant. To Marsh's eyes he was a modern Cambridge Platonist and hence the ideal instrument for promoting spiritual religion in New England. His writings not only manifested all the qualities Marsh admired in the Cambridge Platonists but applied them to the problems of the nineteenth century. Marsh had been planning an edition of seventeenth-century theologians to introduce a new philosophy into American religion, and Torrey testifies that when Marsh read Coleridge's *Aids to Reflection*, he was struck "with the adaptedness of the work to the very end which he had himself proposed. . . . The opportunity which thus offered itself, of introducing both Leighton and Coleridge to the American public, was one, he thought, which ought not to be neglected."[30]

Without attempting here a full treatment of Coleridge's remarkable theology, we can identify those elements most prominent in Marsh's perception of Coleridge's thought. Marsh and Coleridge started out in their searches for a satisfactory theology from similar spiritual convictions. Like Marsh, Coleridge gave instinctive emotional assent to Christian truth, but for years he labored to discover arguments that would prompt rational assent as well.

> I will here record my experience. Even when I meet with the doctrine of regeneration and faith and free grace simply announced "so it is!" then I believe; my heart leaps forth to welcome it. But as soon as an explanation or reason is added, such explanations namely, the reasonings as I have anywhere met with, then my heart leaps back again, recoils, and I exclaim, Nay! Nay! but not so.[31]

A comparison of the routes traveled by Coleridge and Marsh in their progress toward spiritual certainty reveals a significant distinction in their priorities. For Marsh, doctrine always came first. As we have seen, his faith in Congregationalist dogma never wavered. His philosophical energies were directed to finding a system that would justify those doctrines, and he was ready to accept any philosophy that would do so without making a farce of reason.

Coleridge's stance toward doctrine was far less consistent. It has become a commonplace of Coleridge criticism to say that his emotional commitment to Christianity preceded any demands for philosophical rigor. But for all its broad truth, this easy generalization distorts Coleridge's religious odyssey in two important ways. First, it ignores the circuitous route Coleridge took to reach his ultimately orthodox position, a route that took him through years of commitment to Hartlean associationism, to mechanical explanations for human action and even human emotion, and to Unitarianism and a Socinian denial of Christ's divinity. Coleridge's long flirtation with these views, which he later considered antithetical to true Christianity, suggests that he prized philosophical consistency and intellectual respectability far more than the commonplace explanation would admit. Still more importantly, arguments that give Coleridge's emotional need for Christianity priority over his need for rational justification necessarily misconstrue the whole drift of Coleridge's thought. They limit their view to one side of a polarity that Coleridge struggled all his life to maintain in all its uneasy tension. While Marsh was willing to subordinate intellectual rigor to doctrinal stability, Coleridge's dialogue between head and heart had always to be carried on with no hope of an ultimate victor. Coleridge's victory was in the dialogue itself.

This demand for a balance between intellect and emotion placed Coleridge in a peculiar position among theological disputants, one which almost guaranteed that his thought would meet with more confusion and misinterpretation than approval and assent. Theological debate in England as in America depended on the acknowledgment of external authorities (marshaled by Hartley or Paley) often combined with the persuasive power of an almost scholastic logic (in the hands of Newman and others). But by the time Coleridge had developed his mature thought in *Aids to Reflection*, he had decided that all theology that began in external authorities must end in Pantheism rather than in Christian Orthodoxy, and, following Plato, he turned, as Leibniz and Kant had before him, to the primacy of the self, of the personal spirit, as the cornerstone of his faith.

This alternative committed Coleridge to an argumentative strategy with which he was himself partly uncomfortable and which his opponents could hardly be expected to comprehend at all. While they began with the things of the world and ended consistently by positing a Pantheist notion of God as the great sum of all things, the divine validator of a complete and perfect system, Coleridge had to maintain his grip on two worlds, that of things which was the *only* world for his opponents, and the world of the self, of the spirit, of God, which was his own starting place but in which he could not rest as the materialists could in things.[32] The two were intimately linked but did not coincide. Though the material world expressed the spiritual, it did not express spirit fully. In fact, it was one of Coleridge's premises that spirit could never be fully expressed in the objective world, for that would be to make spirit an object. By the same token, spiritual *theology* could never be fully expressed in a completed system, since discursive language and systematic logic led inevitably to a philosophy of things. It was just this view that prompted Coleridge's readers in England and America to label his thought "insubstantial," to fault it for its lack of "solidity," metaphors which identify their differences from Coleridge more accurately than they could have suspected. Coleridge argued, on the other hand, that spiritual ideas were necessarily distinct from the forms in which the world manifests them. It was, he believed, the fatal error of materialist philosophy to mistake manifestation for essence. True ideas, he believed, could never find full expression in objective forms and could not be truly known simply by examining such forms.

At a time when most theologians were arguing over the merits of various evidences for belief in one or another version of Christian revelation, Coleridge took the radical step of abandoning objective verification entirely. The chore for Coleridge was to maintain this view without falling into mysticism with Occam or Boehme, whose views he found unacceptable despite their influence on his own thought. Coleridge maintained that he could not, and would not, offer proofs for his views. Certainty depended, he argued, on personal religious experience beyond the power of human proof or, for that matter, disproof. He proposed a philosophical justification of religious experience for those who *had* such experience, not a *proof* of Christian revelation for those who had not. Proof then, the pivot of theological debate at the time, played no part in his plans. He knew that he could not prove that the world worked according to the Christian dispensation, but he hoped to demonstrate that we must *believe* that it works that way if we are to believe that it works at all. He sought, not to make faith meet rational standards, but to provide a rationale which the faithful could use to fend off attacks on their suprarational beliefs.

Coleridge's philosophy of the two worlds depended on a distinction between two powers of the mind. One, the understanding, rules primarily over the world of things that are identifiable and subject to discursive description; the other, the true or higher reason, rules the world of ideas or spirit. It stands beyond identification or definition and is not subject to generalization precisely because it is the *unconditioned ground* of *all* generalization. Students of Coleridge's philosophy generally agree that his distinction between reason and understanding combines the substance of English Neo-Platonism with terminology from Kant's critical philosophy.[33] But this view ought not to be taken, as it often is, to mean that Coleridge's philosophy simply superimposed Kantian vocabulary on Cambridge Platonist idealism. In fact, Coleridge was dissatisfied with *both*, and using hints from each he established a position very much his own.

The Cambridge Platonists' theology spoke out strongly for a religion of the heart, a practical and personal faith, but because they had not been forced to confront the imposing authority of empirical truths, they saw no reason to account for that authority in their system. They failed therefore to even *make* the distinction between reason and understanding which was so central to Coleridge's thought. Moreover, since Locke had not yet offered his portrait of the mind as a blank canvas, the Cambridge Platonists felt comfortable with a version of reason that combined characteristics of a divine light cast into the mind by God with qualities of particular innate ideas. Kant's thought, in turn, demonstrated two major flaws. Unlike the Cambridge Platonists, he gave insufficient weight to the feelings in religious matters. He was, as Coleridge said, "a wretched psychologist."[34] Moreover, while he formulated for Coleridge just the distinction he needed between two mental powers, reason and understanding, he stopped disappointingly short of investing reason with the absolute authority in spiritual matters which Coleridge needed to nail down his own theological position. In essence, Kant had framed the entire design for Coleridge's house of faith, had built the superstructure, the walls, roof, and windows, and had then left it hanging alarmingly without the foundation that would make it sound and stable.

Coleridge completed this foundation by transforming Kant's reason, expanding its powers beyond the merely regulative (that is, capable of ordering or guiding our perception of reality) until they came actually to constitute reality itself. Such a power effects the direct access to truth on spiritual issues—immortality, God, freedom, the soul—that Coleridge sought. While Kant argued that the practical reason could not produce authoritative statements about reality because it had no proper objects of thought, Coleridge provided his "higher" reason with just such an object, reason itself, the personal "I Am," and ultimately through self-reflection, the divine "I Am."

Coleridge has often been accused of giving a scope to Kant's Practical Reason that cannot be justified within the framework of a critical philosophy. But such criticisms clearly judge Coleridge by the very standards of proof that he wished to supplant. He was engaged in an altogether different sort of enterprise. He repeatedly urged that the only "proof" of the powers of reason was in the *experience* of them. Reason grounded—*made* sense of—all experience, transforming diversity into unity, linking nature and spirit. To the question "How?", Coleridge answered simply, "Look!" Since the links between man and nature and between man and God existed only in the immediate experience of them, they could only be fully apprehended there and could never be adequately described in an objective form. The openendedness of Coleridge's system of thought, its refusal to stand still for logical inspection, is a frustrating but necessary corollary to his view of reason.

A system founded on an alogical, spiritual faculty must appeal for its ultimate verification not to any external logic but to its own generative principle. For all of Coleridge's attempts to delineate its characteristics, his own most successful version was inevitably metaphorical. "Without being either the sense, the understanding, or the imagination, it contains all these within itself, even as the mind contains its thoughts and is present in and through them all; or as the expression pervades the different features of an intelligent countenance." Reason itself never appears whole in the day-to-day world of the understanding. The understanding perceives the world schematically. It divides and categorizes, generalizes and abstracts, and in doing so only confirms our alienation from the world it manipulates, telling us much about the *mechanism* of nature but nothing about its *life*. Everyday perception takes in only manifestation and denies, as we have seen, the very existence of the province of reason. Consequently, all the worldly relationships that owe their explanations to alogical reason appear to the understanding as logical contradictions or absurdities. In fact, as Coleridge said, it is a "test and sign" of *spiritual* reality that it "can come forth out of the moulds of the understanding only in the disguise of two contradictory conceptions."[35]

Here is the source of all the popular objections to Christian doctrine as offensive to logic. Coleridge appealed for doctrinal validity to authority beyond logic, and for conviction to personal experience rather than objective proof. Logic could never convey the truths of reason on which the resolution of apparent contradictions depended. Such truth required a less concrete but more resonant mode of expression. In the *Biographia*, Coleridge remarks that "An IDEA, in the *highest* sense of that word, cannot be conveyed but by a *symbol*."[36] A symbol, by conveying the *experience* of mystery, transcended logic and created a momentary window into reason where logical contradiction assumed a new form that reconciled opposites without dissolving distinctions.

Coleridgean reason revealed the contradictions of the understanding (including that between reason and understanding themselves) as *polar unities*. The barriers that divided man and nature, man and God, form and spirit, responsibility and freedom, finite and infinite all disappeared and these terms appeared as mutually generative, interpenetrating manifestations of the same essential truth. Coleridge's notion of polarity is deceptively similar in appearance to the concept of compromise, but is fundamentally different in its implications. Compromise preserves the logical separation of terms, suggesting a mix of essentially divided elements that cannot be joined without losing something of their natures (black and white mixed to produce grey), a balance achieved only by a certain sacrifice on the part of each member in the interests of unity and harmony. Polarity, by contrast, does not "compromise" (the alternate meaning is instructive) the identity of either pole. There is no blurring of boundaries. Each pole remains perfectly distinct but utterly dependent on the other, without which it could not be said to exist at all. Rather than enclosing or limiting, polarity is creative, expansive, and generative. It produces and enlivens phenomena and opens up a larger world of reference for them, turning mere empirical facts into suggestive manifestations, routes of access to the spiritual powers which alone can give them *meaning.* This was the most important power of reason, to revalue the world of understanding. Without reason, the phenomena of understanding are only fragments. Individuality itself would lack the qualities that distinguish it from mere difference or separateness. Thus reason, which *transcends* the individual, also enables individuality. It is both transcendent and individual, many and one.

This final quality of reason was essential to Coleridge's spiritual motives, and those motives were never very far, were scarcely even distinguishable, from his philosophical inquiries. The demand for unity in the phenomena of consciousness required a unifying power, reason, with aspects both individual and transcendent. Similarly, the demand for unity in the apparent fragmentation of worldly phenomena required the existence of an eternal and immutable One, distinct from the world yet not separate from it. The only way to maintain both the distinctness and the presence of this transcendent One was, to Coleridge's mind, the doctrine of the Trinity—a power both spiritual and incarnate, one and yet also many—that put the capstone on his philosophy and on his emotional need for spiritual conviction. Thus the triune God acts as the ultimate guarantor of Coleridge's settlement of the Cartesian conflict between self and other, converting it into a mutually creative polarity encompassing interdependent modes of the self.

In his reading from Paul to Coleridge, we see Marsh entertaining seriously ideas whose erosive force he simply could not grasp—even when they raised such serious doubts in his own mind—because he could not imagine them apart from his own Orthodox context. He maintained to the end the optimistic conviction that enough knowledge, obtained and applied in the right spirit, would clear up all doubts at last. But Marsh could not foresee either the full difficulty of the problem—the distortions his own mixed feelings would introduce into the discussion—or the multiple appearances of his work as it was viewed from the varied angles of theological dispute. Ultimately these factors played as great a part in constituting the meaning and import of Marsh's *Aids* as did all of its sources.

# 3

## UNDERSTANDING REASON:
## Inventing an American Faith

And Coleridge, too, has lately taken wing,
But like a hawk encumber'd with his hood,
—Explaining metaphysics to the nation—
I wish he would explain his explanation.
—Byron, *Don Juan*

ARSH, LIKE Emerson, first encountered Coleridge in *Biographia Literaria* in 1819, and from that time on he became increasingly fascinated by his thought.[1] In his first letter to Coleridge, on 23 March 1829, Marsh acknowledged his interest and his debt.

> From my first knowledge of your "Literary Life" some ten years ago I have sought, as my opportunities would permit, a more intimate acquaintance with your writings and with your views on all the great and important subjects of which you have treated. . . . I am aiming to introduce some little knowledge of your own views through the medium of a religious journal *The Quarterly Christian Spectator*. . . . In the last number of the Journal alluded to . . . I have a review of Professor Stuart's Commentary on Hebrews, in which I have given a view of the Atonement, or rather of redemption, I believe nearly corresponding with yours, and indeed have made free use of your language.[2]

Coleridge's thought seemed to Marsh particularly well suited to the problems that plagued New England theology. The philosophical center of Marsh's attraction to Coleridge was Coleridge's association of self-knowledge with universal truth, of part with whole, private with public, expanding the power of each individual to apprehend moral and spiritual absolutes. By locating man's moral being in the supersensual faculty of reason, Coleridge endowed each individual with the *immediate access to an unconditioned truth* denied by Orthodox and Unitarian alike. He conceived of *Aids* from the first as an instrument with which young men, especially clergymen, could validate truths attained by individual meditation.[3] His aim, as Charles Sanders argues, was "to catholicize Protestantism without losing what Protestantism had always cherished most—confidence in the power and in the right to inquire."[4] This intention corresponded with Marsh's search for an access to the absolute which did not infringe on intellectual freedom. Marsh valued the individual spiritual perception at the core of Protestant dissent, and he also knew that if individual insight did not produce universal truth, it would end in spiritual anarchy. Coleridge's concept of a supernatural faculty in man analogous to the divine reason guaranteed the universality of truth perceived by individuals.

Coleridge altered Kant's definitions of reason and understanding and applied what had been an essentially psychological system in Kant to religious problems. In doing so he supported Marsh's more narrowly theological efforts to inaugurate a new age of spiritual fervor, to join empirical evidence and faith, and to make religion an active force in changing the world. As Ronald Wells points out:

This distinction [between reason and understanding] . . . was the way out from the inadequacies of the prevailing brand of Lockean philosophy and Scottish intuitionism. The popular philosophy of the day made reflection secondary, if not subservient, to sense. In concrete terms, the currect doctrines seemed to Marsh to exclude any truly spiritual religion because they did not take into account self-knowledge. God, freedom, and immortality had no objective status, because reason was tied down to the understanding of sense data. There was no such thing as a spiritual power differing from nature and yet this idea was central to the Christian faith.[5]

Coleridge reconciled epistemology and spiritual vision, giving man a faculty with which he could perceive universal religious and philosophical truth. Marsh thought that he had discovered this same system in the Cambridge Platonists, but Coleridge applied it to the problems of post-Lockean religious controversy that the Cambridge Platonists could not have foreseen. Marsh's own revolutionary redefinition of reason—the fulcrum on which he tried to balance the elements of a rejuvenated faith—reveals both his desire to resurrect the Puritan religious spirit and his recognition that he could not do so without using the tools of Enlightenment thought that had hastened the demise of Puritanism.

Reason simply did not hold the terrors for Marsh that it had for Thomas Hooker or even for Cotton Mather. Less frightened of its possible excesses, Marsh saw less need than his predecessors to impose systematic controls on it and was content to identify it with reason in the mind of God. Thus he managed to absorb a Puritan vision of reason as a method of perception without the Puritan need to restrict reason within rigid logic. And he could imitate an eighteenth-century confidence in the limitless potential of the mind without the Enlightenment need to confine it to universal principles and agreement with a body of commonly held assumptions. Though Marsh tacitly supported reason with both logic and science, these, too, took new shapes that reflected his methodological bias. Logic became the study of the mind's laws rather than a mechanical system for testing the truth of particular propositions, and science became the perception of the universal moral truths that sustained the world of appearances rather than the observation and analysis of empirical facts.[6] This attention to enlivening spiritual law rather than to mechanical system or material appearance was fundamental to Marsh's need to invoke the spirit of Puritanism while retaining many of the rational biases of the Enlightenment.

Marsh needed both a new formulation of traditional doctrine and *a new and complementary view of the mind*. The conflict he shared with his countrymen was an epistemological one, a contest between different sorts of knowledge. In American theology, Orthodox and Unitarian churchmen impressed by Locke espoused objective sources of religious authority—Scripture and tradition respectively. In the theological quarrels between them, these differing allegiances appeared as the incompatibility of religion and philosophy. Congregationalists distorted current philosophical systems to fit revelation while their Unitarian counterparts evolved doctrine to complement their philosophy, which in turn mirrored their pragmatic view of life.

In the struggle between these two factions, Marsh believed, the powerful psychological appeal of empirical knowledge gave Unitarians an important advantage. Empirical fact, Marsh points out, "impresses itself by the force and evidence of intuition involuntarily upon the mind and never ceases to influence us." Faith, however, is more fleeting. It "quietly shuts itself up in the interior of the soul and springs up only in the depths of our being and is feebly sustained by that reflection in which it manifests itself."[7] Under this disadvantage, philosophy and science would certainly displace ephemeral faith unless religious truth could be endowed with comparable certainty. This was the motive for the spiritual philosophy Marsh would adapt from Coleridge. "The proper business of a philosophising reason is to receive this principle of faith under its protection, to vindicate its claims and to set off faith as clearly as possible in its distinction from knowledge." For, if faith is "confounded with knowledge, faith can only suffer loss."[8]

To oppose the compelling authority of externals, Marsh offers inward truths. It is fruitless, Marsh argued, to seek answers to ultimate questions in external authorities:

The principles, the ultimate grounds of [religion, philosophy, and morals] . . . must be sought and found in the laws of our being, or they are not found at all. . . . It is by self inspection, by reflecting on the mysterious grounds of our own being, that we can alone arrive at any rational knowledge of the central and absolute grounds of all being. It is by this only, that we can discover that princi-

ple of unity and consistency, which reason instinctively
seeks after . . . and destitute of which all the knowledge
that comes to us from without is fragmentary and . . . but
the patch-work of vanity.

Consciousness, Marsh wrote, reveals far more about spiritual
truths and is "far more wonderful than all the phenomena of
the world without."[9] William Paley and his followers made an
industry of using nature as evidence for God's rationality and
conformity to law, and Unitarians gratefully turned his methods against Calvinism. But Orthodox churchmen, Marsh among
them, were quick to point out the dangers of moving from generalizations about nature to generalizations about God. As
Marsh said, reversing Paley, "one cannot pass from the watch to
the watchmaker."[10] A safer, though more arduous, method was
to move from the spiritual in man to the divine source of all
spirit with "the same rules and cautions" used in investigations
of external phenomena.[11] Marsh was advocating nothing less
than a scientific philosophy of the human spirit, a diversion of
the mind's attention from its environment to its own workings,
as a route to direct, rather than second-hand, knowledge of
spiritual truth. "To know ourselves scientifically, or philosophically," Marsh cautioned, "must of necessity be the most deep
and difficult of all our attainments in knowledge." But, in light
of the possible rewards, he insists on the necessity of going on-
ward, "with faith in the human mind."[12]

Marsh's desire to bring philosophy and religion together in
one harmonious system was, at least to his own way of thinking, also a desire to return to the ordered universe he imagined
the Puritans had enjoyed before Locke misled the world into excessive reliance on objective appearance. Yet his insistence on
the compatibility of religion and philosophy and his faith in the
mind bespeak his kinship with liberalizing forces in eighteenth-
century religion that were the flowering of the Enlightenment.
In fact, this stance puts him ahead of eighteenth-century rationalists and abreast of such radicals as the Transcendentalists
in that, like the latter, he acknowledged the essential myste-
riousness of religious truth and desired to expand reason to
meet mystery. He wished to incorporate the historical develop-

ments that Unitarianism and Orthodoxy ignored in a new religious philosophy that would resurrect what Larzer Ziff has called the "a-historical" structure of American Puritanism: antitraditional, individualistic, antiinstitutional, and antiauthoritarian.[13] The conservative factions, on the other hand, whether Orthodox or Unitarian, separated reason and religion because they entertained comparatively mean opinions of one or the other. Calvinists found reason a frail handle by which to grasp religious truth, while Unitarians distrusted religious feeling and found doctrine logically absurd.

Marsh applied Coleridge's reason to the link between subject and object in order to defend Orthodox doctrine from charges of absurdity. While Unitarians denied spiritual mysteries that were not subject to logical analysis, Marsh acknowledged that certain mysteries were beyond human *understanding* but asserted that they ought not therefore to be rejected as false. Instead, they should be illuminated by the inner light of *reason*, which radiated not from sense data but from the individual spirit to reveal a universal order. Coleridge not only helped Marsh explain how Christ could be both God and man, rebutting Unitarian objections to Orthodoxy; he also accounted for the God in each man and in the natural world, uniting God, man, and nature in a philosophically respectable spiritual system.

Marsh laid the foundation for the American version of this new spiritual philosophy by taking reason out of its conventional empirical context and linking it with the divine. Reason, Marsh said, is *not* intellection, it "is the actuation in us, of that universal power which is the real ground and actual determinant of all living action, and one with the power and life of nature."[15] As long as reason depended on empirical knowledge, the mind would remain subservient to nature and could not ascend to spiritual vision. In order to avoid overemphasizing the powers of the mind at the expense of feeling or the authority of the senses which made the mind dependent on natural facts, Marsh had to make reason embrace the qualities of both spirit and nature. He aimed to resolve the split between nature and the mind by uniting the process of self-discovery with the discovery of nature. He avoided uncontrolled subjectivism by employing the empirical reality of nature to restrain the potentially dangerous flights of individual fancy, and he avoided the opposite extreme of materialistic determinism by subordinating those natural facts to their spiritual correlatives in the reason—the fundamental God-given principles of the mind.

He described the products such a system would produce as "the men who shall put to flight the phantasms and hollow abstractions of an unfruitful and lifeless system of speculation, shall lead us to the true knowledge of ourselves, and of that living and spiritual philosophy, which elevates knowing into being, which is at one with the truth of the gospel, and which, beginning with the fear of God, terminated in the adoring love and holy participation of his divine nature." [16] Marsh believed that the universe operates according to a consistent set of spiritual laws, and that faith alone, without the instruction of reason, cannot comprehend those laws. "It is the evil heart of unbelief," he wrote, "that we have reason to fear as the perverter and misinterpreter of truth. . . . We are of the number of those who believe that, in the legitimate and conscientious employment of our understandings and rational powers, we are bound to follow truth with our whole hearts; and that in so doing, even though we might not attain it, we could not be at war with it." [17] The significant phrase here is "whole *hearts*," which Marsh designates to guide our "rational powers"—"hearts" to distinguish the powers of spiritual inquiry from the practical reasoning with which most Americans were familiar, and "whole" to identify them as the powers at the center of our being rather than the whimsical affections.

Marsh's earliest references to Coleridge demonstrate that the interdependence of subject and object, the identity of the thing perceived and the mind that perceives it, was from the first one of Coleridge's greatest appeals for Marsh. In "Ancient and Modern Poetry," Marsh writes, "to our imagination as to our faith what we see is shadow, and all beyond is substance. It is not the visible itself, which we regard, but that, which looks out from 'behind the elements,' and like the bright eye of the Ancient Marinere [sic] attracts and fixes our attention, as by a magic power." [18] This early formulation of the power that Marsh would later call reason, a moral and spiritual sympathy be-

63

tween man and the transcendent reality of nature, suggests the place of Coleridge's philosophy in Marsh's struggle against Locke. Marsh subsumes faith and imagination, religion and art, nature and mind under a spiritual "magic power" with which man can "sympathize," a power in the mind and in nature that joins them in an interdependent unity.

In Marsh's system truth lay in no extreme but in a balanced relationship between nature and the mind, a relationship that consists in "action and reaction."[19] This process implies that the mind develops by its reflections on its own workings in response to external reality. Its powers are called into action by external phenomena. The senses feel, hear, see, smell, and taste; the understanding organizes sense data into knowledge; and reason appears as the mind's awareness of its own ordering principles. Thus, while the highest spiritual faculty of man, the reason, arises in response to the perception of sense data, it does not merely respond to external stimuli without exerting any influence of its own on external nature. Each spiritual potential of the self can be realized only by finding its correlative object in the external world.

It was *crucial* for Marsh to preserve the integrity of both nature and mind in an organic system, steering a course between antinomianism and Arminianism. Arminianism grows from excessive confidence in natural experience interpreted by the intellect, and antinomianism from excessive confidence in the authority of subjective faith, uncontrolled by empirical verification. For Marsh, neither faith nor empirical reason alone was a sufficient authority for religious truth. His Orthodox distrust of the fallen affections made him deny the unaided mind access to immediate knowledge of moral truths. As Wells explains, "Marsh cautions against the hasty conclusion that the soul by itself could release its powers without the presence of external objects. In other words, powers are potential until actualized by their outward, correlative objects. The body becomes the connecting link, the 'transparent medium' through which the objects of sense excite the inner potentialities of the mind."[20] In Marsh's system, man can know spiritual truth because the ordering principles of reason are essentially one with the ordering principles of nature, and the experience of nature actuates the reason in man that distinguishes him from the beasts and links him with God.

Marsh took equal pains to avoid the Arminian idea that the spiritual reason is created by experience. In arguing against the authority of the senses, Marsh writes,

> Whether we have any innate ideas, or the soul be as a piece of blank paper or of sealing wax, on which outward objects make an impress, simply, of their own characters or forms, with other questions of the like kind, will hardly be asked by those who have well considered the general relations here exhibited [between the soul and nature]. It will be seen at once that phenomena of consciousness which have reference to the world of sense, are determined, not *solely* by the *outward object*, but also by the *specific* reaction of the *subject according to the inherent laws of its own nature*.[21]

To find the origins of the reason in experience alone would either imply that man could approach salvation through his own efforts, without divine intervention, or mire him in things, cut off from God.

As carefully as he worked to maintain the distinction between spirit and nature, Marsh ultimately turned to spirit, to the divine, for his authority. He felt more strongly than Emerson the need to preserve an unconditioned supernatural ground for the soul beyond space and time. He viewed Orthodoxy and Transcendentalism as the extremes of religious belief to which all intermediate positions tend. There are, he said,

> but two thoroughly consistent complete systems, and these are, the evangelical system which places the ultimate views of truth and grounds of conviction beyond the sphere of the speculative understanding, in the voice of conscience, and the perishing need of a spirit fully awakened to a sense of what it needs; and for the other system, that, confiding in speculative conclusions, explains away in the last resort the authority of conscience and terminates in a consistent Pantheism. I very much

fear that [Boston Transcendentalists] mean nothing more than the opposite of sensualismn and still have a wide space between them and the spiritualism of St. Paul.[22]

Marsh strove to preserve the free will and individual identity by asserting the fundamental independence of human moral powers from their correlative objects in nature, and by finding their ultimate correlative in a personal God.

The ultimate aim of the relationship between the mind and nature was spiritual. According to Marsh, reason seeks its true home in heaven rather than in the natural world into which it is born:

> For as the life of the body begins in an unconscious orga-
> nization whose inherent principle, with its whole process
> of development, according to the law of its nature, are
> [*sic*] in the unconsciousness, so the principle of our in-
> ward life, the life of the soul, has its first dawning, its first
> actuality, and the whole process of its development, in
> consciousness. But that consciousness is awakened, and
> its materials furnished, by the agencies of our organic
> life. The organic cravings of the body awaken the first
> feelings of the soul. . . . Yet in the consciousness of the
> self and the reference of these affections to self, there is a
> new principle of life, it must be remembered, distinct
> from the life of the body, and having its own laws of
> action.[23]

Marsh's division of spirit from nature bespeaks his Orthodox antimaterialism and emphasizes his conviction that man can reach God only by exploring the self, not through empirical knowledge of nature.

This *hierarchical* notion of the interaction of mind and nature reveals a subtle but significant divergence from Coleridge's philosophy of reason based on *polarities*, one which suggests that Marsh had strayed several steps from his Orthodox intentions down the pathway to Transcendentalist philosophy. By defining reason as one member of a polar interdependence, Coleridge preserved the authority of both the creative mind and brute fact. Marsh, too, cherished this balance, but he was *less* committed than the poetic Coleridge to things, and *more* committed to divine authority, so he subsumed understanding in the supreme reason, absorbing in the process, things into God. With this movement into God the world loses its individuality and begins to resemble the undifferentiated spirit of Emerson's Oversoul.

Reason was, finally, a philosophical justification for personal religious experience, and by stressing practical religious experience over abstract metaphysical speculation, Coleridge helped Marsh to defuse the doctrinal controversies that had driven so many laymen into skepticism or Unitarianism. Marsh was convinced that abstract speculation on the fine points of dogma would only lead laymen into error and confusion. He followed Coleridge in distinguishing between philosophical speculation, on the one hand, and personal spiritual participation in faith, practical living religion, on the other.[24] To comprehend the Christian mysteries in their true light, Marsh taught, the believer must abandon abstract speculation and apply doctrine to his own experience. In one instance, Marsh contrasts historical knowledge of the crucifixion to "the inward experience of the crucifying of the old man and of the awakened energies of the new and spiritual life. . . . Only so far as I am crucified with Christ," Marsh explained, "only so far, I say, is Christ any thing for me, either in his own death or his life."[25]

Coleridge's *Aids* helped Marsh alter the current view that religion is a set of doctrines (propositions subject to logical analysis), redefining it as a system of truth (descriptions of undeniable fact) which, when rightly apprehended in the reason, is one with the truth of philosophy.[26] Doctrines that may seem absurd in the abstract become incontrovertible, Marsh argues, when applied to the practical experience of the believer. In regard to the apparent contradiction between divine omnipotence and man's free will, Marsh acknowledges that "turn it as you will and state it as you may, for the human understanding the difficulty is still there and still incomprehensible. . . . The apparent contradiction arises from the incommensurateness of our finite understandings. . . . But . . . I will say in a word that each individual is concerned with the doctrine only as it is *practical* and of *immediate reference* to his *own character and condition*."[27] Marsh asserts that "as the powers of our natural life have their correlative objects in the natural world, so that which is spiritual in us must seek and find its correlative in the spiritual."[28] Belief leads to understanding because "with the awakening of the subjective there is a necessary presentation of the objective and a commensurate conviction of its reality."[29] Coleridge's philosophy served Orthodox doctrine by permitting Marsh to skirt logical paradox in order to stress the emotional and spiritual gratification doctrine could convey, a strategy that effectively disarmed Unitarian objections to Orthodox doctrine without falling back into enthusiasm.

Marsh believed that a rational faith needed dogma, the objective expression of the divine will and the theological analogue of Christ, to control its potential subjectivism. Like the seventeenth-century Puritans, he saw God's truth as one and unchanging and wished to express it in a consistent system that would accurately represent the divine will. For Marsh, as for Andrews Norton, contradiction does not issue in a higher truth, but in absurdity. A rational faith requires a systematic statement of religious truth, and the doctrines of the Christian church incarnate the ordering principles of the universe in just such a system. Marsh's new metaphysical justification for the discredited Orthodox doctrines of free will, redemption, and the Trinity aimed to retain the traditional form of Christian dogma. Therefore, like Edwards, he defined sin as the domination of the unregenerate will by selfish rather than spiritual ends. But where Edwards had submitted the will to natural determinism, Marsh tried to preserve its freedom by distinguishing the supernatural will from the natural faculties of man. "That self-affirmed and self-conscious I," he says, "is a higher birth, a principle of higher and spiritual energy, and having its proper relations to a world of spirit."[30] In describing the fall of the will into nature, Marsh says,

> The understanding, reflecting and reproducing in its own abstract forms, the fleeting experiences of the life of nature, its wants and its tendencies, seeks, in the false and notional unity which by reflection it forms out of these, its own center and principle of action; seduces the will into the pursuit of the ends thus determined; and thus the spiritual principle is brought into bondage to the life

of nature. . . . It has thus become a self-will, not governed by the spiritual law, but by a principle originating in itself, and bringing it into subjection to the law of sin, the self-seeking principle of the mere individual nature. . . . In this fallen state it is still self-determined, since it is not determined from without, but by an inward principle.[31]

Although the will acts only according to its own spiritual principles, it falls because those principles direct it to seek ends provided by the understanding, and the understanding invariably prescribes natural rather than spiritual ends.

Despite Marsh's own conviction that reason had enabled him to avoid natural determinism, it is difficult to distinguish conclusively between his notion of the will and Edwards's. Since Marsh's fallen will, like Edwards's, must invariably pursue natural rather than spiritual ends, Marsh's argument that his will is free because it acts on a spiritual principle sounds more like a rhetorical evasion of the problem than a real solution. Although Marsh asserts that the will is a self-determined spiritual agency, influenced, but not controlled, by natural events, he describes its operation in terms almost identical to Edwards's. Marsh observes that once the will has fallen, "it cannot rise to the pursuit of a higher end and the obedience of a higher law, for it cannot rise above itself, its inward principle, and being in bondage to a law of nature obey a law above nature."[32] To Edwards, Marsh's assertion that the will is not passive, and that "the grounds of its determinations are in the character of the will itself," would have sounded Arminian, while his contention that the enslaved will is powerless to rise above natural determinism without divine aid, that it can exercise its freedom only after grace when it acts in accordance with divine law, would have seemed Orthodox.

Yet the affinities between the two are still more instructive. In 1843, Henry James, Sr., wrote to Ralph Waldo Emerson, "I believe Jonathan Edwards *redivivus* in true blue would after an honest study of the philosophy that had grown up since his day make the best reconciler and critic of philosophy."[33] While Marsh may not have been Edwards reborn in "true blue," they were remarkably alike in motives and methods. Like Edwards, Marsh believed that prevailing church policies catered to the layman's emotional comfort at the expense of his spirit. And like Edwards, he tried to enlist the most advanced philosophy of the day in the service of Orthodox doctrine. Marsh called on diverse intellectual sources—seventeenth-century heretics, the Anglican Church, Calvinism—but, in place of Edwards's affection for English empiricism, he offered the new German metaphysic as it was interpreted for him by Coleridge, and this departure was crucial since it was Edwards's theology as it had been passed down by Hopkins, Emmons, and others that Marsh set out to revise. Inspired by Locke, Edwards continued to divide the senses from the understanding, which was subordinate to, and subject to persuasion by, the senses. By doing so, he preserved the division between spirit and mind, between spiritual being and intellectual knowing, that trapped man in his own mind and frustrated certainty about the external world. Marsh on the other hand, joined faith and understanding under the aegis of reason, offering a metaphysical foundation for the optimism that previously had rested on the mere assumption of an orderly universe. He applied dynamic views of the mind to Congregationalist theology, reestablishing that optimism on the grounds of a sounder philosophy and preparing for its growth to cosmic proportions in Emerson's hands.

Marsh's dissatisfaction with the particulars of Edwards's theology would mislead, however, if it obscured the crucial similarity in their thought, one which makes Marsh just the nineteenth-century Jonathan Edwards that the elder James called for. Although Edwards and Marsh based their two systems on contradictory philosophies, both aimed finally not to revise doctrine but to offer a new *method* of spiritual insight and thus to alter fundamentally man's access to God. The tradition from which both Marsh and Edwards sprang constructed faith like a bulwark of doctrinal blocks piled one on the other according to a complex logical system. While this theological fortress had served well in the threatening world of the sixteenth century, both protecting and controlling its inhabitants, by Edwards's day a less threatening world of greater promise encouraged greater reliance on personal experience. By revising Calvinist theology, Edwards hoped to reconcile Puritan dogma with modern epistemology, stable form with change, a system resting on man's helplessness with one that assumed his power to order his world.

To effect this reconciliation, Edwards offered a new mode of perception, a spiritual sense that was superior to all the rest not because it provided a sixth and additional sense, but because it totally revised the original five, organizing them according to a new principle that opened up the world to the believer in a new way. This faculty of spiritual sight links Edwards closely to Marsh by prefiguring in Lockean terms the reason Marsh derived from Coleridge. Marsh and Edwards did not offer new articles of faith; their alterations were not of doctrine, but of the mind and spirit that transformed faith itself, substituting a new method of apprehending religious truth for adherence to a system of theological propositions, and thereby endowing existing doctrine with a new vitality. In Edwards's and in Marsh's hands, religion became less a system than a process, less a form of belief than a way of being.

Marsh tried to plug the remaining logical gap in his own system with conscience, which provides the only hope to a soul enslaved to nature. But in the process he only moved toward the opposite extreme. "God has not left us," Marsh says, "like the brutes that perish, to the dominion of sense, and the blind impulse of nature."[34] God has placed in each man a spiritual principle that can "present itself to us as a commanding and authoritative law of duty, claiming our unconditional obedience and prescribing to us an end paramount to the ends of nature."[35] The conscience is God's revelation of His divine being to man, and as such "is the only true ground of our conviction of the reality of anything spiritual."[36] In this view, conscience replaces Scriptural revelation as a way of knowing God's will, opening the door to antinomianism and moral relativism. Conscience represents "God in the World." "To lose this," Marsh said, "is to lose ourselves, to become the abandoned slaves of circumstances, to betray the trust which God has committed to us, and to lose our souls."[37] But Marsh did not explain any better than Edwards how we are to identify the claims of conscience or distinguish them from those of the appetites or affections. Because Marsh's conscience resides in the mind and lacks even the qualified historical authority that nineteenth-century Biblical criticism had left to Scripture, it strays very near the uncontrolled subjectivity that he deplored in the Unitarian moral sense. The conscience is also the "schoolmaster" of the soul,[38] demanding obedience to the highest spiritual laws, teaching man when he strays, and remaining unsatisfied until the human will has become one with the divine will.[39] By insisting on indwelling moral law, Marsh usurped for man the spiritual authority that Edwards had vested solely in God.

Marsh's version of the Christian Trinity represents as it did for Coleridge the culmination of his efforts to explain both the unity between nature and man and the link between man and God. It seems more successful than his views of the free will or the conscience largely because the symbolic and alogical nature of the Trinity excused Marsh from having to measure the adequacy of his explanation against logic. The Trinity is a mystery and a miracle, the cornerstone of Marsh's faith as it was the fundamental absurdity to the Unitarians. In Marsh's system, Christ mediates between man and God, and his mediation is both religious and philosophical. He not only atones for our sin, He also embodies the attributes of both matter and spirit. God, the reason, knows Himself in Christ, the will. Christ, in turn, objectifies the Father and makes reason active in the world. These two are made one by the Holy Spirit, which is faith. Marsh's innovation was his notion that the human consciousness could strive through faith to imitate God's perfect unity of reason and will, producing a human analogue of the divine nature.

Neither Marsh's nor Coleridge's thought is best seen as an independent philosophical or theological system. Each developed in its particular context and had its life only there. One might say that the problems of New England theology had been created as theology became abstracted from its generating circumstances, as New Englanders tried to protect it from change despite changes in New England *life*. Certainly, Marsh had never approached Coleridge (or, for that matter, any of the metaphysical questions that Coleridge addressed) with the rigorous philosophical system, the *intellectual* posture, that Coleridge himself assumed. Like Edwards, Marsh wanted to *use* a sophisticated philosophical system to prop up an existing theological form. But neither realized that their doctrinal systems were not immune to change despite their ties to what they conceived as a timeless divine will.

Marsh's union of dogma and philosophy transformed *both*. Orthodox doctrine filtered through Romantic philosophy and emerged free from strictures about human helplessness and fundamental limitation and also from reliance on the authority of a literal text. Coleridge's philosophy, when applied to the Congregationalist need for renewed access to divine truth and reassurance that Christianity was a "personal" faith, gave up the intellectual tone Coleridge had so scrupulously maintained and, chameleon-like, began to assume the colors of a Christian theology. Analogues between the divine and human mind, intellectually and metaphorically satisfying, did not meet Marsh's doctrinal need for effective relationship between man and God. So reason became associated more closely with the divine mind and less with the human. It became a power distinctly *spiritual*, rather than a sophisticated ordering principle of the intellect as Coleridge had viewed it.

As MARSH applied Coleridge to his own theological doubts and saw them fade away, he became certain that Coleridge could resolve the same conflicts in American religion if only his ideas could reach the American public.[40] Already, he said, *Aids* was "with a few exerting an influence that will help to place the lovers of truth and righteousness on better philosophical grounds."[41] But in its English edition *Aids* did reach only the few, and of those still fewer could comprehend Coleridge's difficult principles and unfamiliar language. Marsh understood Coleridge because he had prepared himself for what he would find there. Paul, the Cambridge Platonists, and the German faith philosophers had introduced him to ideas that Coleridge had, after all, gleaned largely from the same sources. But even scholars like Hodge at Princeton, who agreed that American faith needed a spiritual transfusion, had not educated themselves, as Marsh had, to receive it.

Since they had not thought to prepare themselves, Marsh set out to open their minds to the new vision (to his mind the old vision in new dress) that Coleridge offered.[42] At first Marsh's plans included only a review of *Aids* similar to his review of Stuart's *Commentary on Hebrews*, but by the Spring of 1829 he had concluded that an article on *Aids* could not do justice to Coleridge's philosophy and decided instead to republish *Aids* itself in an American edition. "My object," he said, "will be chiefly to point out the bearing of his metaphysical views on

73

theology in this country. Warm disputes are growing up here which I think his views if understood would wholly supersede and I am anxious to lay hold of anything that may give circulation and influence to the work."[43]

This decision to republish the whole work reflects Marsh's sensitivity to the American philosophical temper in general and America's limited appreciation of Coleridge in particular. William Charvat concludes from attacks on Coleridge and appreciations of the French eclectics printed in the *Christian Examiner* and other journals before 1829 that "New England wanted a clear and comprehensible metaphysics, and . . . a morally vital and persuasive philosophy."[44] The operative terms here for our purposes are "clear" and "comprehensible." In the first quarter of the nineteenth century, most American theologians and intellectuals missed these qualities in Coleridge.

To overcome American objections to Coleridge, Marsh added notes to Coleridge's text that clarified its difficult passages, tailoring them to readers less familiar with philosophical discourse. He also appended passages from Coleridge articles in *Blackwood's Magazine* and *The Stateman's Manual* that amplified the crucial distinction between reason and understanding—the idea Marsh was most anxious to plant in the minds of his audience. Most important of all, Marsh introduced Coleridge's text with a long "Preliminary Essay" that defended Coleridge's style and applied his thought to American issues. This essay was intended to counter American objections to Coleridge by demonstrating his applicability to the theological needs of both Unitarians and Congregationalists. Marsh sought to persuade Congregationalists that reason need not dilute religious fervor, and Unitarians that religion offers truths inaccessible to the senses.

By accommodating Orthodox dogmatics, Unitarian rationalism, and evangelical fervor in the "Preliminary Essay," Marsh hoped to build a religious platform with the stability of revealed Scripture, the expanse to contain intellectual inquiry, and the strength to withstand powerful religious feeling. Marsh himself was a sort of amalgam of New England religious perspectives. His own Orthodoxy would not allow him to compromise the doctrine that man is a created and dependent creature of God, that his highest ends are not in this world but in the next, and that although he is obligated to reach for them, he can never succeed without Christ's intervention and God's grace.

Yet coexisting in his heart with this Orthodox feeling of helplessness was a confidence in intellect and in man's power to shape his life and world that marks Marsh as a man of the nineteenth rather than the sixteenth century. He was, after all, an educator himself and a product of the finest education available in his day. This training led him to espouse a vision of progress and of the mind's powers that historically had subverted dogmatic constraints. And overlaying both his dogmatism and his confidence in intellect was the sort of unsophisticated piety that had traditionally fostered both doctrinal heresy and antiintellectualism. Although Coleridge seemed to Marsh the solution to these conflicting impulses in his own mind and to the similar factional disputes that fragmented American religion, his attempt to outline that solution in the "Preliminary Essay" created more problems than it resolved, and its influence thoroughly frustrated his expectations.

Marsh's efforts to resolve in nineteenth-century terms the conflict between dogma, morals, and piety carried his thought from Orthodoxy toward Romanticism and from Coleridge toward Emerson. His strategies in the "Preliminary Essay" soften the difficulties of Coleridge's theology and dramatize the intellectual conflicts out of which Transcendentalism was born. As Marsh responds to the opposed biases of his different audiences, the essay frequently lapses into self-contradiction, and it achieves the appearance of unity only by sacrificing philosophical precision. These assertions, however, should not be taken as criticisms of Marsh's work so much as descriptions of the necessary consequences of his attempt to speak to several audiences at once on the merits of a hybrid philosophy.

The confidence in human freedom that had gained strength since Edwards and the energies of Marsh's personal faith combine in the "Preliminary Essay" to produce a language of antinomian transcendence while, at the same time, blurring the distinctions that had held antinomianism within Orthodoxy. This language was uniquely suited to the needs of certain young Unitarians who had already been freed from the restrictions of doctrine and who shared Marsh's interests in the subjective experiences that had been shunted aside by Locke. The various elements that Coleridge brought together in *Aids*—the Church fathers, seventeenth-century Christian Platonism and mysticism, eighteenth-century German pietism and idealist philosophy, and English Romantic poetry—underwent in Marsh's hands one more transformation. He shaped them to the nineteenth-century version of theological conflicts that had both troubled and defined American culture since Massachusetts Bay Colony set itself up as a City on a Hill. In trying to inscribe the infinitely thin doctrinal line between rational and spiritual religion, Marsh created a document that would lend itself to interpretations far removed from any he had intended.

BOTH Coleridge's philosophy and Marsh's explication of it in the "Preliminary Essay" revolve around the concept of reason, and Marsh's attempt to define reason epitomizes the resonant difficulties of the essay as a whole. Marsh begins by acknowledging the distaste for rational religion that was a part of his own Orthodox upbringing. "By a philosophical view of religious truth," he writes, "would generally be understood a view, not only varying from the religion of the Bible . . . but at war with it; and a rational religion is supposed to be of course something diverse from revealed religion."[45] As a first step, Marsh had to convince suspicious conservatives that Coleridge was not out to overthrow from within the doctrines that Unitarianism had attacked from without under the banner of reason. Accordingly, Marsh argues that, far from contradicting the truths of revelation, Coleridge's thought defends them against detractors who use false philosophies against them. In bold type to add force to his point, Marsh asserts that Coleridge's only purpose is "A PHILOSOPHICAL STATEMENT AND VINDICATION OF THE DISTINCTIVELY SPIRITUAL AND PECULIAR DOCTRINES OF THE CHRISTIAN SYSTEM." Marsh describes the instrument of this defense as a reason with qualities far different from those that Congregationalists or Unitarians knew. Not only is this reason compatible with religion, Marsh argues, but "CHRISTIAN FAITH IS THE PERFECTION OF HUMAN REASON."[46] Coleridge proves "that religion passes out of the ken of reason only where the eye of reason has reached its own horizon—and that faith is then but its continuation."[47] The definition of reason that Marsh offers in this early stage of his argument reflects his desire to accommodate conventional Orthodox attitudes about the role of the fallible human mind in religious inquiry. Thus, Marsh strictly limits the reason. He subsumes it in faith, suggesting that doctrinal revelation has the final authority on spiritual matters and, most important, that Coleridge desires simply to bring man's errant philosophy into conformity with established religious truth.

In its next stage, Marsh's examination of reason and religion shifts slightly in emphasis to further reassure Orthodox ministers that reason does not threaten their cherished beliefs. He assures his audience that Coleridge's reason is not the cold, empirical faculty that banishes religious feeling along with the mysteries of doctrine. On the contrary, it recognizes that mystery and welcomes it as a necessary part of religious experience. "It may meet the prejudices of some," he says, "to remark farther, that in philosophizing on the grounds of our faith [Coleridge] does not profess nor aim to solve all mysteries, and to bring all truth within the comprehension of understanding. Truth may be mysterious, and the primary ground of all truth and reality must be so." "Rational," Marsh then says, "is most spiritual."[48] And with that statement he begins to move away from the safety of Orthodox doctrine, drawn by his equal attraction to the potential powers of the mind. He could have said "spiritual is most rational" and preserved the primacy of doctrine over mind, but he does not, and such apparently insignificant changes of direction prove decisive in the thicket of theological controversy.

At this point in Marsh's attempt to reconcile intellectual powers and revelation, intellect begins to take the upper hand. The origins of this shift lie in Marsh's discomfort with the blind submission to doctrine recommended by so many of his colleagues as a retreat from the Unitarian onslaught. Such blind faith in Scripture seemed to him, as it would have to the Puritans, a refusal to use God's gift of reason. "If we do not . . . adhere to reason," he says, "we forfeit our prerogative as rational beings, and our faith is no better than the bewildered dream of a man who has lost his reason."[49] But while the Puritans insisted on the *effort* to understand through reason, Marsh urges its *authority*. As Marsh attributes more power to reason, faith becomes conditional. Marsh asserts that, though we may believe what "*passeth all understanding*, we *cannot* believe what is *absurd,* or contradictory to *reason."*[50] This reason begins to have more in common with the analytical "common sense" of Unitarianism than it has with the servant of faith Marsh described earlier. To avoid a know-nothing approach to theology and to avert religious enthusiasm, Marsh turns in the "Preliminary Essay" to intellectual authority, just as the Unitarians did, and, as it did for the Unitarians, Marsh's analytical reason would soon sprout wings and take off into the transcendental ether.

Marsh was not satisfied with a merely analytical power, however, and his desire to give reason an authority that is spiritual as well as empirical impels him, at this point in his argument, to a highly unorthodox expansion of the rational powers. Marsh's reliance on the mind to provide him with a route to God grew from his dissatisfaction with spiritual knowledge that depended, as nineteenth-century Unitarianism and Congregationalism did, on external authority. He demanded a self-validating system, an internal authority providing its own proofs, in which the absolute ground of existence and the ground of *knowledge* of existence would be one. By discovering in reason the arbiter of the highest spiritual truths, Marsh effectively reversed the Puritan relationship between reason and Scripture. The Puritans employed reason as a servant of Scripture, responsible for comprehending and validating revealed truth. Although Scripture was occasionally obscure or resistant to reason, it was unthinkable that the two could be in direct conflict except through error born of man's imperfection.

Earlier in the "Preliminary Essay," Marsh has construed reason in a limited sense, first as a servant of religious truth and then as a voluntary process of intellectual examination. But in his zeal to obtain immediate access to unconditioned truth, he abandons both doctrine and intellect and piously relies on indwelling spirit. It was this concept of spirit that became the heart of his personal religious faith and made him attractive to Emerson and the other Transcendentalists. Significantly, there is no boundary between his description of an empirical analytical reason and his reinterpretation of reason as an absolute authority. One springs directly from the other, as if in his fervor the reason needed only to be released from the restraints of doctrine to spring full-blown to the height of its powers. In the space of one sentence Marsh blends two crucial ingredients: the

78

authority of reason ("it is impossible for us to believe on any authority what is directly *contradictory* to reason and *seen to be so*,")[51] and a redefinition of reason itself from an analytical faculty to a "power of intuitive insight in relation to certain moral and spiritual truths."[52]

Marsh's transcendent reason opens a direct line between man and God that, potentially at least, bypasses Scripture entirely. This is a new version of the antinomian vision. Although Marsh does not claim converse with the Holy Spirit as Anne Hutchinson did, his position has the same effect. It supplants the authority of revelation or tradition with that of something akin to unaided intuition. In these circumstances, Scripture serves reason. "The design of revelation is obvious," Marsh says, "namely to develop faith into distinct consciousness and therefore into reason."[53] Like nature, Scripture has no authority of its own. It has become a correlative object for faith, eliciting its powers and encouraging its development into reason. Yet the importance of Scripture should not be minimized—like nature it is essential to spiritual development. Marsh believed that the universe operates according to a consistent set of spiritual laws, and that faith alone, without instruction, cannot comprehend them. Scripture develops faith into reason, and reason makes order out of the apparent chaos of life. By subordinating both Scripture and nature to reason, Marsh neatly subsumes the opposed parties in New England theological controversy—Unitarianism and Congregationalism—within a more comprehensive position. Their oracles prove to be necessary but insufficient aids to spiritual knowledge, which is finally achieved only through the insights of the individual mind.

Although Marsh perceives the radicalism of his new position, this does not keep him from expanding transcendent reason to the fullest extent. Even God's truth must conform to the individual's intuitive insights. "We necessarily attribute to the supreme Reason," he writes, "to the Divine mind, views the same, or coincident, with those of our own reason. We cannot, (I say it with reverence and I trust with some apprehension of the importance of the assertion) we *cannot* believe that to be right in the view of the Supreme Reason, which is clearly and decidedly wrong in the view of our own."[54] Defining reason as a faculty of divine insight, Marsh elevates it to absolute authority in all spiritual matters. Man's mind becomes a standard to which even scripture and doctrine must conform.

It is easy to see how such notes as these might draw a deep response from Emerson as he read the "Preliminary Essay." They lent support to his belief that religious truth must be found in the soul or nowhere at all. Most telling was Marsh's summary definition of reason itself and its crucial distinction from understanding. Although Marsh deliberately leaves the full exposition of this distinction "to the work itself," he points out that reason constitutes a supernatural element in man— "that *image of God* in which man alone was created of all the dwellers upon the earth, and in virtue of which he was placed at the head of this lower world . . . that which is the being of the soul, considered as anything differing in kind from the understanding."[55] The understanding, on the other hand, is "the faculty judging according to sense," a faculty of "abstracting and generalizing, of contrivance and forecast," which "we are expressly taught belongs to us in common with the brutes."[56] Here was the likeness of man to God, his participation in divine spirit, and the promise of a higher world of perception above the demeaning empiricism that Unitarians set as the limit of human potential. Only Marsh's typically Puritan insistence on the distinction between man and nature would have rung false to Emerson, and that would have been easily enough ignored by so selective a reader in the rush of inspiration from the rest.

Marsh himself was not entirely blind to the radicalism foreshadowed by the view he developed in the "Preliminary Essay," but his struggles to maintain an Orthodox posture simply recall the conflicting allegiances to dogma and intellect that provoked his flight into intuition in the first place. In trying to limit reason, Marsh slips into a circular argument that only confirms the complexity of his position and fails to bring reason and revelation any closer together. In respect to "the peculiar doctrines of the Christian revelation," Marsh writes, "the Author assigns to reason only a negative validity. It does not teach us what those doctrines are, or what they are not, except that they are not, and cannot be such as contradict the clear convictions of right reason."[57] Not only is this statement confused, but in its final apparent assertion of rational authority it recalls Unitarian attacks on trinitarian doctrine. Throwing up his hands, Marsh avoids further trouble by referring the reader to the fuller statement of Coleridge's views on the subject in *Aids* itself.

Unable to balance the authorities of intellect and revelation, Marsh returns his attention to the religion of the heart, confirming in the process his bias for experimental over speculative religion. He argues that the ultimate grounds of faith cannot be found, as Congregationalists and Unitarians proposed, either in doctrine alone or in the frigid halls of philosophy. Doctrine is suspect, and the best philosophy can do is prove "the doctrines of the Christian faith to be rational, and exhibit philosophical grounds for the *possibility* of a truly spiritual religion. The *reality* of those . . . states of being, which constitute experimental or spiritual religion, rests on other grounds."[58] Faith cannot be explained or defined: "'Christianity is not a *theory*, or a speculation; but a life. Not a philosophy of life, but a life and a living process.' It is not, therefore, so properly a species of knowledge, as a form of being."[59]

But, more important for our purpose, Marsh's essay locates religious authority in the experience of the individual believer rather than in any doctrinal system or external institution. In doing so, it implicitly provided ammunition for Ripley and Parker in their running battle with Norton over the miracles question. Marsh's assertion that religion is either a personal experience in the depth of the soul or it is nothing was one of the most appealing elements of *Aids* to the Transcendentalists. They read Marsh to mean that religious faith or belief in Christian truth cannot rest on testimony that Christ worked certain miracles and hence carried divine authority. It must rest on the response those truths evoke from the heart. Faith, Marsh taught, is indistinguishable from the self—not something we *know*, but something we *are*, the ground of our being. These statements reflect only one extreme in the continual swing of Marsh's thought, but they are crucial, as we shall see later, for they opened the territory that Transcendentalism would soon settle permanently.

Marsh showed Emerson everything he needed. Kant had separated sensation from reason, arguing that the mind knows only phenomena. Coleridge had altered Kant, making reason constitutive rather than regulative, a power of intellectual insight into noumenal truths, a route to the absolute. Marsh converted this power of insight from a process of intellectual reflec-

tion on the inner workings of the mind to an intuitive harmony
between the mind and the divine spirit, and Emerson extended
that harmonious sympathy to include all of nature.

HENRY MAY has argued that "ambiguity is, for an American
thinker, the major key to influence,"⁶⁰ and certainly that standard (if no other) would place Marsh in company with Edwards, Emerson, or Dewey. His attempt to unite conflicting elements of American thought in *Aids* produced a document that
mirrored those conflicts more than it resolved them. The "Preliminary Essay" is remarkable in that it both anticipated and
actually helped to create subsequent developments in the intellectual battle for spiritual authority between revelation and
mind. In trying to erase divisions between rational and spiritual religion, Marsh engendered an ambiguous new philosophy
rather than a faithful exposition of Coleridge's thought. It is a
microcosm of the controversy between Calvinism and Unitarianism, and like that controversy it produced a new and un-
wanted offspring. In his determination to do justice to all sides,
to fully acknowledge the claims of both mind and spirit, Marsh
avoided polemic. In order to reconcile doctrine and common
sense, he imported elements of European culture that had been
neglected in America and added an altered version of Coleridge's philosophy filtered through his own experience of theological life in New England, and this mixture underwent a sort
of chemical reaction, producing a statement of the mind's powers that carried subversive implications.

Much of what has generally been called Marsh's "influence"* on Emerson, Alcott, and Ripley was, in fact, an elabo-

* The version of influence enacted in the works I discuss here differs
from that developed by Harold Bloom (*The Anxiety of Influence: A Theory
of Poetry* [New York: Oxford University Press, 1973] and *A Map of Misreading* [New York: Oxford University Press, 1980]) in that it is more narcissis-
tic than oedipal. Marsh and his readers do not seem to "kill off" their intellectual predecessors to make way for their own prose. They seem, in fact,
never to really "see" them at all, at least not during the formative stages of
their own intellectual development. They see, instead, what they take to
be concrete expressions of their own still inchoate views. These visions, as
I argue throughout these chapters, often have little to do with what we

rate and inevitable exercise in creative misunderstanding. We might with justice argue that Marsh did not *provide* Emerson with the distinction between reason and understanding. He offered a definition of reason distorted by the tensions of the controversy it was supposed to resolve, and Emerson in turn read/misread it as an answer to his own philosophical needs. In his more deliberate moments, Marsh construed reason as intellectual self-examination, a power of inward ordering that reflected the principles of universal order. Moreover, because Emerson viewed the mind through Unitarian lenses, he naturally overlooked the fact that Marsh's reason and the truths it revealed were available only to the *regenerate* mind, the mind that had benefitted from Christ's intercession. Marsh continued to believe that natural man and nature itself needed to be redeemed.

This Orthodox attitude toward nature guided him even when he seemed closest to the Transcendentalists. His brief discussion of language in the "Preliminary Essay" must have been one of the most suggestive passages for Emerson as he began the long process that would produce *Nature* in 1836. Defending Coleridge against charges of obscurity, Marsh argues "that he uses words uniformly with astonishing precision, and that language in his use of it . . . becomes a living power, 'consubstantial' with the power of thought that gave birth to it, and awakening and calling into action a corresponding energy in our own minds."[61] Marsh makes words the objective forms of spiritual thought and suggests that such language can evoke corresponding powers in the reader. Hence words mediate between the universal spirit in two minds. This notion was a giant step toward Emerson's famous declaration in *Nature* that "Words are signs of natural facts . . . particular natural facts are symbols of particular spiritual facts . . . Nature is the symbol of spirit." But the difference is significant too. While Emerson used nature as a middle term between spirit and language, Marsh moved directly from one to the other. Nature held no power of its own. His mediator was Christ, who appeared in the mind as reason. Marsh entrusted language with the task of

would call (perhaps equally self-deceptively) a "rounded" or "objective" view of the works in question. Perhaps the word "ambiguity" is only our excuse for this necessary and self-projecting misreading.

83

communication and praised it in proportion as it conveyed spiritual truths with "precision." It is one of the greatest ironies of his story that the ambivalence of his "Preliminary Essay" would attract the Transcendentalists, who valued language for its power to evoke the ineffable, and move them to laud Marsh's *Aids* as one of their greatest sources of inspiration.

# 4

## With Tyrannous Eye:
## The Problematics of Influence

What we are, that only can we
see.
                    —Emerson, *Nature*

M ARSH, OF COURSE, did not have Transcendentalism in
mind when he wrote his introduction to *Aids* in 1829.
He aimed it at quite another audience and, blind to
other possible interpretations, he believed that the "Preliminary Essay" had removed all obstacles to Coleridge's acceptance by American readers. Marsh's version of *Aids* differs from
Coleridge's in ways that describe the temper of the times in
America. It communicates a less rigorous, less consistent critical philosophy, aims for a more practical morality, and appeals
to native American individualism much more strongly than
does the *Aids* alone. It converts the difficulty of Coleridge's language into an advantage by reinterpreting it as a mark of his
depth, simplifies the essential elements of his philosophy, and
applies that philosophy to American issues.[1]

Although Marsh's edition did not remake American theology
as he had hoped, it did revise opinion among American theologians and critics about the value of Coleridge's writings. Charvat notes that "in America his career as a philosopher . . . began

in 1829 with James Marsh's Burlington edition of [*Aids to Reflection*]."² Because of Marsh's efforts, it was as a philosopher that America knew Coleridge best and appreciated him most. If some reviewers, like Frederic Henry Hedge, deplored the apparent lack of system in his writings, they did so because they felt it obscured the truth Coleridge's writings contained, and if some conservative theologians still disagreed with him and thought him a "fool," they could no longer simply disregard his writing as meaningless. R. H. Dana fairly represented the post–1829 attitude toward Coleridge's thought in the preface to his *Poems and Prose Writings* (1833). "The man who is unable to enter into the deep things of Coleridge," he asserted, "though he may pass for an alert dialectition [*sic*], must no longer think of dictating from a philosopher's chair. To profess to differ from Coleridge may be safe, but to profess to hold him incomprehensible, would now savour less of a profession than of a confession."³ News of Coleridge's growing American reputation seems to have made its way back to England where it particularly pleased Coleridge himself. Richard Monckton Milnes recalled that "in the course of conversation the poet asked us if either of us intended to go to America. He said 'Go to America if you have the opportunity; I am known there. I am a poor poet in England, but I am a great Philosopher in America.'"⁴

*Aids* was widely read, brought Marsh a certain amount of personal recognition, and altered America's opinion of Coleridge as a philosopher and poet, but it did not revolutionize the theologies of its readers. Marsh foresaw this possibility when he first considered editing *Aids* and blamed it on the fact that American readers had not been properly prepared for Coleridge. Marsh had prepared himself for Coleridge by discovering Coleridge's image in Paul, in the Cambridge Platonists, in the Germans, and in English Romantic poetry, and he wrote his "Preliminary Essay" to *Aids* similarly to prepare his readers. Marsh's introduction did give his readers *access* to Coleridge's thought for the first time, but only by irrevocably altering Coleridge in the process.

The story of *Aids* in America is not so much that of its acceptance and "influence" as of its appropriation and transformation into shapes that neither Coleridge nor his American editor would have recognized.⁵ While Marsh's ambiguous discussion of philosophy and religion and his suggestive definition of reason quieted his readers' objections to Coleridge, they did so not by reconciling Americans to a faithful portrayal of his philosophy, but by painting his thought in such broad strokes that American readers could interpret it to confirm any assumptions they brought to it. In fact, Marsh did not so much reconcile his audience to Coleridge as transform Coleridge to meet the expectations of his audience. With few exceptions readers saw in Coleridge a distorted, but still provisionally acceptable, version of their own views.

Marsh's "Preliminary Essay" conditioned every reader's view of Coleridge's text. Apart from Marsh's essay, Coleridge's thought was beyond the grasp of most of these early readers, and when with Marsh's help they saw it at all, they could do so only through the reconstituting medium Marsh provided. Marsh's formal contribution had been to "Americanize" Coleridge by applying his thought to social and theological issues familiar to his American readers. But by doing so, Marsh inevitably misled them. By putting Coleridge into a familiar intellectual context, a context in which Americans could *read* him really for the first time, Marsh encouraged them to see Coleridge as familiar rather than as a figure who might revolutionize the very terms and conditions of their discourse. As a familiar object in a familiar context, Coleridge could be read in familiar ways. Thus Marsh's readers failed to see that Coleridge's *Aids* was a text of a new sort, one that *changed* its context and required in the process a new sort of reading. Marsh's readers realized his own worst fears and saw only the Coleridge that Marsh's introduction and their prior theological and philosophical preconceptions permitted. As a result, their responses to *Aids* expressed their own assumptions rather than Coleridge's thought. In responding to *Aids* they revealed themselves.

MARSH's Orthodox readers, veterans of numberless theological debates, read *Aids* as just one more doctrinal tract. They remained unconvinced by, even oblivious to, all Marsh's strategies in the "Preliminary Essay," and praised or condemned Coleridge's theology according to its compatibility with their own dogmatic positions. Charles Hodge, for one, admitted his appreciation of the *motives* behind Marsh's defense of spiritual religion but felt "bound" to point out Coleridge's dangerous divergence from Orthodox views of the atonement. He correctly identified the participation of *Aids* in a growing tendency to substitute human agency for dependence on God. But in this respect he lumped Coleridge together with Unitarianism, and where he distinguished between the two he did so, again, on narrow doctrinal grounds alone. He argued that both cast aside the Orthodox doctrine that Christ died to satisfy divine justice and assumed that the effect of Christ's death on man was subjective. This position, he continued, changes "the whole system of the Gospels . . . instead of sinners depending on what Christ has done . . . he is taught to look to himself."[6]

For all his interest in reading German literature, Hodge was primarily a theological scholar and his habitual doctrinal outlook blinded him to the larger consequences of importing English Romantic thought into America. Hodge looked to Scripture and to church doctrine not only as his final but as his *only* arbiter, and he was blind to the possibility of a discourse that did not seek its validation there. The implications of Coleridge's reason and of his organicism escaped him entirely, a symptom perhaps of the inflexibility that shackled the old order and made it so unappealing to a new generation that wanted to think for itself.

Surprisingly, however, even those clergymen and educators who praised *Aids* were no more sensitive to its implications than Hodge. Some had developed doctrinal views similar to Coleridge's independently in their own struggles with similar issues. Many of these, like Alonzo Potter, had been teaching similar doctrines for years on such issues as man's free will and moral accountability. Potter asserted that Coleridge's ideas would become "the American philosophy" and that they were "destined, to effect a new era in Moral and metaphysical philosophy,"[7] a prediction history would bear out, though not quite as Potter expected. Despite their approval of Coleridge, these readers simply enacted a liberalized version of Hodge's viewpoint. They had been unable to cling to the traditional doctrine of Congregationalism and had turned instead to views that sustained faith in their own spiritual power. The doctrinal propositions that Hodge condemned as heterodox they greeted with satisfaction as "admirable and unanswerable."[8] In short, though they were on the opposite side of the doctrinal fence from Hodge, they were no less the prisoners of doctrine than he.

As might be expected, Marsh was most apprehensive about the reception of *Aids* among his former teachers at Andover, and with some cause. As Marsh explained to Coleridge, these influential ministers not only remained unconvinced by *Aids*, they were incapable, at least initially, of apprehending its true drift. Marsh resigned himself to the fact that many of the older theologians, like Leonard Woods and Moses Stuart, would never "comprehend its true character."[9] Stuart affected a complacence similar to that which Marsh had condemned in his "Preliminary Essay" as one of the most debilitating side effects of Lockeanism. He did his best, according to C. S. Henry, to "choke the spirit of reflection by ominous warning of the moral danger of it," and he clung stubbornly to Scripture and denied the power of reason to do anything more than identify God's revelation. "'The office of reason,' [Stuart] cries, 'is solely to interpret the Bible' by which he really meant that his students should 'interpret the Bible just as I do'."[10] Stuart's unvarying scorn for Coleridge was untroubled by any first-hand knowledge. Henry remarked that although Stuart himself repeatedly stumbled off of the narrow Orthodox path in his careless rambles into philosophy, he nevertheless jeered at Coleridge because, Henry said, "forsooth [Stuart] has occasionally *looked into* his books at the Bookstores, and elsewhere, en passant and 'didn't understand him'!!"[11] Between them, Woods and Stuart mounted a stubborn resistance to Coleridgean influence at Andover. Coleridge was never among the theological writers assigned for study, and Stuart repeatedly condemned German "Mysticism"[12] and sneered at Coleridge's thought as "a new and somewhat modified form of Pantheism."[13]

Woods's response, however, proved more interesting than Marsh had expected. Like Hodge's and Stuart's, his apprehension of *Aids* was essentially doctrinal, but he was, apparently at least, only mildly disturbed by Coleridge's doctrine and aimed his criticism elsewhere. Like the canny theological debater he was, Woods opened his letter to Marsh with praise for Coleridge's spiritual intent and admiration for his "mind of mighty grasp."[14] Woods professed to agree with more of Coleridge's theological views than his reading of Marsh's introductory essay had led him to expect and suggested with condescending good humor that either Coleridge's ideas were not so unusual as Marsh seemed to think, or that he himself was more heterodox than he had imagined. In part, we may trace this apparent receptivity to Marsh's perfectly genuine, but nonetheless tactical, association of Coleridge with the Cambridge Platonists, to whom any Calvinist could feel more akin than he could to contemporary empiricists. Woods himself expressed a special affection for these writers who, he thought, should be the model for the tastes of modern students.[15] But, in fact, Woods was far from heterodox and he knew it. He was a moderate member of a decidedly conservative faction, and in his comparison of *Aids* to Marsh's "Preliminary Essay" he managed both to chide Marsh for making more of Coleridge than he was worth, and, more pointedly, to warn him of the distance he had wandered from Orthodox doctrine into radicalism in his "Preliminary Essay," a distance even greater than that of the views he was trying to defend.

Woods's remarks on Coleridge's doctrine were designed to trivialize *Aids* and to make the Orthodox position seem comfortably unassailable. Though he could not grasp Coleridge's crucial definitions of reason and understanding, he was, nonetheless, distrustful of their possible larger effects on Orthodoxy, warning of "consequences unutterably gloomy and dreadful"[16] should they be generally accepted. This forecast seems more foreboding than the causes as Wood described them warranted, suggesting that perhaps there was more at stake here than Woods wanted to admit. Woods was no less steeped in doctrinal scholarship than Hodge or Stuart, and he was as incapable as they of comprehending Coleridge's thought. What he understood he deemed only slightly at odds with conventional dogma. So complete, however, was his immersion in the doctrinal perspective that he could not imagine the possibility of another fundamentally different approach, and anything that strayed significantly from the traditional verities was beyond his ken. He disguised his objections to Coleridge and his failure to comprehend him by concentrating not on doctrine but on serious rhetorical matters, that is, on what he describes as Coleridge's tendency to obscure simple truths in difficult phraseology—a sin against the Holy Ghost in the eyes of a Puritan minister.[17] In effect, he reinterpreted modes of belief that he could not comprehend as errors of expression that he could.

Woods's strategy suggests that many Orthodox ministers who were willing to accept the spiritual truths Coleridge offered but balked at his rhetoric misunderstood his more fundamental drift, one that divided him from the rationalism of the early church and linked him to the Romantics. Coleridge suggests that truth does not exist apart from language, that the verbal symbol, not the literal word and the decorative trope, is the fundamental vehicle of knowledge and persuasion. His Orthodox readers failed to see that Coleridge's meditative method was not a means to persuade others but a discipline for creating knowledge and for creating a self in a process of becoming. Marsh himself may well have overlooked these differences, partly because he saw in Coleridge a reflection of the Cambridge Platonists and an older, purer spiritual religion, and also because Coleridge himself encouraged this misunderstanding by attaching himself to Archbishop Leighton. If Marsh had known, however, what Jonathan Edwards seems to have known when he tried to incorporate Locke into Calvinism—that the mind cannot throw out what it has once used to arrive at its present state, that one can not recapture the pre-Lockean Eden but must build on Locke (especially since Marsh himself had passed through Locke and the Scots to his present position)— he might have realized that in taking on Coleridge he was inevitably committing himself to a kinship with Emerson and a whole strain of radicals rather than joining the legions of enlightened reaction.

*Aids* found its most fervent champions among Orthodox youths who had not yet settled into a doctrinal system, especially those whom Marsh himself had prepared for Coleridge through his teaching at the University of Vermont. A number of these young men were at Andover when *Aids* appeared. For them, German thought was not the novelty it had been for Marsh only ten years earlier. The lines of conflict between Orthodoxy and Unitarianism had been drawn still more sharply in the intervening years, and the deficiencies of each seemed even clearer to them than they had to Marsh. The works that had drawn Marsh to Coleridge were more familiar and influenced them even more strongly. Most importantly, these young would-be Orthodox ministers, like the future Transcendentalists in Boston, were just beginning to move out of their intellectual adolescence into maturity, and their teachers, striving to hold them within the faith, provided an obvious surrogate parental authority against which they could rebel. Full of such zeal, Coleridge's younger followers espoused *Aids* and Coleridgean philosophy as the manifesto of their ecclesiastical revolution. Letters from Marsh's friends and ex-students at Andover between 1830 and 1834 record a bitter struggle between young champions of Coleridgean metaphysics and the formidable professors who were determined to exclude it.

An initially small group of students, led by Vermont graduates, capitalized on the predisposition toward spiritual religion among Andover students in the 1830s to increase Coleridge's influence. The opposition of the seminary authorities made this a delicate undertaking, and Coleridgeans at Andover were careful to release Coleridge's philosophy into the intellectual atmosphere slowly so as to avoid alarming conservatives. Although Coleridge remained little known at Andover as late as 1833, students were eager to read his works. B. B. Newton, a Vermont graduate at Andover, told Marsh that "there is not a copy of *Aids* to my knowledge in the seminary except those *we* brought—*none* in the libraries, where there should be fifty copies and they would be read *now* if they were there."[18] Despite these difficulties, Newton was encouraged in his efforts by the growing popularity of *Aids* at Yale, where "quite a number of the students and several of the tutors were *firm Coleridge men*."[19]

Two years later, Coleridge's supporters had worked a great change at Andover, not only consolidating his influence among the students but even insinuating it among his adversaries on the faculty. Coleridge's thought had become a common subject of discussion, and the ideas advanced in *Aids* could, on occasion at least, stand up to established doctrine. Newton told Marsh that Dr. Skinner, Professor of Homiletics at Andover, was "alive to Coleridgism" and, despite continuing doctrinal objections, "admits Coleridge a *great* and *wonderful* man." Even Leonard Woods himself had "materially . . . changed his manner of presenting certain truths."[20]

Yet even with the help of Marsh's teaching, the Coleridgeans at Andover were so caught up in their crusade to spread Coleridge's *philosophy* that they themselves failed to absorb its less systematic implications. Despite Marsh's attempts at impartial mediation, Coleridgeans had been defined by the Orthodox as an opposition party and so regarded themselves. Newton protested Marsh's distaste for partisan debate when his voice alone could lend authority to the cause. But, in arguing his case, Newton adopted a standard of judgment—public opinion—that thwarted Coleridge's most fundamental aims and that could not have been better chosen to offend Marsh's sensibility. "The fact is," Newton pleaded, "you in reality, i.e., as the public understands it—belong to a *party* and there is a Coleridge *party* as much as there is any other party in the land."[21] Newton was certain that without Marsh's active participation Coleridge's cause could not succeed, but he failed to see the point of Coleridge's philosophy apart from theological politics.

Newton's readiness to reduce Coleridge's American disciples to simply another voice in New England religious factionalism (not to mention his identification of reality with public opinion) reveals his selective assimilation of Coleridge's and Marsh's philosophy. With all the enthusiasm of youth, Newton urged Marsh to help form a religious party that would publish its own party journal and eventually even found its own college to promote Coleridge's thought in America. He could not understand Marsh's reticence and complained that Marsh's scruples about what amounted to theological party politics undoubtedly would inhibit the spread of Coleridge's thought in New England religious circles.[22] Marsh refused to answer Newton's call for a party leader because he viewed such methods not only as useless but as counter-productive. Newton's institutional aspirations misconstrued Coleridge's intention by pinning hope on the effects of a mass movement. Coleridge's materialist opponents could employ schools, journals, and political organizations in behalf of their views because their metaphysics limited them to the senses and to external cause and effect. But Marsh foresaw a spiritual awakening, an inward and individual awareness of a supernatural existence beyond natural causes. Party and social pressures could not touch the part of a human being where this change must occur. Only the individual could reach it in the depths of his or her own being.

This misapprehension of Coleridge's intent by some of his

strongest supporters makes Marsh's confidence in Coleridge's future among younger Americans seem ill-founded. Raised in an intellectual context saturated with disputation, competing authorities, and factionalism, these young theologians could not free themselves to imagine a way of talking about faith in which these features played no part. In the hands of these theological firebrands, the philosophy that Marsh imported to end American religious factionalism became the banner of still another religious faction. Where could Coleridge hope for a proper reception if he could be so profoundly misinterpreted and misapplied by those who should have been his most faithful practitioners?[23]

ODDLY enough the sympathetic reception that Marsh failed to receive from his own students and colleagues came, with certain important modifications, from his Unitarian opponents. But it did not come from the Unitarian establishment, for the older generation in Boston can hardly be said to have received *Aids* at all. Almost to a man Unitarians rejected it out of hand as hostile to their most cherished principles. As Marsh predicted, most Unitarians rested too comfortably in Scottish philosophy to disturb themselves with the uncompromising introspection Coleridge prescribed. Marsh scorned the "arrogance and pride of understanding" that encouraged Unitarians to "mistake a shallow system, which they have learned to comprehend, as containing all that is to be comprehended, while in fact it contains only their own notions."[24]

Though few Unitarians acknowledged Coleridge's value, one or two voices in the Unitarian community welcomed Marsh's edition of *Aids to Reflection* and spoke in its defense. Charles Follen, the first Professor of German Literature at Harvard, was himself in—but not of—the Unitarian camp. Follen was something of a radical in staid Boston society despite the status conferred on him by his marriage to Eliza Lee Cabot. He had been run out of Germany for his political radicalism, and although his learning made him welcome in Boston intellectual circles as an interpreter of German culture, his idealist theology, inspired by Kant and Fries, made him suspect. Follen was radical enough himself to accommodate radicalism in others, and his lifelong familiarity with German philosophy prepared him for

Coleridge's philosophical innovations. He envisioned a great future for *Aids*, which, he said, "has done and will do much to introduce and naturalize a better philosophy in this country and particularly to make men perceive that there is much in the depths of their own minds that is worth exploring, and which cannot be had cheap and handy in the works of the Scotch and English dealers in philosophy."[25]

Also somewhere on the fringe of the Unitarian community was Richard Henry Dana. Dana was himself a highly respected writer and journalist and a founder of the *North American Review* (although his tastes were too Romantic for his colleagues and his audience, who ultimately forced him to give up his editorship). He was Orthodox in his theology, though his Orthodoxy was, like Marsh's, colored by a fascination with German philosophy and Romantic literature, and he did his best to encourage a more spiritual attitude among his Boston neighbors. Consequently Dana received *Aids* with great enthusiasm and sent Marsh his hopes that it would hasten the downfall of Lockeanism.

> You must by this time, Sir, be satisfied that what you
> have done to bring Coleridge into notice in this country
> has not been in vain. The deeps are moved, and must swal-
> low up quick the brawling, shallow, rambling stream of
> Taylorism, and the artificial, formally cut canals of the
> other system. The Bible . . . will be applied to that which
> it was intended to meet. . . . The endeavor will at last be
> given over to apply its great principles of Love and Truth
> to a sort of mechanico-metaphysico-automaton—dubbed
> man.[26]

Dana and Follen brought similar pietist backgrounds to *Aids* and shared assumptions much like those that helped Marsh to republish the work in America. They welcomed it not as a new theological manifesto, but as a particularly forceful expression of their own views, which were, like Marsh's, focused on an essentially conservative resurrection of Orthodoxy rather than on a radical restructuring of faith, society, or art. Their influence lay in their ability to invest Marsh's spiritual philosophy with some of their own respectability, making it, if not more acceptable to Unitarians in general, at least more likely to be read by those who might welcome its influence.

THE Transcendentalists alone imbibed the distinctive character of Marsh's work, absorbed its life, and left the dry husks, the vestiges of worn out conventions, to continue their two-hundred-year-old process of decay. Freed by their Unitarian training to ignore its doctrinal preachings (thereby earning Marsh's lifelong disapproval), they were able to discover in its spiritual epistemology a new method for gaining access to experiences left out of account by the prevailing metaphysic. The Transcendentalist reception of Marsh's *Aids* both reveals a common theme beneath the apparently diverse attitudes held by these men and identifies more precisely the differences among them as each put Marsh's work to his own uses. In contrast to their more conventional Unitarian contemporaries, the Transcendentalists without exception greeted the *Aids* with the greatest enthusiasm and credited it with a major role in forming their philosophical outlook.

The Transcendental genius was acquisitive and selective. It extracted from other systems the ideas it could turn to its own purposes without regard for the integrity of the system as a whole. From Marsh, Transcendentalism acquired no single idea, no specific proposition or article of belief. The Transcendentalists took the method central to Marsh's thought, and placed it at the center of their own. Marsh's *Aids* was, as William Charvat has said, "the beginning of American Transcendentalism in its more abstruse manifestations."[27] While individual Transcendentalists may have sketched out their fundamental assumptions and identified their motives before they read *Aids*, it provided them all with terms about which their own still only half-formed beliefs could cohere. Coleridge supplied the spiritual epistemology that could make Transcendentalist assumptions active and communicable.

Marsh's method offered a new epistemology, an alternative way of knowing, to replace the discredited authority of Scripture and the sterile dictates of the senses and of tradition. Although this method was associated with a variety of complementary ideas, particularly with the organic metaphor, it was primarily a promise of immediate access to absolute truth, an assurance that man need not be bound to dogma or limited to the second-hand testimony of abstract scholarship. With this promise came a new and ambitious individualism. Marsh's method provided a way of answering immediately questions that once would have been answered by appeals to established authorities—the church, state, Scripture, or science. In the process, it gave the common man—not the saint, not the churchman, not the scholar—previously unheard-of authority. It was, thus, a major step in the growth of the self that had been an American preoccupation for two hundred years.[28] As one side-effect, Coleridge's method guaranteed that there would be no unifying authority about which Transcendentalist views of *Aids* (or of anything else for that matter) could cohere. For each Transcendentalist, *Aids* established its meaning in the context of his or her own particular motives and preconceptions (a process which was itself particularly characteristic of Transcendentalist thinking), and *Aids* cannot be said to have *had* any meaning independent of those contexts. Some Transcendentalists measured *Aids* against European philosophy, but many others lacked the philosophical expertise needed to measure it at all. Still others were personally committed to a more pragmatic view. The sketches that follow dramatize the diverse intellectual positions that determined Transcendentalist responses to *Aids*. They investigate the ways in which differing perspectives on *Aids*—technical philosophy, philosophical naivete, French eclecticism, mystical idealism—reshaped its meaning and altered its implications, probing and unfolding the Transcendentalist method it conveyed.

ALTHOUGH *Aids* must share with numerous other works the responsibility for encouraging Transcendentalism,[29] Alexander Kern's view seems just: "it is only a little too strong to say that Coleridge furnished the spark which set off the intellectual reaction: the American publication by James Marsh . . . of Coleridge's *Aids to Reflection* in 1829 and of *The Friend* in 1831 was a crucial effort."[30] *Aids* offered the Transcendentalists the philosophy they hungered for, and with Marsh's emendations of Coleridge, *Aids* spoke to Transcendentalist ears in just the intuitionist and antiauthoritarian tone that would best invoke their inclinations and prejudices. Coleridge's system precipitated the interaction of previously isolated ideas and united individuals who habitually prided themselves on their independence from any group. Kenneth Cameron asserts that "Marsh's 'Preliminary Essay' has an interest all its own. It was itself a trumpet blast against the metaphysics of John Locke as well as a commentary on contemporary thought in the United States. Marsh called attention to a growing dissatisfaction with prevailing opinions on man and man's will."[31] The Transcendentalists ranked high among the dissatisfied, and *Aids* ignited their impulse to convene and share both their complaints about the old system and their aspirations for a new and better one.

This power to unite the stubbornly independent Transcendentalists was, in part, a result of the aphoristic style of *Aids*. The Transcendentalists habitually praised the moment of insight, the luminous idea, over the systematic argument. The literature of Transcendentalism sticks in the memory as a collection of powerful phrases from *Nature*, Alcott's "Orphic Sayings," and Thoreau's *The Service*. Such writing appealed to the Transcendentalists, as it did to Marsh, precisely because it subverts logical argument. It suggests or inspires, leaving ample latitude for meditation and elaboration by the reader. More coherent, systematic statements chafed readers who preferred to find their own truths and balked at swallowing anyone's ideas whole. The Transcendentalists were not, however, fully reconciled to the apparent disunity of the aphoristic style. The stylistic traditions of Puritan preaching were far from dead to them, and they lamented their inability to master a more obvious and conventional organization. Such allegiances account, in part, for the superficially logical structure of Emerson's *Nature* and for his famous complaint that his paragraphs are collections of "infinitely repellent particles." Men, too, Emerson said, were "infinitely repellent orbs," a fact that the Transcendentalists lamented and strove mightily to overcome. When they could not, prevented by their cherished individualism, they simply shifted their emphasis and said with Coleridge that "the greatest and best of men is but an aphorism."[32]

F. O. Matthiessen has pointed out the significant similarity between this perception and the Transcendentalists' identification of the word with the thing. Aphorisms were powerful because they could disclose the unity of apparently diverse thoughts. Aphorism overcomes superficial fragmentation by tapping unity of spirit, and like spiritual unity, the unity of Transcendentalist writing is not formal. It exists not on the page but in the mind of the reader, where it lives, like nature itself, in the "integrity of impression created by manifold . . . objects."[33] The Transcendentalists cherished aphorism and proverbs as momentary insights into unconditioned experience. In *Aids*, Coleridge makes absolute statements that transcend both their own superficial disunity and the reader's awareness, in more analytical moments, that they require qualification.

IN THE fall of 1836, the Transcendentalists were eager for such statements. Frederic Henry Hedge recalled that in September,

> Mr. Emerson, George Ripley, and myself, with one other, chanced to confer together on the state of current opinion in theology and philosophy, which we agreed in thinking very unsatisfactory. Could anything be done in the way of protest and introduction of deeper and broader views. What precisely we wanted it would have been difficult for either of us to state. What we strongly felt was dissatisfaction with the reigning sensuous philosophy, dating from Locke, on which our Unitarian theology was based. The writing of Coleridge, recently edited by Marsh, and some of Carlyle's earlier essays . . . had created a ferment in the minds of some of the young clergy of that day. There was a promise in the air of a new intellectual life.[34]

Hedge's charter membership in the Transcendental movement, and the Transcendentalists' habit of designating themselves the Hedge Club because they met whenever he came down from Bangor to Boston, have obscured the fact that Hedge was a relative conservative among his Transcendentalist fellows. In many ways he more closely resembled the elder Channing than he did Emerson. It was on Hedge that Channing pinned his hopes that the Transcendentalists would remain within conventional Christianity, and when those hopes were dashed and Transcendentalism moved away from Unitarianism, it moved away from Hedge as well. As the years went by, Hedge minimized his participation in the movement, characterizing himself as an intellectual radical but an ecclesiastical conservative. Like Channing, whom he revered, Hedge was willing to give any idea a hearing in pursuit of truth. But, again like Channing, he managed to keep a tight rein on the energies of his questing intellect and so to contain it within the rather broad theological territory of Unitarianism. Hedge's later standing within the Unitarian community as editor of the *Christian Examiner* and president of the Unitarian Association is a mark of his lifelong intellectual breadth and liberality. He managed to wield influence in both the Transcendentalist and Unitarian camps and never attracted the kind of criticism that Convers Francis received when he abandoned Transcendentalism for the comforts of a Harvard professorship.

Hedge's intellectual liberality along with his philosophical sophistication colors his response to Coleridge's *Aids* as it does all of his religious thought. In reading Coleridge, Hedge had an advantage enjoyed by no other Transcendentalist; he had spent five years in Germany before entering Harvard and had a firm grip on German philosophy. Hedge came to Coleridge, not as a novice seeking initiation into the mysteries, but on even terms. As a result, his response to Coleridge carried weight in the early days of Transcendentalism. In 1833, before the *Christian Examiner* was closed to liberal views, Hedge wrote the first review of Marsh's *Aids*. Hedge himself later called it "the *first word*, as far as I know, which any American had uttered in respectful recognition of the claims of Transcendentalism." Emerson called it, characteristically, "a living, leaping logos."[35]

In the essay, Hedge displays the fruits of his German study, a critical and analytical attitude toward philosophy and theology. Both his criticism of Coleridge and his own writings on theology and ethics demonstrate a Kantian delight in classification, breaking down man's moral nature, his aesthetic perception, and his intellect into faculties, qualities, powers, or forms.[36] In addition to making Hedge an ecclesiastical conservative, this love of system put limits on his appreciation of Marsh's version of Coleridge, which subsumed understanding and sense in reason, blurring the distinctions that Kant had so painstakingly drawn. Hedge criticized Coleridge for neither presenting an accurate interpretation of Kant's system nor completing one of his own.[37] Behind this philosophical difference of opinion, however, lies a deeper religious disagreement, one that helps to distinguish Hedge from Marsh on one hand and from Emerson on the other. Hedge's distaste for Marsh's union of man's faculties under reason reflects his own habitual insistence on a clear separation between phenomena and spirit, between science and religion. These are the very realms Marsh's philosophy was intended to unite, and Hedge's scrupulous limitation of each to its own sphere suggests his continuing ties to eighteenth-century rationalism.

More than either Marsh or Emerson, Hedge put the entire responsibility for the spiritual life on man. Unlike Emerson, he separated man from nature, which, he wrote, is "inexorably conditioned and conditions us."[38] For Hedge, external nature had no moral power of its own. It was not infused with spirit. Nature was an inhibition which man must overcome in his own spiritual development. The communion Emerson discovered in nature Hedge had to find elsewhere, and he turned to (or more accurately never turned away from) Scripture. He defined Christianity as reliance on revelation and placed Emerson and Thoreau outside the circle of Christianity when they found revelations all around them and denied that the Christian revelation was unique or essential. Hedge, who was probably better prepared than anyone else to recognize the difficulties of Marsh's system, avoided those difficulties by separating his philosophical speculations from his religious convictions. While this careful separation of intellect and faith may show a less than inspiring intellectual courage, it seems also to reflect his informed, and probably justifiable, suspicion that Transcendentalist philosophy was ultimately incompatible with traditional Christianity.

Yet Hedge aligned himself with the Transcendentalists and parted from Unitarianism (and from Marsh's Orthodoxy) by making man the meeting place of the natural and the spiritual. Hedge believed that natural and spiritual were simply two stages of the same humanity. With Emerson he accused Christianity of stressing the "religion of the cross," of atonement and afterlife, when it should turn its attention to the kingdom of heaven within.[39] Hedge approved of Coleridge primarily because of Coleridge's attention to the inner spirit, and that is the issue he elaborated on in his pioneering review. Like Marsh, Hedge argued that the proofs of Christianity lay in experience rather than in philosophy, but he went further, pushing Transcendentalism over the edge of reticence, by asserting that understanding of Transcendentalist philosophy could come only to those who had raised their minds to transcendent heights. With this essay, Hedge signaled the end of Transcendentalist apologetics and the beginning of a new and more aggressive strategy.

As HEDGE later recalled, Coleridge's writing was most influential among the younger Unitarian clergy, who worked enthusiastically against the prevailing system in hopes of replacing it with a better one. Coleridge's premise that the inner powers of the mind could reveal absolute truth helped them avoid the skeptical conclusions of Lockean epistemology and bolstered their native confidence in the mind. As R. H. Dana wrote to Marsh, "there is something in Unitarianism wonderfully adapted to make a mind vain of its untried powers. The young are like the insane—they are unconscious of any limits to their powers."[40] James Freeman Clarke spoke for this "insane" younger group, acknowledging his own debt to Coleridge and *Aids*:

> It was about the time of our senior year that Professor Marsh of Vermont University was reprinting Coleridge's "Friend" and his "Aids to Reflection" and his "Biographia Literaria." . . . Coleridge the philosopher confirmed my longing for a higher philosophy than that of John Locke. . . . Something within me revolted at all . . . attempts to explain soul out of sense, deducing mind from matter, or tracing the origin of ideas to nerves, vibrations, and vibratiuncles. So I concluded I had no taste for metaphysics and gave it up, until Coleridge showed me from Kant that though knowledge begins *with* experience it does not come *from* experience. Then I discovered that I was born a transcendentalist.[41]

The Unitarian tradition did not encourage profound metaphysical speculation and most of the Transcendentalists were satisfied, like Clarke, to rest on the simple premise that knowledge is elicited from the mind by experience, without entangling themselves in the mechanics of this process or in its implications for religion, society, or art. Like Hedge, Clarke clung to the institutions and theological dogma of Christianity. But he could not rest content with Lockean attempts to make man a mechanical creature, and *Aids* provided an alternative to barren sensation for him and for his Transcendentalist colleagues. Clarke and others like him did not read *Aids* for a systematic philosophy. They were not philosophers. They read it for assurances that theology was not limited to common sense, and to rationalize doctrines they had cherished in their hearts all along.

Young men like Clarke extracted from their reading of Coleridge a resounding and uncomplicated proclamation that absolute truths lay within rather than without in empirical science and scholarly authority. But several students of the growing "New School" were less satisfied than Clarke with Coleridge's subjective route to salvation. Although they were repelled by the deterministic mechanism that lay at the end of the Lockean philosophy, at the same time they had been brought up in it and it colored their outlook, creating a demand that truth be ratified by some objective authority. These Transcendentalists sought a way of incorporating the conviction of scientific fact into religious experience. Among the lesser lights, for example, W. H. Channing objected to the "egotheism" of some of his associates.[42] His own brand of Transcendentalism was unformed and vague, but it was in every way less individualistic than the familiar principles of Emerson or Thoreau. Channing recognized the divinity of mankind as a whole rather than that of any individual man, and he hoped to organize mankind into social units that would reflect the order of the divine mind. For such men, Coleridge's reflection was distasteful, even self-indulgent, and they turned to sources of more practical inspiration—Fourier in Channing's case.

Stronger minds within the movement housed their desires for an absolute objective truth in a more fully developed system, and most often they turned not to Coleridge but to the French version of Kantian philosophy in Victor Cousin. Alexander Kern has said that Cousin's "eclecticism had a widespread vogue among the Transcendentalists because, using the

Kantian system in a way which was easily comprehensible, he rescued innate ideas while still retaining some of the empiricism of the English school."[43] Most prominent of Cousin's disciples among the Transcendentalists were George Ripley and Orestes Brownson, who seem to have used Cousin much as the Unitarians used Scottish realism or, more remotely, as the Puritans used Ramus. In each case the object was a simple, comprehensible philosophical system that would provide easy access to metaphysical certainty at once intuitive and objective. Given Cousin's oversimplification of Kant, it is surprising that he should find followers in two of the most powerful intellects among the Transcendentalists. This attraction to a simplistic philosophy demonstrates the pertinence of Brownson's own well-known assertion that Transcendentalism was "really of American origin, and the prominent actors in it were carried away by it before they formed any acquaintance with French or German metaphysics; [which] is the effect of their connection with the movement, not the cause."[44] The Transcendentalists had, for the most part, formed their views before they read the works we generally call their sources. The broad outlines of their thought were already firmly drawn, determined by their individual turns of mind, and each attached himself to the thinker who best fit his own existing motives, without particular regard for the technical philosophical merit of his system.

Clearly, Coleridge did not complement Ripley's temper so well as did Cousin. Ripley's enthusiasm for Marsh's *Aids* was tempered by his characteristic desire to *verify* religious truth. Therefore, he was understandably dissatisfied with Coleridge, who made it a point to deny the possibility and even the *desirability* of verification. To Ripley it looked as if Coleridge left the concrete foundations of truth in doubt, though he provided an eloquent refutation of Lockeanism and a moving statement of idealism. In his "Introductory Notice" to *Specimens of Foreign Standard Literature*, Ripley correctly attributed "the remarkable popularity of Mr. Coleridge as a philosophical writer" to his awakening of "inward powers,"[45] but he had reservations about Coleridge's own philosophy. "Mr. Coleridge cannot satisfy the mind whose primary want is that of philosophical clearness and precision. He is the inspired poet, the enthusiastic prophet

104

of a spiritual philosophy; but the practical architect, by whose skill the temple of faith is to be restored, cannot be looked for in him."[46] Ripley's typically American distaste for Coleridge's difficult language and complex philosophical argumentation seems unworthy of a scholar of his talent and attainments, and it is likely that behind his insistence that philosophy must speak to the mind of the common man lies the distrust of subjectivism and love of system that distinguished Ripley from Emerson and later inspired Brook Farm and Ripley's other attempts at social reform.

Ripley's criticism of Coleridge did not, however, prevent him from valuing Marsh's efforts to popularize Coleridgean philosophy. On the contrary, he welcomed any system that seemed to work against Locke. In 1837, he responded to Marsh's works by asking him to translate a German work of his choice for *Specimens* "with an introduction and notes similar to your valuable commentaries on Coleridge."[47] Ripley was well aware of Marsh's theological conservatism, and he deftly combined apology with encouragement as he sought Marsh's assistance. "We are heretics and radicals ourselves: so much must be confessed; but we have large sympathies with ideal conservatives in church and state; and some individuals of that character feel that they can write with us and for us without compromise or inconsistency."[48] He assumed a general commonality of interests with Marsh without losing sight of their areas of disagreement. "I have ventured to make some distinct references to your Edition of the 'Aids to Reflection,'" he said, "and also to exhibit a view of Coleridge in which I cannot hope for your sympathy. However, I am sure that we are both laboring for the same object; and if you can make Coleridge instrumental in the restoration of a spiritual philosophy among our countrymen, I will à l'autre hand for Cousin."[49]

The reality of the sympathy Ripley imagined he shared with Marsh is open to doubt. Nothing draws the lines of difference between the two more sharply than Ripley's own statement of what he takes to be their common aim: to "spread a more generous culture and the illustration of clearer and more healthy relations between man and man."[50] Although Marsh would not have denied the worthiness of such ends, they would have struck him as incidental to the true goal—personal spiritual growth. Once again, Ripley's emphasis is objective and social rather than subjective and individual.

Yet, both Marsh and Ripley were evidently able to overlook these differences, or at least to subsume them in a mutual respect that was a measure more of the generosity of their minds than of particular philosophical agreements. Ripley's letters seem to have been part of a continuous correspondence with Marsh beginning in 1837, and they apparently met more than once during Marsh's visits with Dana or Channing. The letters also imply that Marsh expressed some interest in Ripley's project, and he may even have considered undertaking a translation of one of several writers he mentioned to Ripley as possible subjects. But ill health after 1835 made Marsh incapable of sustained effort, and he never began the project Ripley had suggested.

In Ripley's response we see the peculiar fact that Marsh's *Aids* was least appreciated by those Transcendentalists with whom he had the most in common. Ripley shared Marsh's philosophical bent, his affection for formal and historical Christianity, and, most important, his belief that religious truth must come from a source outside the self. Like Marsh, he argued that absolute reason was not and could not be one with the self and urged selflessness as the proper path to divine knowledge. Both Ripley and Orestes Brownson valued Cousin for this formulation of a "Reason not ourself," an objective absolute authority that was not subject to personal vagaries.[51] In this one respect, the Cousin school of Transcendentalism was closer to Marsh, who also defined reason as a divine element in man separate from the personality, than it was to Emerson. Brownson, for instance, greeted Emerson's "Divinity School Address" with concern about Emerson's possible pantheism. "If there be no God out of the soul, out of the me," he said, ". . . then there is no God."[52] In their search for an authoritative faith, Ripley and Brownson always gave greater credence to historical religion than Emerson did. Brownson's remarkable odyssey through almost every conceivable version of Christianity suggests both a certain failure of belief and a willingness to follow a philosophical system to its logical consequences. At one stage of this intellectual journey Brownson espoused Cousin, but it was the same

need for an objective absolute authority that gave his radicalism its economic and social cast and drew him finally into the
Catholic church.

AT THE opposite extreme from the objectivity of Ripley or Brownson stood Bronson Alcott, and of all the Transcendentalists
none voiced his debt to Coleridge so emphatically or with such
unqualified enthusiasm. Although Alcott acquired a copy of
Marsh's *Aids* soon after its publication, he did not read it until
two years later, when he was running a school in Germantown,
Pennsylvania.[53] Before this time Alcott had not read widely, and
what he had read served, he said, merely to bind him more
firmly in "the thralldom of sense into which I had been enticed
by the morbid food of English literature."[54] His reading of Coleridge freed him from this servitude and opened up new worlds
of the mind. "No writer ever benefited me more than he has
done," Alcott asserted; "the perusal of *Aids to Reflection* and *The
Friend* forms a new era in my mental and psychological life."[55]
Odell Shepard calls *Aids to Reflection* with Marsh's commentary
and notes the work that "led Alcott to abandon the philosophy
of John Locke and made him a Transcendentalist."[56] Shepard
points to Alcott's voluminous marginal notes in his copy of *Aids*
as proof that the work "never ceased to stimulate Bronson Alcott. Four years after the first perusal," Shepard continues, "he
was reading it for the fifth time, and fifty years later it was still
on the list of his annual reading."[57]

As the leading spirit of the more mystical side of Transcendentalist philosophy, Alcott welcomed Coleridge's elevation of
inner powers over external truth and his connection between
human reason and unconditioned ideality. He acknowledged an
allegiance to Coleridge most unusual in a Transcendentalist
who sought all truth in the depths of his own heart. "Were I to
name any modern 'master,'" he said, "it would be him. I could
belong to the church as this is portrayed in his thought, and
cannot but wonder at the neglect which his writings receive at
the hands of theologians of every shade of orthodoxy. He is a
college in himself and fairly comprehended, would render sects
and schools superfluous."[58] Alcott preferred Coleridge's philosophy to the innate ideas of the French eclectics, whom he eventually found "too shallow" for his purposes, and to Kant, who

still limited man's knowledge to sensible experience. Far from being inferior to Kant, Coleridge was for Alcott "the greatest and indeed almost the only representative of spiritual philosophy among modern metaphysical thinkers."[59]

Even forty years later, long after the Transcendentalist wave had subsided and near the end of a life devoted to reading and solitary reflection, Alcott still revered Coleridge as "the first of English thinkers," the best possible study for theological students "alike for depth and for subtlety of insight." "All sects," Alcott wrote, "are in his books . . . of modern teachers, he may be styled 'the Divine.'"[60] This last distinction reveals a crucial difference between the visionary Alcott and the more scholarly Hedge or George Ripley. For while the latter concentrated on matters of form (Hedge criticized Coleridge as an inadequate interpreter of Kant, and Ripley regretted the lack of clarity and system in Coleridge's philosophy), Alcott cared less for formal system than for inspirational assertions that compel assent, less for critical philosophy than for spiritual epiphany. He interpreted Coleridge's philosophy as proof of man's capacity to know spiritual truth immediately and certainly—a proof that Kant's system had denied him.

EMERSON's understanding of *Aids* is more difficult to assess for, unlike Alcott, Emerson acknowledged no "master" or school and denied all influence but inspiration. He took from other writers only those phrases that spoke to something in himself, giving credit not to the writer but to the universal truth that lay in his own soul awaiting revelation. Emerson read widely and eclectically, selecting from each writer only those ideas that he could use and virtually ignoring the rest.[61] As Rene Wellek has noted, in the profusion of Emerson's reading he had access to assorted original and translated texts of German philosophy and therefore did not necessarily require the mediation of Coleridge.[62] Yet, especially for Emerson, access to a text did not necessarily ensure mastery of its substance, and often Emerson's journals do not begin to reflect his engagement with a work until years after his first reading of it. The date of Emerson's first contact with Coleridge is uncertain. As an undergraduate at Harvard he read and disapproved of Coleridge's poetry, and in 1819 he checked out the *Biographia Literaria* from the Boston Library Society, but returned it only two days later. Emerson may have seen *The Friend* before he read Marsh's edition of the *Aids* since Sampson Reed secured a copy of the 1818 London edition in three volumes and began circulating it by 1826. Nevertheless, Coleridge does not appear frequently in the journals and letters until the end of 1829, when Emerson first read Marsh's *Aids*. So, while Emerson may have encountered much of Coleridge's writing before he read Marsh's edition of *Aids to Reflection*, this early reading does not seem to have made much of an impression on him.

Of course, it would be foolish to claim for any work definitive influence in Emerson's intellectual development. Marsh's initial appeal surely lay in his Platonism, his antiempiricism, and his insistence on experiential piety—ideas Emerson already held by 1829. By the same token, Marsh alone does not account entirely for Emerson's tendency to find moral import in natural law—a concept he found in Thomas Taylor's translation of Plato and in such native examples of natural religion as Cotton Mather's *The Christian Philosopher* and Charles Chauncey's *Benevolence of the Deity*. Yet between late 1829, when he first read Marsh's *Aids*, and 1838, Emerson mentioned no writer as frequently as he did Coleridge. Kenneth Cameron finds Coleridge "preeminent among the teachers of Emerson"[63] and attributes the increasing maturity of Emerson's philosophical thought between 1829 and 1838 to his almost continuous study of Coleridge's works. Many of Emerson's early sermons explore themes traceable to *Aids*. Especially prominent among these are reliance on the "inward eye," the power of childish perception, the virtue of self-knowledge, and the idea that knowing is being or becoming. *Aids* also provided the germ of Emerson's evolutionary theory in Coleridge's assertion that "all things strive to ascend and ascend in their striving."[64]

Emerson first read Marsh's *Aids* during a period of desperate search for a spiritual system that would raise his idealist faith into knowledge. He took up *Aids* and *The Friend* at almost the same time, and initially he preferred *Aids*. To his brother William he said that he had read "Coleridge's *Friend*—with great interest; Coleridge's '*Aids to Reflection*' with yet deeper."[65] His greater early interest in *Aids* stemmed almost certainly from Marsh's simplified interpretation of Coleridge, which conveyed the distinction between reason and understanding in terms akin to those Emerson had learned from Plato. This distinction provided the missing piece for Emerson's idealist philosophy.

In the first flush of his encounter with this original and important idea, Emerson wrote enthusiastically to his aunt, Mary Moody Emerson, outlining the new principle, and in a second letter defended Coleridge against his American detractors:

> People wag their heads, and say, I can't understand Coleridge, yet [Coleridge] is only one more instance of what is always interesting, the restless human soul bursting the narrow boundaries of antique speculation and mad to know the secrets of that unknown world, on whose brink it is sure it is standing. . . . I say a man so learned and a man so bold, has a right to be heard, and I will take off my hat the while and not make an impertinent noise. At least I become acquainted with one new mind I never saw before. . . . Then I love him for he is no utilitarian, nor necessarian, nor scoffer, nor *hoc genus omne*, tucked away in a corner of Plato.[66]

Since Emerson's first letter to his aunt has been lost, his technical understanding of Coleridge at this time remains uncertain, but by now it ought to be clear that the standards of formal philosophy are inappropriate measures for the impact of Coleridgean thought on a reader like Emerson. Although Emerson was not totally ignorant of Kant's version of reason, he, like Marsh, preferred Coleridge, who removed the Kantian division between the mind and the world. "Coleridge alone has treated the mind well," he said.[67]

During this period, Emerson studied the notions of reason and understanding obsessively and used *Aids* as his primary text because it dealt more fully with this subject than Coleridge's other works. In May 1834, Emerson inquired of his brother Edward, "let me ask you do you draw the distinction of Milton, Coleridge, and the Germans between reason and understanding [?] I think it is philosophy itself."[68] In December, still reading *Aids* and *The Friend*, Emerson remarked that "Mr. Coleridge has thrown many new truths into circulation."[69] At this time *Aids* and *The Friend* receive about equal space in Emerson's journals and letters, but after 1836 *Aids* seems to have sunk in Emerson's estimation while *The Friend* rose.

This change in Emerson's opinion almost certainly grew from his increasing dissatisfaction with the more technical, rigorously philosophical quality of *Aids*. Emerson aspired to an unconditioned knowledge of the ideal that exceeded the limits of Kant's reason, and those limits appear much more distinctly in *Aids* than in Coleridge's earlier writings. Those passages in *Nature* which follow Kant more closely seem to show the influence of *Aids*, but in general the more systematic *Aids* was a victim of Emerson's desire to interpret reason in semimystical terms that could find more support in Coleridge's earlier writings and in Carlyle. *Aids* contained the most faithful exposition of reason in the Kantian sense, and once Emerson had formed his own distinct notions of the powers of reason and *Aids* had exhausted its inspirational usefulness, Emerson came to view it as "the least valuable" of Coleridge's books.[70] But during that important period between 1833 and 1836 when *Nature* and Emerson's concept of reason were taking shape, *Aids* always lay by him on his work table.

The version of reason that Emerson found in *Aids* was intended by Marsh to reflect and reinforce his Orthodox theology. In Marsh's concept of the hierarchical relationship between reason and understanding, regenerate reason subsumed understanding and turned it from selfish to godly ends. Marsh acknowledged the *apparent* fragmentation of human experience and the authority of worldly forms only to absorb all fragmentation, all transient earthly forms, into a divine unity, the one eternal form of God. He united the powers of the objective world (understanding) with those of the spiritual reason, resolving human chaos into divine harmony. He did so, however, only by discounting at last the authority of the self, subordinating it to God and to a reason that resided in the mind as God's representative, not as an inherent faculty. Marsh still clung to the Puritan vision in which fallen nature and divine grace were interacting but decidedly separate realms. The divine sustained nature without becoming a part of it. In such a system, one which includes original sin, the source of truth cannot be human, it must be divine, and if it appears in man it must be a divine addendum available only through God's grace.

111

Emerson first began to re-form the concept of reason in his own image during the emotional crisis following the death of his first wife, Ellen. It was then that his thought began to cohere and that he first used reason and understanding in a manner akin to Coleridge's. "It would be well . . . ," he mused, "to . . . make a catalogue of 'necessary truths.' *They* are scanned and approved by the Reason far above the understanding. They are the last facts by which we approximate metaphysically to God."[71] While this statement suggests that Emerson had absorbed Marsh's notion of reason as a power of spiritual insight into unconditioned truth, it already shows a distinctly Emersonian stamp. Instead of describing understanding as a lesser part and servant of reason as Marsh does, or as a polar *unity* with Coleridge, it *divides* reason from understanding, banishing the latter to sensual perdition and elevating the former to spiritual God-head. By separating reason and understanding, Emerson traded Marsh's hierarchy for dichotomy. This step forced him to value alternately either the form or the spirit, but it gave him no way of uniting them and threatened to leave him always moving restlessly from one to the other.

By interpreting reason as a means of insight into unconditioned truth available even to unregenerate minds, Emerson discarded the last instrument of mediation between man and God and thereby cast off all restraint on the authority of the self. Having discarded the barrier that original sin placed between the realms of nature and grace, Emerson could no longer distinguish absolute from natural truth. Truth could, on the contrary, comprise a natural form of the mind which would reflect the divine nature as no natural power ever could for Marsh. Emerson made reason his own, not an ambassador from heaven empowered to impart the Lord's will, but a power of individual insight. Previously, interpretation of experience had been controlled by accepted standards, by absolute and universal values codified in Scripture or in the church or social institutions. Now the last of those standards was brushed aside, clearing the way for the possibility of a truth that did not depend on external authority but was constantly created between the individual and the objects of his experience. With the same stroke that made man supreme in his universe, an unquestionable authority, Emerson altered the very meaning of "authority" itself. Without Marsh's link to the external and absolute authority of God, reason became a part of the mind, subject to all the influences that sway the fancy and bias the judgment. Looking for some control over this potentially wayward reason, Emerson turned to nature as a repository of unconditioned truth with which the mind must be in harmony, but even nature was too quixotic for Emerson's needs, and he was never able to quiet his suspicions that the absolute dictates of reason might really be tempting whispers of personal whim.

Such an admission, with its implicit denial of *all* forms, was one that neither Emerson nor any of the other Transcendentalists was prepared to make explicit. Not unlike Marsh, the Transcendentalists wished to enliven the old forms with a new and transforming spirit. Even in the "Divinity School Address," which unfolds Emerson's most energetic attack on formalism in religion, he concluded by enjoining his listeners to "let the breath of new life be breathed by you through *the forms already existing*" (emphasis mine).[72] Transcendentalist thought derived much of its character from this desire to preserve stable forms despite its commitment to a method of inquiry and insight that denied the possibility of such stability. The often unspoken assumption that man can *create* as well as *perceive* divine truth informed the social schemes of Ripley and Brownson, who were convinced that truth was both objective and objectifiable and were determined to realize that truth in a social institution like Brook Farm. Emerson could not agree with Ripley that truth was objective, and he was often unsure that it was universal. Although at times the insights of reason seemed divine inspirations, truths that passed through him as a medium to reach the world, at other times they seemed new and personal revelations, absolute truths that were true absolutely for him alone and for a certain time and place, but which had limited value for others. For both Emerson and Ripley, truth became, potentially at least, a matter of man's creation, a matter of art.

MARSH's readers worked their own art on his text as Marsh had on Coleridge's, recreating it as they read, producing a new text blended of two parts preconception and assumption to one part authorial intent. None of them saw the *Aids* Marsh had seen when he published it. Orthodox divines viewed it as com-

113

mendably spiritual but heterodox and possibly dangerous. Unitarians defensively scorned it as muddy and mystical. Even Marsh's friends and students failed to apprehend its fundamental significance, trumpeting it as the banner of a new theological faction or emasculating it to defend Marsh's Orthodoxy. Only the Transcendentalists, who cared little for its Orthodox intentions or its systematic metaphysics, seized on its elaboration of the mind's power to find truth in its own depths and absorbed its true message by adopting its method. Marsh's attempt to apply his healing system to America's theological ills produced a protean text that frustrated the desires that had engendered it as it opened the door to a new form of religious radicalism.

The potential consequences of the creative authority that Marsh invested in the mind is nowhere clearer than in these responses of Marsh's readers to his own text. From the perspective of external authorities that Marsh wanted to supplant, what I have described as intellectual analogues and transformations would have appeared as originating source and influence. But the view of the mind Marsh created out of Coleridge and others and offered up to the uses of his American readers displaced authority from the empirical past, where it could be fixed, defined, and verified, and thrust it into the shifting present and the Romantic consciousness, where it mandated an unparalleled variety of interpretation in shifting contexts. Thus the speckled history of the American reception of *Aids* expresses better than anything else the revolutionary implications that the work itself half (but only half) concealed.

# 5

## FROM EDWARDS TO EMERSON:
## The Romantic Mind and Social Forms

'The Circumstance is Nature. . . . We have two things,—the circumstance, and the life. Once we thought positive power was all.
Now we learn that negative power, or circumstance, is half. Nature is the tyrannous circumstance, the thick skull, the sheathed
snakes, the ponderous, rock-like jaw.'
    —Emerson, "Fate"

TRANSCENDENTALIST radicalism chose a traditional end, the
discovery of a new route from man to God to replace the
one science and scholarship had closed. This was Marsh's
aim as well and the root of his kinship with Emerson. Getting to
God had always been particularly difficult for American Protestants, who lacked the religious mediation—institutional and
symbolic—that moved Catholics between man and God. In
place of interceding saints, Papal infallibility, and the historical
continuity of the church, the Puritans had only Scripture to illuminate their spiritual way. By the nineteenth century, German Biblical criticism had torn down even this last spiritual
landmark, and the tortuous arguments of conservatives like Andrews Norton only dramatized the weakness of their position,
while their abstruse scholarship turned Scripture into an obscure historical document open only to the diligent scholar.
    Traditionally, religious mediators had served a double pur-
pose. They acted not only as spiritual *guides* but also as *curbs*
on the human will. Christ, the archetypal mediator, bridged the

115

void between man and God. He completed an incomplete system, making up for the sin in man that divided him from his creator. By measuring the distance between imperfect humanity and divine perfection, external mediation stressed human inadequacy, by contrast, and muted rebellious impulses with the firm assurance that man cannot know his own best interest, that truth resides in heaven, not on earth. Scripture provided an authority validated by its divine origin which could control dangerous subjective impulses so that they would not lead the soul away from God into mere eccentricity. The necessity of ordering one's spiritual life to imitate Scriptural models had been one of the most important restraints on the growing power of the self in the Renaissance, and the need for such constraint was still more acute in nineteenth-century New England, which retained and even expanded Enlightenment optimism about the power of the individual mind. On all fronts, the demands of the "I" were more insistent than ever, hence more frightening and more in need of control.

It was just such a controlling, *conservative* mediation that Marsh was trying to provide. He offered his philosophy to reconstruct, not to weaken, the ties between men and social institutions that empiricism had severed. Marsh himself was far too deeply committed to established forms, too much the Orthodox churchman, to nurture unrestrained ego. Using reason, he attempted a compromise between detached external authorities and the dangerous heresy of original personal revelation. He even modelled his union of the mind and society on traditional theological structure. Locke's influence, Marsh imagined, had divided Christianity into three parts, depriving each of the power it had generated in union with the other two. Reason, the principle of divine order, dwindled to mere analysis of empirical fact when separated from doctrinal incarnation and spiritual elevation. Dogma, the incarnation of divine will, was reduced to a mean and unjustified Scriptural authority without the overarching design of reason and the vitality of faith. Faith, the passion uniting abstract reason with its doctrinal incarnation, became unbridled religious enthusiasm when deprived of its proper objects.

Marsh wanted to reunify them in a religious system modelled on the Trinity. In Marsh's theological trinity, each member

116

would partake of the others while retaining its own distinct identity and function. This revitalized religious system would reconcile all three of the currently opposed religious parties, uniting Unitarian reason, Congregationalist legalism, and Evangelistic passion—making the earthly church an institutional analogue of the triune God. Yet, lovely as this model seemed to Marsh, its beauty was mostly symbolic, and it could only imitate a vanished form that it could never actually renew. Worse still, it made a place *within* traditional Christian forms for notions that ensured their final demise. Like all of Marsh's conservative impulses, it was a gesture back toward a tradition that it had irrevocably left behind.

Marsh's practical inability to harmonize his own antinomian and Arminian impulses, his competing allegiances to personal spirit and objective form, vastly complicated his attempts to instill spirit into social institutions. He could neither banish his antinomian self into the Rhode Island wilderness nor accept its subservience to the testimony of the senses. To meet his need for a personal yet absolute authority, he moved the previously external authority of God into the mind itself, making the dictates of the individual spirit divinely authoritative.

It was, in a sense, the antinomian heresy fulfilled. If each man can discover divine truth in himself, the need for social controls becomes unclear. When the route to God is through the self rather than through the world, institutions should, in theory, exist solely to further this quest by increasing freedom for self-reflection and self-development. They are good only as long as they strive to make themselves obsolete, to create a society of saints, a national gathered church guided by mutual participation in the divine will and therefore free to dispense at last with artificial institutional forms. Earthly institutions of all kinds ought to function as contexts for individual salvation, as objective representations of universal principles, as correlative objects to draw forth the latent power of the individual so that man can learn, grow, and finally free himself from institutions and stand alone.

In practice, however, imperfect institutions, those in the real rather than the ideal world, proved far from passively accommodating. The loss of theological mediation, which meant greater spiritual authority for the individual, prompted earnest

117

believers (Marsh among them) who were naturally still unsure that their newly acquired powers would guide them aright, to make social institutions into secular versions of the old mediatory authorities. Despite his intentions and the logical implications of his theology, Marsh could not avoid seeing social institutions as alternate routes to God. Thus, the lack of spiritual mediation in the early nineteenth century ended by conferring unprecedented spiritual authority on *both* the individual *and* institutions, making the conflict between the two sharper than ever.

From the perspective of Marsh's *intentions*, however, his writings on religion, politics, education, and art may be seen as steps in a continuing effort to reconcile particulars and the universal. As a man of faith, Marsh naturally aimed always toward the universal and located authority there. And it is the nature of the universal to be distinct from particular social forms. Marsh's ambition to enact the divine will in conditional social institutions recalls the risky Puritan passion for tropes—metaphorical readings of the divine will in worldly events. The relationships Marsh perceives between universal truth and particular social institutions are strained because they are essentially *metaphorical*. In the absence of Scriptural mediation, Marsh could not resist the temptation to indulge in such metaphorical system building, but the consequences were unpredictable and proved disastrous for Marsh's conservative purposes. By constructing metaphorical relationships between social institutions and universal values, Marsh added new uncertainty to the location of authority, freeing it to shift with varying circumstances—making authority conditional rather than absolute. In other contexts, such as art, where particular content drops away, metaphorical truth takes on a unique, absolute authority of its own, one that certifies the validity of *symbolic* relationships.

In practical social contexts, Marsh's thought shows a distinct bias in favor of the solid and particular truth. This bias inheres in his impulse to *enact* the divine will rather than simply to read or know it. While knowing suggests greater capacity for revelation and directs the mind or spirit toward its own workings and the intangible, doing is by definition concrete and turns the mind outward toward the particular. Consequently, the institutions Marsh cast as mediators repeatedly imposed their *own* authority on spirit rather than offering spirit access to divine authority. Each social form twisted spirit in a characteristic way, frustrating its supernatural inclinations. Each offered its own version of universal truth, provided a different estimate of the good. In each context, the mind acquired a different sort of authority, markedly altering its own powers and its access to divine truth.

Marsh not only failed to bathe social institutions in the light of his harmonious universal vision, he repeatedly found that existing forms—the social conventions and expectations of nineteenth-century New England—redefined his own position. Circumstances did not just mechanically inhibit reform, they actually imposed themselves on his mind and altered the terms in which he could perceive social problems and their possible solutions. In practical social controversies, individuality and law never appeared to Marsh in the reconcilable terms they assumed in his theory of the mind. Individuality, too, often looked disturbingly like anarchy, making Marsh support rigid authority to preserve social order. When the individual did not immediately threaten church or state, forms and traditions appeared as repressive impediments to personal growth, and he fought them with an antinomian fervor. Consequently, his thought on the cultural controversies of his time mirrored those problems more than it resolved them.

It has been said, though still perhaps not with sufficient emphasis, that American Romanticism had its roots in American religion. It might even be said that it embodied a secularized version of theological impulses. But it is more difficult to determine the nature of those transformations that brought American Romantic literature out of church doctrine. Both attempt to give objective form to supernal truth, to supply, in Emerson's words "a ground unconditioned and absolute" for worldly experience. But they disagree radically about the location of their sanctioning authorities. In Marsh's search for absolute spiritual authority—from religion, the original center of American culture, to art, which increasingly preoccupied American intellectual life in the nineteenth century—he explored the power of objective institutions to embody spiritual impulses. That exploration illuminates more than simply the varied and conflicting

119

opinions and attitudes of a New England theologian struggling with the issues that all thinking New Englanders faced in his day. In it we can make out the intellectual stages that mark the transformation from submission to rigid doctrine to unconstrained creative expression. The balance between individual and social authority shifted with the varying circumstances Marsh faced, and these fluctuations describe the essential patterns of stress in the ideological shift from Puritan faith to Romantic aesthetics.

Marsh was no less artful a reader of his own work than was his audience. As his fears and motives changed with changes in social context, the key terms of his view of human authority changed as well, in both their associations and implications. Synchronically viewed, then, meaning becomes a function of context rather than of definition or historical inheritance. The often sought-after movement from Puritan to Federalist to Romantic to Modern appears here, not as a function of historical development leading neatly to ourselves, but as a relationship among social contexts, assumptions, and motives, which combine to shape meaning cut loose from absolute moorings.

## THE CHURCH

Marsh was, above all, a churchman. He had been touched by grace in his youth and moved to serve God in the world. But the 1830s were a troubled time for the church. New England was convulsed by theological uncertainty. Conservative churches were too often empty formal structures without the spontaneous feeling that enlivened faith. Desperate for religious *feeling*, many laymen forgot religious *authority*. Fleeing the dogmatic discourses of Orthodox ministers, they turned to evangelical preachers who were not hedged in by church conventions and could offer them more palatable fare. Transcendentalism was only one of a spate of radical sects that arose to give voice to the religious affections. The Second Great Awakening, still a matter of recent memory, had stirred up swarms of Anabaptists, Quakers, Shakers, Dunkers, and Comeouters, all eager to re-form American faith.[1]

Many ministers who were sensitive, as Marsh was, to the moribund state of New England theology were more than willing, as Marsh was not, to accept the *appearance* of piety in lieu of the reality. They welcomed anyone who could bring their parishioners to life. Several invited Jedidiah Burchard, a popular New England preacher who gathered a considerable following in Vermont in 1835 and 1836, into their churches, where he enjoyed a considerable success. Like popular evangelists from Charles Grandison Finney to Billy Graham, Burchard was a powerful speaker who charged the atmosphere with emotion to sweep listeners into confessions of faith. Burchard ostentatiously cast aside the formal steps designed to guard the religious order from the feelings of its own members. To the ministers' delight, he managed to lure the disenchanted back into the churches and created all the appearances of a new revival of faith. But by delivering the converting power into the hands of laymen, he made salvation a procedure rather than a miracle.

Burchard's apparent success did not blind Marsh to his subversion of traditional religious authority, but to oppose him Marsh had to give new power to social forms and take the first step in the movement away from intellectual security within absolute authority. He asserted the exclusive right of the trained clergy to interpret spiritual truth, and more important, he identified the *institutional church* as the worldly form of faith. Marsh was predisposed to see the universal in the forms of Congregationalism simply because the forms of the church defined and constituted Marsh's own notions of the universal. The church not only offered the earthly form of the divine will, but in Marsh's mind it was the *only* concrete form God's will had ever taken, making the two indistinguishable for him and encouraging him to see church principles as absolute. For Marsh's purposes, the church order was the earthly type of the divine order and commanded the same allegiance. Yet we can see that Marsh's loyalty tends to blur the crucial boundary between universal authority and particular expressions of it.

At bottom, Marsh was defending the rational form of faith itself as it was expressed in the church. God *was* reason, and faith must be rational. He feared that Burchard aroused the worst elements in his listeners by ignoring the rational will that was crucial to the process of redemption. Those who scorned consistent beliefs, who circumvented solid church forms, would fall into heresy (as he believed Emerson had done), substituting their private whim for the one absolute and universal will. To H. J. Raymond he wrote,

> The whole of Boston Transcendentalism I take to be rather a superficial affair and there is some force in the remark of a friend of mine that the "Dial" indicates rather the place of the moon than the sun. They have many of the prettynesses of the German writers, but without their manly logic and strong systematizing tendency. They pretend to no system or unity, but each utters, it seems, the inspiration of the moment assuming that it all comes from the universal heart, while ten to one it comes only from the stomach of the individual.[2]

Although he acknowledged (with some reluctance) that true faith can exist apart from doctrine, he insisted that, ideally, doctrine and spirit, form and substance, are wedded in an organic whole according to God's will. Earnest believers who strayed somewhat from Orthodoxy in a sincere and humble search for God did not threaten the Christian church as a whole and were, moreover, undoubtedly good practicing Christians. If however, the church did not necessarily carry the faithful *to* God, Marsh feared that itinerant evangelists or such lecturers as Emerson threatened to lead their listeners *away* from true faith with deceptive promises of a surer and easier path to divine truth.

Behind all of Marsh's work since Andover, he said, was "the paramount desire of apprehending and teaching aright the true principles of spiritual or evangelical religion, as distinguished from those systems which preclude the spiritual, as Unitarianism or generally rationalism on the one hand, and fanatical counterfeits on the other."[3] Marsh's response to Burchard's methods reveals that he distrusted fervor when it threatened clerical authority or challenged established church procedures. When piety was taken up by hostile forces outside the church, Marsh perceived its unsettling implications far more plainly than he could in the context of his own abstract philosophy.

Yet, the stridency of Marsh's reaction to Burchard seems entirely out of proportion to any real danger posed by one itinerant preacher. Burchard drove Marsh into uncharacteristic fits of emotion. Burchard's theology, Marsh raged, contained only "the crudest conceptions," his arguments the "most palpable contrivances." His teachings on regeneration were the "shallowest trash," the "most undigested crudities," and "the merest brain-dribble."[4] Marsh was not alone in his ire. Many of his colleagues feared the end of the church as they knew it if influences such as Burchard were not suppressed. He was for many "a noxious animal among the churches—a vermin—a pest."[5]

The truth is that Marsh and others made Burchard the correlative object for New England's ecclesiastical difficulties. He was the occasion for their anger, rather than its real target. As Marsh's friend Willard Childs reminded Marsh, "I fear that if Burchard should leave the state, the evil of which Burchardism is only a symptom, will remain." He suggested that Marsh's real interest lay not so much in "cutting off the 'fingers'" as in using Burchard to give New Englanders "a clear insight into the nature of the morbid state of the 'body ecclesiastic' which had produced it, trusting that if a general state of health could be restored, the excrescence would be soon cast off without difficulty or danger."[6] Marsh hated Burchard because Burchard represented the sickness of his own church and seemed a harbinger of New England's theological future if existing institutions did not once again make a place for piety. But, as always, it was the spirit and not the forms that Marsh wanted to alter. His inability to imagine that the old forms might be incompatible with a new spirit suggests both the conservative potential of his philosophy as a weapon of ecclesiastical reaction and his own ignorance of its radical implications in other fields.

Marsh built his case against Burchard as he did against Unitarianism and Orthodoxy, on the evangelist's reliance on empirical assumptions. Burchard had started out as a disciple of Charles Grandison Finney, and Marsh seized on this connection, following it back still further to Burchard's and Finney's common debt to Nathaniel Taylor.[7] By preaching group prayer as a means of grace, Burchard stepped over the doctrinal line into Arminian heresy. His practices implied the "perfect ability of the sinner to repent and do all God required of him without conditions or limitations"[8] and defined redemption as an act of the will on the part of the sinner requiring no divine intervention. Marsh's philosophical opposition to Locke taught him that the spirit could not be formed by worldly influences, that it was not subject to natural causation. Burchard's success stemmed, Marsh argued, not from any unusual spiritual force or from the special working of God in the hearts of his listeners, but from "natural causes put into operation on psychological principles, without supposing any spiritual element in the whole process."[9]

This "psychological" approach to conversion had a long tradition of American theology, one that was strengthened both by native American faith in experience and by the Orthodox impulse to institutionalize faith in the natural world. This impulse had been subtly reversed by men like Solomon Stoddard, who substituted the influence of institutions on the spirit for the influence of spirit on institutions. Stoddard replaced the traditional Puritan view of communion as the seal of the bargain between God and his elect with a new view of communion as a converting ordinance in order to swell church membership. The actual result, however, was a radical transformation of communion. This communion was not sacramental as in the Catholic Church—the communicant did not participate in the real body and blood of Christ. Rather, its significance was symbolic; it was a sign of Christ's suffering, and its function was psychological—to turn the emotions toward God.[10]

Although by 1800 Stoddard's methods had given way to Edwards's in most Congregationalist churches, they set a precedent for less deliberate, less professionally certified practitioners like Burchard, who actually took a further step, placing the converting power in the hands of the congregation itself.[11] The common note implicit in Stoddard and Burchard was an accommodation to practical needs at the expense of traditional church forms. In a time of flagging faith, church membership became an end in itself rather than an outward sign of an inward spiritual transformation. The outward signs assumed their own value. Ministers prized the form of a church for its own sake, without regard to its substance, and measured success by the number of bodies in the pews on Sunday rather than by the far less tangible piety of the spirits in those bodies. As Stoddard marks the first subtle inroads of Enlightenment standards of judgment into New England religious thought, Burchard reveals the firmness of their grip in the early nineteenth century and the inability of many New Englanders—even those in the ministry—to consider that there might be others.[12]

These ministers abandoned that rigorous strain within Christianity that presupposes the absolute opposition of practical and spiritual values. From the lives of the martyrs on, Christian literature taught that appearance is a lie, that wealth is poverty, weakness is strength, death is life. Marsh had learned the deceptiveness of appearances from Paul only to find that it made him an anomaly in 1836 as similar convictions did the Transcendentalists. Most of Marsh's contemporaries could not understand why he was horrified when Burchard and his supporters proudly defended their crusade by counting the converted masses. Such evidence, they protested, surely proved Burchard's spiritual power. While Marsh, sensitive as Edwards had been to the ambiguous validity of revivals, did not deny the possibility that some individuals in Burchard's audience had genuine conversion experiences, he did object when Burchard's system was approved merely because it appeared to have been *effective*. In the line of Mather, Edwards, and Emerson, Marsh argued that the spirit cannot be measured in numbers. It moves in harmony with divine precepts that can be neither confirmed nor denied by men. "Where are we to stop," he asked, "in the career of experiment if experience is admitted to have convincing force to justify such violations of all order."[13] External appearances, Marsh insisted, often deceive the unaided understanding, and he argued that Burchard's faith in appearances would "set us afloat upon a boundless sea of *novel and untried experiments*, and substitute the *shallowest empiricism* for all that has been regarded as fixed and established in the principles and practices of the church of God." Men must "judge," Marsh said, "according to truth and righteousness, i.e., principles a priori established in the unchanging verities of reason and the word of God." "Is there any other safe course?" he asked rhetorically, and answered predictably, "I cannot believe there is."[14]

Marsh's theological adventurousness was directed in ecclesiastical matters to conservative ends. Here his radical faith in universal reason reinforced his institutional conservatism as he used the forms of the church to control errant religious impulses and stave off ecclesiastical anarchy. Marsh argued that empiricism leads eventually to a total breakdown of moral and religious standards and undermines the church in which those standards reside. These abstract motives neatly complemented his more practical interest in defending particular church procedures that had, over many years, maintained the precarious balance between spiritual enthusiasm and church authority. He insisted that church conventions were the only guides men could follow to avoid metaphysical doubt and reach God.[15] In casting them aside, Burchard invited chaos, condemning the spirit to wander without direction or hope.

Marsh's investment here in the security of the church form rather than in the ordering power of individual reason aligns him with Protestant thinkers in both England and America who sought refuge from spiritual uncertainty in religious institutions.[16] Just as Marsh sought security in the historically authorized forms of Orthodox Congregationalism, many Protestants—notably John Henry Newman, Orestes Brownson, and Marsh's collaborator in publishing the *Aids*, George Allen—fled the spiritual anarchy which they discovered at the root of Protestantism and sought security in the Catholic and Anglican churches' claims to infallibility through a direct historical link to Christ and hence to God. Marsh could not become a Catholic, but he did endow the church with a symbolic power akin to that of Rome, and thus he may be seen as part of an American corollary to the Oxford Movement in England.

Although the Oxford Movement incorporated aristocratic biases and an aestheticism that may seem, at first, far removed from Marsh's democracy and practicality, both deployed a higher spiritual law to combat the forces of secularism in personal and social affairs, both asserted the satisfactions of obedience to that law, both found historical antecedents in primitive Christianity, both espoused the translogical, unconditional powers of the mind, and both valued "practical" (that is, experiential) rather than "speculative" (abstract) religion. Protestants who fled to Catholicism did so because they saw the *first step* into individual interpretation as a fatal one, ending inevitably in utter relativism. Or as Orestes Brownson said, "Protestantism ends in Transcendentalism."[17] In religion, this relativist impulse encouraged procedural controls on the potentially rampant individual will, and in this respect Marsh's position was no different than that of the Puritans, who in their struggle to secure an institutional form for their faith often had to repress the very spiritual fervor that supported that faith. The difference was that after two hundred years of increasing secularization in America, the church's formal restraints had lost their potency and seemed artificial or merely symbolic. Moreover, the pressure on them was heightened by the force of a cultural bias that for the first time favored individual authority and by a view of the mind (one that Marsh had helped create) that validated individual spiritual perception.

In order to defend the forms of the church against this pressure, Marsh had to invest them with an authority far greater than they had been designed to sustain. Church procedures had been established not to cause conversion but to offer the context in which it could occur. In a religion short on mediation, the church was intended as a minimal mediator between man and God. It exercised the controlling but not the facilitating mediatory power. It could not represent divine authority on earth or provide a direct historical connection to God through Christ. It offered a *way*, not a *means*, of grace, and the difference is crucial since it deepens the rift between spirit and form and makes grace work directly from divine to human spirit within a worldly form that is beneficial but in no way sanctified. The church provides a free place, a context in which spirit can grow, one that guides spirit and prevents it from straying *away* from God but does not help bring the spirit closer to God. Understandably, in doubtful times the faithful began to seek an easier path and to ignore church traditions that only seemed to bar their way.

Like Edwards, Marsh wanted to preserve institutional controls over the evidences of election and ensure the purity of his faith, and to do so he had to relocate spiritual authority, elevating the church institution far above its individual members.[18] Although this step was sanctioned by Marsh's belief that the church was the earthly type of the divine order and could claim direct access to spiritual authority, his next was more radical. Congregationalist ministers had always been merely well-educated members of the congregation with no special sacramental power. In practice, however, the church *was* its *ministers* (this was just the danger of seeing the church as the earthly form of divine spirit), and the authority Marsh conferred upon the religious institution easily transferred itself one step farther away from the universal and into the world to dress the pronouncements of a few privileged individuals. Ironically, Marsh's efforts to secure the church led to unprecedented individual power, a power that might seem benign enough here, but which would stretch itself more freely elsewhere.

Marsh argued for clerical authority over untutored spiritual insight with a vigor that makes him sound like a Puritan saint inveighing against Anne Hutchinson. He asserted the unique and irreplaceable authority of ministers to provide spiritual guidance for laymen. The Burchard affair, he declared, was "precisely such a case as demands the higher knowledge and superior insight of the clergy to guard the people from the influence of deceitful teachers and delusive doctrines."[19] In effect, Marsh redefined the relationship between minister and flock, minimizing the rational powers of the laity and stressing the practical significance of doctrine which, in its full speculative complexity, laymen could not comprehend. In fact, ministers must protect laymen from speculative knowledge that might shake their simple faith. "It is important," Marsh said, "and a part of their responsible and especial duty, to keep from the people all those agitating questions which the people cannot act upon intelligently, and leave their minds, as far as possible unexcited by them."[20] He endowed the minister with both special *knowledge* of divine truth and superior *insight*. The relation of the minister to the laity should be, Marsh said, "one of watchful superintendence and guidance and spiritual authority on the one side, and of confiding and reverential docility on the other."[21] A minister must use his authority to prevent laymen from the meddling in speculative theology which "puffs up the ignorant and inexperienced with a vain confidence in their own understandings or their own fancied experience in spiritual things, and leads them to undervalue, perhaps to censure and deride, those to whom they ought to look up with humility and reverence."[22]

By conferring nearly divine authority on a ministry that had historically been viewed as one with its congregation, Marsh imposed authoritarian hierarchy on Congregationalist brotherhood and injected elitist politics into discussions of church order. This attempt to defend church forms—the worldly forms of faith—had a nearly contradictory effect, transforming the church from a spiritual institution (the instrument of spirit in the world) into merely another political agent that had to compete with other social institutions for the allegiance of the people.

The language Marsh brings to bear on the argument is that of the upper class defending its standards against the unruly masses. Similar terms were leveled against Roger Williams, Paine and Hamilton, Wesley, Jackson, and Emerson. Burchardism, Marsh said, is "extravagance," "pride and conceit," "levity and vulgarity," "hypocrisy," "ignoran[ce]." Church principles, on the other hand, are governed by enlightened "conscience"; they are worthy of "confidence"; they are "good," "grave," "solemn," "useful," and above all, "safe."[23] From the Cambridge Platonists, Marsh had learned to portray God as divine reason. But in this context, reason acquired connotations of breeding, social convention, and intellectual training that it lacked elsewhere. Man approached this rational God only insofar as he was himself orderly and acquiescent. When he acted in a mob he reduced himself to the level of the animals.

Elitist claims to clerical infallibility naturally brought protests from Burchard as similar pronouncements by Andrews Norton had from Ripley. "Many rise up," Burchard proclaimed, "and say the 'conversions are *all* Spurious.' The individuals incur an awful responsibility who sit with their arms folded and make such statements. What do they know about it? 'O, its all fanaticism—new measures—trash—we alone are wise and wisdom will die with us.'"[24] Burchard's portrayal was all too accurate. When the church order was threatened, Marsh did not hesitate to characterize the intellectual capacity of laymen in terms that sound almost precisely like Andrews Norton's essentially political insistence on the authority of the educated elite. "There is some evil in the religious as in the political world" Marsh said, "in appealing to the people on subjects which speculatively considered are above the comprehension of the community at large, and in regard to which their only safety is found in *trusting* the wisdom and sound principles of men worthy to be trusted on such subjects."[25]

This conservative confidence in the intellectual and spiritual superiority of the clergy represents a departure from his early years at Andover, when, in the midst of metaphysical uncertainties of his own, he entertained a deep-seated nostalgia for a simple faith uncomplicated by speculative doubt. At Andover, Marsh distinguished between the clergy and common men by describing the simple layman as better off and perhaps even closer to God for not knowing of the learned controversies surrounding theological matters:

> The simple, unlearned Christian, who knows only his Bible and daily reads that with an unquestioning confidence in the more simple truths which he reads . . . may well be in some respects the envy of the puzzled though learned man of books. He goes on in the even tenor of his way, with his head at ease. He knows nothing of the ten thousand distracting questions, the harrowing doubts and maddening skepticism that dry up the heart and seethe in the brain of the unfortunate student who has ventured past the consecrated limit of his traditional faith and looks back on it with the cool eye of critical investigation.[26]

In this description, the "puzzled though learned man of books" is surely Marsh himself, and his envy of simple piety can be taken as a measure of his own theological distress. While the younger Marsh preferred spiritual simplicity to metaphysical doubt, in his more mature thought he rejected spiritual ignorance in favor of metaphysical certainty. This reversal might most charitably be viewed as a product of his longing for the simplicity he had irrevocably lost to his own theological investigations. As he struggled against skepticism toward philosophical salvation, using the very tools that had brought about his fall—they were the only tools left to him—he lamented his loss and yearned for the theological innocence he felt obligated to protect in his parishioners.

Marsh's longing for lost innocence barely conceals a rather romantic vision of the minister's lot. Not only is faith *easier* for the simple layman, but knowledge is a burden to its possessor and brings with it a responsibility to guide the less knowledgeable. Puzzling out the rational form of faith was the job of lonely scholar/ministers performing Christianity's highest and most painful mission, making faith *apparent* in the world so that their simple parishioners would possess it in spirit. Years later, Marsh still believed that "the more simplicity, the more immediate and unquestioning assurance there is in the reception of doctrine on the simple authority of conscience, the less of speculation and of speculative doubt about it, the better for the ends of the gospel in the application of all its truths."[27] This is the halfway point to Emersonian antiinstitutionalism and a giant step toward antiintellectualism. That Marsh should have raised this distinction in the process of defending a learned clergy against the inroads of evangelism is particularly ironic, for what he gives away in this defense—the distinction between objective and subjective authority—is far more crucial than what he protects.

By recommending ecclesiastical institutions as a curb on the restless lower class, we see Marsh reenacting the outcry of Arminian ministers against the excesses of the Great Awakening. The ministry had never approved less restrained manifestations of the spirit; shaking or speaking in tongues smacked of direct revelation and heresy. During the Awakening such excesses had contributed materially to the growth of Arminianism in the cultured congregations of Mayhew and Chauncey in Boston. The kinship between Marsh and the eighteenth-century Arminians is far from unconscious. Like his friend L. L. Tilden, Marsh was convinced that Burchard's successes demonstrated that a "revolutionary—not a reforming, spirit is abroad."[28] And significantly he turned to Charles Chauncey's anti-Awakening tract, *Seasonable Thoughts on the State of Religion in New England*, for lessons in dealing with the current unrest. Burchard's supporters, in their turn, saw Marsh's arguments as rationalism pure and simple, evidence that Marsh was afraid to offend his Boston friends. In Middlebury, where Burchard was a huge success, Marsh was accused of "truckling to Unitarianism" and even of Unitarian sympathies of his own.[29] Although, in Emerson's hands, Marsh's reason supports an inner light philosophy, testifying to the divine insight in even the most common mind, Marsh controlled this democratic tendency with a conservatism typical of liberals confronted by the spectre of irrational mob rule, deriding the natural inclination of laymen to trust their own experience.

Thus in his opposition to Burchard, we have seen Marsh resembling, paradoxically enough, both the Arminian critics of the Awakening and Jonathan Edwards, its champion. The explanation lies in the fact that by Marsh's time evangelists, faced with lifeless doctrine and church inhibitions to salvation, had given up antinomian associations and moved, like their urban Unitarian counterparts, toward an Arminian insistence on taking salvation into their own hands. Just as Nathaniel Taylor, Burchard's spiritual grandfather, adapted Arminian principles to Congregationalist theology, Burchard, following Finney, adapted them to evangelism. Burchard was, to Marsh's eyes indulging in an *Arminian* enthusiasm, creating an equally odd hybrid in Marsh's authoritarian pietism.

The determining factor here is context. Marsh's religious position was not monolithic. It really was not a "position" at all but a vision, a way of seeing that produces differing interpretations of experience in differing social and intellectual circumstances. In Marsh's debate with Unitarianism, his pietism was most prominent because the form of the *mind*, the way of *knowing* religious truth, was on trial, leading Marsh to give the individual mind access to absolute authority. With Burchard and evangelism, the issue was the form of the *church*, the shape and efficacy of church practices—a matter of institutional authority—and in demanding conformity to established procedures, Marsh assumed an essentially political posture and made the church into a political institution designed to preserve theological order among its members. This peculiar schizophrenia was as close as Marsh could come to the Puritans' ideal of a union between subjective faith and institutional expression. But in the nineteenth century this effort could not produce a truly spiritualized society. It tended instead to move authority out of heaven entirely and into the natural world of institutions and the individual minds of a privileged few. *Divine* authority receded from the world with the politicization of the church, and a new battle was joined between the authority of the mind and the controlling force of social institutions.

However Orthodox Marsh may have been by training and habit, it is remarkable that he could avoid seeing the tendency of Coleridge's reflective method to undermine rather than reinforce the clerical authority that had mediated between Scripture and the parishioner as it resuscitated the radical individualism latent in Protestant—and particularly in American Protestant—thought. In offering it, Marsh not only weakened the power of the Orthodox clergy, he gave the Transcendentalists the means to rebel against Unitarianism, which, for all the professed liberalism and antiestablishmentarianism of its early zeal, had become by 1829 an exclusive sect governed by an educated elite. Marsh repeatedly played unaware into the hands of Emerson and his school, whose developments of Marsh's ideas the Vermont divine scorned as atheistic. At every stage Marsh built better (or worse) than he knew.

## THE STATE

In church polity, Marsh had invested divine authority in a worldly institution, the church, and watched it become political. When the same authority seems necessary in politics, political institutions assume some of the qualities of the divine. Marsh's conservative response to Burchard's assault on the church reflected his intuitive awareness that popular spiritual enthusiasm breeds evangelism in religion and revolution in politics. As Alan Heimert has shown, the evangelical forces of the Awakening lent themselves later in the eighteenth century to the forces of political rebellion.[30] The antiprelatical language of rural Congregationalism easily adapted itself to the political purposes of the revolutionary polemicists, Paine and Adams, and conjured in the fading light of America's theological ideals a new vision of a chosen society proclaiming the primacy of individual rights over government authority. Just as Arminian ministers damned evangelism for its real or imagined excesses despite their envy of its spiritual zeal, their successors doubted the political wisdom of the common people who had been given so much power in the new system even as they prized the intellectual freedom from which that system took its life. For decades after the Revolution, such men remained skeptical about the attempt to translate democratic impulses into stable political forms.

For all his faith in the individual mind, Marsh was filled with such doubts, and he took the involvement of Americans in a minor Canadian uprising, the Canada Rebellion of 1836–37, as a deplorable example of rash action unrestrained by calm rational judgment.[31] Marsh closely associated his views on the Canada Rebellion with his opposition to religious enthusiasm.

"I was not more clear and decided in my own convictions in regard to Burchardism, than I am in regard to this, or more confident of the result as to the calm decision of sound and unprejudiced minds."[32] In each case, Marsh acted to prevent forms of anarchy, spiritual and political. Once again we hear the voice of reason speaking against passion, implying that feeling obscures truth rather than revealing it. His instinctive defense of institutional order in terms that deny the romantic impulses he indulged elsewhere suggests that in political as in ecclesiastical affairs Marsh was unable to make established forms express the ever-changing, developing needs of individuals. In politics, the laws that protect social order repeatedly infringed on the freedom of individual citizens, while individual freedom uncontrolled by law became license and threatened the stability of the state.

In one key way, however, the political problem was doubly acute; unlike religion, politics provided precious few precedents, few absolute guidelines, to support Marsh's authoritarian position. Coleridge had supported a national church to link spiritual authority and the authority of the state, enlivening political forms and endowing them with divine sanction. In America, such a view was out of the question. So, while Marsh disapproved of political disorders just as he did religious enthusiasm, he had to justify his position with markedly different arguments. While Marsh could endow the church with authority as the earthly type of the divine will, he had difficulty justifying *a priori* principles in politics. The relationship between divinity and the state was metaphorical at best. But the consequences of confusing God's universal authority with the necessarily conditional authority of the state are not metaphorical at all, they are profoundly practical, for conditional authorities change with time and circumstances, shaking the foundations of established social forms.

At first, Marsh seems to have taken a line against the Canada Rebellion based on universal principles as he had against Burchard. He complained that "there is little use in a discussion that looks directly and constantly at the change of one's opinions in reference to a particular case when they have been made up and the feelings enlisted. The only way to arrive at truth is by the study of principles with no other reference to particular cases than a perfectly disinterested one for illustration and example."[33] The culprits here are feelings derived from "particular" experiences, and they are to be restrained by "distinterested" reason and the study of principles. If the common citizen cannot be trusted to give rational form to the state, then the state must be invested with its own form. "The laws and institutions of the state are the reason objectized and fixed in positive forms or express the dictates of the universal reason as applied to the outward correlative and relations of the people. They are the objective spirit."[34] In politics, Marsh took the mere existence of institutions as proof of their divine endorsement as though they had come directly from God, disregarding for the occasion their human genesis. Yet, Marsh's apparent conviction that spirit finds its objective form in political institutions erects a perplexing barrier between those institutions and their actual creator, man, who is himself incapable of realizing spirit in the world. In linking governments and divine reason, Marsh intended to control political emotions as the church controlled religious feelings. Yet, so convincingly empowered, the state becomes the alienated measure of its citizens.

In order to justify this authority Marsh formulated a conservative version of the organic relationship between individuals and government which he used elsewhere to support individual rights, but he found the success of *this* organic union in its ability to fulfill the aims of government. The universal prevails over the particular, which "cannot obtain its highest potence otherwise than with and by the highest perfection of the whole."[35] In civil polity, Marsh valued the stability and authority of government and its capacity to provide direction for the unreasoning public.[36] Hence, in his organic unity of state and citizens he subordinated the individual wishes of the latter to the policies and integrity of the former. "To say that individuals may do what the government cannot sanction," he wrote, "that we have a right to do as individuals what we are bound not to do as a people and a nation is, according to my philosophy, in direct contradiction to every sound principle of public morals and sophistical upon the face of it."[37] The government must assume responsibility for and hence control over the actions of each in-

135

dividual citizen since, "if one individual may go into Canada without violating the laws of neutrality and of this country then 100 nay 1000 or 100000. Thus our citizens might actually conquer all the British provinces while the Governments are in a state of profound peace."[38]

Here we see Marsh significantly altering the balance of power between spirit and world. While his argument that the state simply objectifies the individual wills of its citizens is analogous to his belief that the church objectifies spirit, the authority of the state cannot be spiritual *or* universal. In supporting that authority, Marsh shifts his terms from the *universal* to the *general* (the objective analogue of universality), from a divine form to a worldly one. And when universal becomes general, the particular becomes the individual forms of the minds of citizens. What had been, in religion, a hierarchical expression of the universal *in* the particular becomes, in politics, a formative opposition *between* competing worldly powers—society and the individual.

Although Marsh tried to maintain an apparent connection between the political order and universal principles, he had to admit that politics calls for a more pragmatic standard of judgment than he applied in theology. In an ideal state, spiritual principles would guide political actions as they do spiritual, but, as Marsh frequently reminds us, men are far from perfect. The immediate threat of rebellion and disorder highlighted for Marsh the unfortunate limitations of a social reality in which American citizens acted rashly without considering the consequences of their actions for the state. Marsh sympathized in spirit with Rousseau's premise in the *Social Contract*, that government should conform to universal principles shared by each of the citizens, but he felt that Rousseau erred "in advocating as practicable a form of government which could only be applied to man . . . when divested of his sinful nature." In a sinful world, government had to act expediently, and Marsh looked for a government of reason only when men had attained "a higher and more elevated station of human perfectability."[39]

The lack of a divine source for political wisdom forced Marsh to argue from experience in sharp contrast to his attack on Burchard, suggesting for the first time in his thought the necessary primacy of *things*, of particulars, of immediate experience in a

world without an absolute ground. When a supporter of the rebellion urged reason in its defense, Marsh retorted that

It must be determined not by mere abstract principles
whether a revolution would be desirable for Canada but
by a careful and thorough examination of the character
of the people by the lights of past experience, by the exercise of that sound and deep political wisdom which few
possess.[40]

Somehow Marsh managed to maintain the conservative *tone* of
his arguments against religious enthusiasm while he completely reversed his substantive position. Judgments must still
be "careful and thorough," "sound and deep" and right judgment still belongs to the few rather than the many. But the
validity of "general" or "universal" principles which Marsh so
adamantly maintained to prevent the church from being set
helplessly adrift on the "boundless sea" by Burchard's deceptive empiricism have fallen suddenly into doubt. "Universal
principles" have become "abstract," and dangerous empiricism
dons new respectability as the "lights of past experience."

Of course, political decisions have been pragmatic in all
ages. Winthrop quoted Plato to justify social innovation in Puritan New England only to condemn him as pagan when those
innovations failed. Marsh's position here is unique neither for
its expediency nor for its inconsistency with his earlier view. Its
interest lies in the fact that the reliance on experience that remained *implicit* in Marsh's defense of the clergy has become *explicit* for the first time in his views on political order, creating
the potential for a new and troubling union between Marsh's
willingness to admit that authority is not absolute, that it
comes with experience, and his central philosophical conviction that authority lies in the mind itself. Together these notions
make possible the conclusion that authority is not divine and
absolute but finally both human and provisional—a matter of
unfolding art.

In his shift from universal laws of reason in religion to
the lessons of experience in social questions, Marsh reenacted
America's transition from a nation of saints to a saintly nation,
from theology to politics. As the influence of the church in so-

ciety narrowed with the decline in its constituency, the church-man's greatest weapon, his ability to appeal to a higher stan-dard, could no longer be applied outside of the church walls, and as we saw in the Burchard affair, its application even within them had become questionable. The primacy of spiritual principles was not so evident, even to a minister, as it had been two hundred years earlier, and to fill the gap, the authority of man-made (as opposed to God-made) forms became more po-tent. Marsh's preference here for particulars over general prin-ciples reversed the typical Puritan bias for inductive over de-ductive reasoning, a bias that he shared with them in spiritual matters. By elevating the authority of experience over general principles in politics, Marsh took a giant step toward Transcen-dentalism and its inclination to seek truth through particulars, a strategy that has been described as an essential characteristic of the Symbolist imagination.[41] Marsh once again stood be-tween two traditions, using the newly wrought tools of one to repair the crumbling walls of the other.

MARSH's fear of lawless revolt did not weaken his belief in social reform. But he had little patience with attempts to legislate so-cial harmony or to create it artificially, and he rationalized his impatience by raising the authority of individuals over that of institutions. When Marsh faced social reform rather than revo-lution, his fear of anarchy gave way to an oddly conservative brand of individualism, antiempiricism, and antiinstitutional-ism—conservative in the sense that it opposed radical attempts to make over society in accordance with an ideal vision, and countenanced gradual and cumulative, rather than radical, change. Although Marsh repeatedly argued for progress, he meant by it what Emerson appears also to have intended,[42] that individuals raise themselves to a state of spiritual fulfillment within a preordained and completed system. This vision makes no room for radical innovation, proposing instead the gradual fulfillment of a preexisting ideal. According to Marsh, progress occurs when growth in the souls of individual citizens leads eventually to harmonious social relationships.

It is important to distinguish this notion from the equally conservative Unitarian version of progress in which society is transformed gradually by the influence of its virtuous members.[43] The latter describes virtue as an upper class quality, related to—perhaps indistinguishable from—formal education and breeding. The virtuous elite exercises its influence mechanically, shaping the forms of society to its ideals, acting as both guide and example to the less fortunate masses, reforming them in its own image. Marsh's view, shared by Emerson, though not necessarily by other Transcendentalists (Ripley, Brownson, Parker), more closely resembles the gradual formation of a gathered church. The reform of institutions follows as a natural consequence of the spiritual reform of individuals. Change is internal and spiritual before it is externally apparent, and (following Pauline tradition) it can appear as readily in society's meanest as in its most elevated members. It is essentially anti-formal, a matter of spiritual expression rather than imposition, independent of learning or manners, and immune to external influence. Therefore, Marsh disapproved of utopian experiments that promised to reform society *en masse* by the influence of group pressure and denied any means for the abolition of social ills but the instruction of men in the truth.

Marsh ridiculed utopianism for the very Christian reason that it blindly ignores the all-too-apparent weakness of man in its zeal to cultivate his strengths. To Henry J. Raymond, one of his former students and the founder of the *New York Times*, Marsh said,

The schemes cherished in New York are very nearly of the same character, I suppose, as those which Mr. Ripley and others are going to commence near Boston on the first of April (an ominous day); . . . Those engaged at Boston are men, so far as I know, of good spirit, and as well qualified to realize such schemes as any men can be who are visionary enough to entertain them seriously at all. Ripley says it requires men of Christian spirit, above the grovelling selfishness of the world; and the grand error I take to be in the hope which he indulges of finding men in this world sufficiently under the law of pure reason, or even sufficiently raised by divine grace above the selfishness of human nature, to live together on such terms as they propose. Every scheme of social existence that does not assume the principles of self-seeking, as

giving law practically to the conduct of men in their intercourse with each other, and form its arrangements on
that assumption, will and must fall. . . . These reformers
. . . hope to redeem the world by a sort of dilletanti process, to purge off its grossness, to make a poetical para-
dise in which hard work shall become easy, dirty things
clean, the selfish liberal, and a churl a churl no longer.[44]

Such schemes as Brook Farm seemed to Marsh at once irrational and impractical. He believed that institutions could be
no better than the fallible men who made them and that, while
governments could restrain the excessive *actions* of the un-
educated and irrational public, no institutions could change
their *souls*. Therefore, to reform society one must first reform
the individual minds of its citizens. Like the Puritans, Marsh
distrusted external evidences of internal transformation. He
wanted society to reflect the divine will, but he balked at attempts to create a heaven on earth. The utopia-builders erred in
aspiring to work a spiritual change in the souls of their followers by natural means. Their later espousal of Fourierist
principles suggests that the ideal society is shaped by human
schemes rather than the divine will.[45] In their implicit faith that
spiritual salvation depended on favorable social conditions,
Ripley and Brownson paved the way for social Darwinism and
literary naturalism.

Marsh delegated the task of preparing the minds of men
for the inward working of the divine spirit to Christian faith.
He considered faith an eminently practical system because it
worked to overcome the evil in man instead of assuming his be-
nevolent nature against all the evidence of Scripture and experience. He told Raymond:

the great purpose of Christianity [is] to redeem men from
the bondage and limitations of the natural self-will, and
bring them into that spiritual freedom in which each
shall do freely and from the heart that which is for the
best good of all—in which the universal shall overpower
and control to its own higher ends the individual and
self-seeking principle in each. But Christianity is, and
professes to be in a state of continuous warfare with the

natural will of man and with the spirit of the world, which is the natural will generalized. In this view Christianity is a perfectly rational system—its means are adapted to its ends—it assumes the facts as they are, and works accordingly—waving a mighty weapon, and sweating great drops of blood.[46]

This vision of a crusading church becomes suspect, as we shall see, in light of his arguments against church involvement in the abolition movement. Like Emerson's self-reliance or Edwards's "true virtue," Marsh's reason is a capacity latent in all men but one which only a few achieve, and then only with the greatest difficulty. Yet, Marsh, like Edwards or Emerson, tends in theoretical discussion to stress its potential and minimize the difficulty of attaining it. Instruments of reform, the church, the *Dial*, Brook Farm, always seem more effective in their conception than in practice, where social forms prove inhospitable to the ideals which inspired them.

THE demonstrable inability of the church to deal effectively with slavery reflected still more clearly both the growing power of particulars and the corresponding weakness of general principles, carrying Marsh into a new reliance on the individual that recalls the nurturing rather than the controlling powers of the mediatory church. It marked the failure of the Puritan dream of a godly nation guided by a socially active church and confirmed the division between spiritual principles and political necessity. The church could no longer arbitrate national morals. Cultural events had divided spirit and law into sovereign spheres, and Marsh declined to try to rejoin them for fear that if religion ventured beyond the narrow bounds of its remaining territory even that might be lost.[47]

In the 1830s and 1840s, the slavery question was being debated with increasing vehemence among New England intellectuals. Nearly all agreed that slavery was morally wrong, but individuals differed widely in their grounds for this belief and even more widely in their feeling about abolition. It was clear to all that slavery was a dangerously divisive issue. To those who, like Marsh, were dismayed by the already existing divisions in society, who were trying to resolve the conflicts that separated Congregationalist from Unitarian, New Haven from Andover from Princeton, New England from the middle states from the South, the slavery issue was pure poison. The church, Marsh felt, already squabbled internally over too many spiritual issues. To involve it in a dispute over slavery might overtax its already shaky structure. So beset by internal problems, the church seemed incapable of dealing with the complexities of modern life. Marsh tried to isolate it from those complexities, but in the process he enfeebled it still further and frustrated his own desires to put spirit back into common life.

Marsh's views on slavery were elaborated at the annual convention of the Vermont Congregationalist churches in September 1840, when that body was urged to draft a letter to the Southern churches enforcing the evils of slavery. With so many local problems before the convention, Marsh was vexed that "our time should be thus occupied year after year with a matter so alien as this is from the appropriate business of the convention."[48] He insisted that "the evils of slavery are worldly evils, evils pertaining to the worldly condition of men and to their civil relations in the state."[49] The business of the church, he argued, is not with worldly evil—poverty, slavery, injustices—but strictly with spiritual evil, with sin. Worldly evils are a matter for governments to remedy.

Marsh's view of the complete separation of church from this social issue implies that the world is simply not the place to enact spiritual principles. In fact, Marsh looked for dire consequences of attempts to do so, citing "the destructive and outrageous inferences of the French and of the ultraabolitionists—denial of parental authority—the woman question." Thus, he continued, "Christianity is made a worldly system and identified with civil and political institutions to the destruction of both."[50]

Clearly, the conditional context of politics forced Marsh to shrink the power of Christianity to an astonishing degree, until faith could retain its spirituality only by isolating itself from the world. By implication, the survival of Christianity depended not only on its ability to maintain the high ground of absolute authority in worldly debates, but on its dexterity in avoiding such debate altogether.

Yet Marsh was far from insensitive to the evils of slavery. On the contrary, governmental inaction and the impotence of the church drove him to rely on the individual to solve the slavery problem. One of Marsh's strongest motives for opposite action by the Vermont churches was his fear that Northern pressure along with abolitionist protest might drive those Southerners who, at heart, opposed slavery into an unwilling defense of southern institutions, thus actually subverting the cause of abolition. Marsh's years in the South had given him a perspective on slaveowners that most of his Congregationalist colleagues could not share. His experiences there had confirmed in him a hatred for slavery, both for its effects on the slave and, at least equally, for its effects on the slaveholder. If he better understood the evils of slavery, he also better understood the men, black and white, who were caught up in its complex workings.

Marsh had difficulty condemning as sinners the tasteful and refined gentlemen he had met in Virginia. Like Booker T. Washington, and for much the same reasons, he was far more inclined to pity them as victims of their heritage.[51] He knew that not all slaveholders were evil men. Like most ministers of his time, Marsh was less ready than his Puritan predecessors to judge the spiritual state of his fellows. Sin, he argued, in the tradition of Jonathan Edwards, is subjective rather than objective, a matter of intent not of acts, and as a result, he was unable to say which slaveholder might deserve condemnation and entirely unwilling to condemn the institution as a whole on spiritual grounds.[52] He counted on more enlightened southerners to take the lead in freeing the South from its greatest burden. In contrast to his attitude toward social disorder, Marsh hesitated here in a moral context to impose institutional controls on the individual spirit. In Marsh's view, social institutions, the state and the church should not meddle in matters of conscience. He continued to defend existing social forms, but he justified this defense, not by the greater wisdom of a social elite, but by the inaccessibility and primacy of individual spirit.

These significant shifts in strategy had a still more significant side effect. They effectively placed man's spiritual fate in his own hands. Moral authority could now reside in the individual mind, where it would be immune to conventional influence. Under such conditions, social change could be viewed as a process of education. It would require the transformation of individual minds and spirits rather than of institutions. Marsh saw his own role as a social reformer in this way. One of his fondest ambitions during his stay in the South had been to combine his educational talent with his preference for secluded study and writing in work as a pamphleteer against slavery.[53] It was the Southern *mind* that needed attention, and if that were brought to see the truth, institutions would naturally follow. The result of such education would be a harmony of minds and spirit, a nation united on truly Christian principles, the fulfillment of America's moral promise.

WHEN Marsh did take pen in hand and found himself free of constraining social realities, he unfolded a literary vision of American society that contrasted sharply with the conservatism of his pragmatic response to immediate social crises. In describing the American character, he took up a rhetoric of national and spiritual destiny that has characterized literary portrayals of America from Cotton Mather to Emerson to Teddy Roosevelt, a rhetoric characteristic of the American literary imagination.[54] In his dedication of the new chapel at the University of Vermont in 1830, Marsh depicted America as a promised land and Americans as the modern chosen people, a national gathered church of believers. In the process, he blurred the distinctions between church and state that he so scrupulously maintained elsewhere, making at once a politics of religion and a religion of American national politics.

Prefiguring Emerson's "American Scholar," Marsh discounted, in this new context, the oppressive authority of the state and celebrated the future of the American individual and of the American people as a whole collectively dedicated to individual fulfillment. "We can hardly, indeed, be said to be subjects of any state, considered in its ordinary sense, or body politic with a fixed constitution and a determinate organization of its several powers. But we are constituent members of a community in which the highest worth and perfection and happiness of the individual free persons composing it constitutes the highest aim and perfection of the community as a whole."[55] Here Marsh could unfold his theoretical view that institutions are the servants of individuals, obligated to promote their natural tendencies and to aid them in reaching individual perfection, not masters engaged in restraining the forces of an unruly rabble. In literature, where imaginative inspiration rather than public safety was the standard of value, the controlling responsibility of the state gave way. The state seemed almost to disappear, remaining only as the instrument of the individual will. Like his early optimism about his personal social relationships, however, this was a literary ideal rather than a practical program.

Marsh knew too well that the ideal society could never be established in all its perfection in this world. Although he believed that society generally provided a reasonable latitude for individual action, his own frustrated aspirations showed him that it often inhibited or even crushed originality and freedom of expression. The utopias Marsh envisioned, unlike those artificial social forms constructed by men like Ripley, lay at the end of a more arduous journey out of the world of appearance and into the individual spirit. His were not mere transient social utopias but the immutable utopias of the mind. The ideal commonwealth, Marsh said, "would be realized where the powers of reason were unfolded in all the members of the community. Where all were self-controlled by the indwelling law of conscience, and where the personal well-doing and well-being of each results in the harmonious coagency, the ever-living combined energy and social happiness of all. This, I am well aware, is an idea which belongs either to poetry or to religion. It can be contemplated only in the ideal creations of the poet, or in the city of God."[56]

America no longer held out its early promise. Earthly social forms of all kinds were disqualified as embodiments of the divine spirit that also represented the highest human potential. Man's hopes, even Marsh seemed to say, would be fulfilled *only* in heaven, not in the promised land that the new world had both figuratively and literally *been* to the Puritans. By removing his ideal to heaven and to the mind, Marsh hoped in his conservatism both to preserve it and to defuse radical impulses to social change. But his suggestion that social forms only imperfectly represent human perfection bodes ill for those forms when their increasingly limited authority must strive to restrain the growing demands of the self. In a sense, this abdication of worldly responsibility denied the promise of the New

World frontier decades before Turner announced its official closing, and although American promise would be celebrated as an ideal too long after Turner, it is essential to mark here the cultural circumstances that deprived that ideal of its substance.

America's mission was great as long as it was also God's mission and sanctioned by his authority. But the transfer of authority to the individual dissolved the bond that had united individual and social salvations. Without the divine presence, which cast individual and society as analogous participants in one spiritual quest, the two fell into opposition, contesting for authority and pursuing separately such goals as they could invent for themselves. Though writers like Emerson and Whitman could still make gestures toward a national salvation, they made them most often in defiance of social forms, and despite their initial optimism, they, like Marsh, could finally look forward only to the potent but provincial reality of art.

## EDUCATION

EDUCATION, which recasts the mind and spirit rather than the social structure, seemed to Marsh as it did to Emerson "the only sure means of permanent and progressive reform."[57] And it was in education that Marsh came nearest to his ideals for a free yet orderly institutional expression of spirit. Just as the aim of the church in social issues is spiritual education, colleges, Marsh believed, should foster the development of the whole man, intellectual and spiritual. In social and political terms, Marsh's educational theories were no less conservative than his political views. He was less anxious to question or alter the structures and values of society than he was to raise the lower classes (intellectually and morally, if not politically or economically) to the level of the upper classes. American education had been designed as a vehicle for conveying and preserving existing values. Harvard College itself had been founded under the radical shadow cast by the antinomian controversy to champion doctrine, carrying Puritan gospel unpolluted to later American generations.[58] In a democracy, however, education became responsible for refining the unreasoning masses, preparing them to take up their democratic burden, and integrating them into a harmonious society.

Whatever their consequences, none of Marsh's innovations had aimed to encourage a tyranny of the individual. By investing authority in reason, Marsh did not mean to loose all restraints on the mind. On the contrary, he imagined an authority more absolute *because* it was more deeply personal. He aimed to retain more coherent and forceful controls on the individual whim by replacing external influence as the agent of restraint, substituting internal discipline. Thus the controlling authority would be an inherent *part* of the self rather than an artificial bond which was imposed on the self and could be thrown off in wild rebellion. Yet this step endowed the mind with a self-governing authority never granted elsewhere. It permitted the mind to drift free from the firm moorings of externals, of society, to set its individual course and thus to project for itself its own developing form.

These transformations were possible because the context of education blended issues that the political motives of church polity and social order kept distinct. Marsh's movement into the individual mind in politics had been motivated by his desire to *avoid* social conflict, to flee the arena of public debate for the relative safety and stability of individual conscience. The individual mind was acknowledged in politics only to portray political reform as a process of conservative education, an alternative to revolution. In education, the American democratic ideal actually encouraged, even insisted upon, the individual's right to self-governance, turning external authorities into tyrannical oppressors. Such sympathies with self-direction might prove radical enough applied with Scottish Common Sense attention to externals, but together with reason—a power that pierces through things directly to the enlivening spirit—Marsh's educational ideals threatened still greater problems than he had originally been trying to avoid. Reason freed the educating mind from the imposition of preconceived external goals to become its own guide, pursuing its own course experimentally since even the mind's authority cannot know where it is going before it gets there.

Education provided a more suitable medium for a reliance on the mind's authority than religion or politics largely because the consequences of education as interpreted by the educators themselves seemed uniformly safe and desirable. Education was in the business of producing reasonable men, and the Nortons and Bowens and Wares were hard pressed to see how that could be threatening. It was largely the growing, though often unspoken, confidence in the powers of the mind that made educational theory hospitable to individualistic impulses in the early nineteenth century, and made those impulses more acceptable among the intellectual elite than they were in religion or politics. Even the Unitarians, despite their adherence to traditional educational practice, urged with James Walker that "it is not among the proper or legitimate objects of education, either in religion or anything else, to inculcate an implicit or blind faith, to bind down and enslave the soul to a fixed creed, or to dictate . . . what the mind shall think, feel, or believe. . . . Education . . . does not consist in putting things into the mind, but, as the name implies, in bringing things out." [59]

Of course, Walker is more interested in refining existing faculties than in nurturing latent powers. Nonetheless, education proved a stepping stone to still more radical formulations of the mind's powers for those more inclined than Walker to question the fundamental assumptions behind their faith. Conservative educators could not have anticipated a new definition of reason itself, one which would make teaching and learning a potentially radical activity. By formulating a spiritualized reason that combined cool intellect and spontaneous inspiration, Marsh implicitly surrendered his allegiance to traditional authorities in church, state, and school and loosened some of the existing institutional controls on the growing and potentially disruptive authority of the self.

From the first, this attitude put Marsh in conflict with the prevailing educational principles in New England, which promoted institutional authority. Although, in theory, New England educators adhered to a humanistic educational program that would develop native talents and abilities, in practice they followed the traditional routine of rote learning and mechanical recitations and concentrated more on maintaining discipline than on encouraging independent inquiry. [60] Even at Harvard, law dominated education, leaving little room for enlivening feeling. Frederic Hedge complained that Harvard professors would "hold [their] subject fast with one hand, and pour knowledge into him with the other. The professors are task mas-

ters and police officers, the president, the chief of the college police."[61] Although even Transcendentalist rebels like Hedge or
Ripley were quick to admit that their professors had been earnest and sincere in their search for truth, they complained that
truth once found had been enforced as law. And in a sense there
was good reason behind this rigidity. The values instilled at
Harvard and elsewhere were those that made society and its institutions *work*. They were essential to it, guaranteeing that the
debate over educational method would be far from merely
academic.

Authoritarian dogmatism seemed more lifeless than ever to
Marsh in education, where he entertained a typically Romantic
distaste for mere imitation and an equally typical attraction to
intellectual spontaneity that he denied in matters of church
polity and politics. Even during his early days at Dartmouth,
Marsh complained that classes "seemed too formal" to permit
the lively exchange of ideas.[62] Later, in his first year at the University of Vermont, he recalled the deficiencies of his own education under the old regime. "For several years and nearly from
the time of leaving College," he said, "when I found myself compelled to begin again at the very foundation, I have been fully
convinced that very essential changes were necessary in our
whole course of early instruction. In many cases I have no
doubt the present system is rather an injury than a benefit to
the scholar since it confirms and flatters with the appearance of
learning many who if left more to themselves would sooner become their own teachers."[63] Although the "present system" fills
the head with facts, Marsh insisted, true learning is not a fixed
or unchanging state that can be attained simply by the acquisi-
tion of knowledge.

To most American educators, education meant leading the
student out of the darkness and into the light already occupied
by the instructor and other educated, socially useful citizens.
But it could also suggest, as it did to Marsh, an entirely new educational method, one which implied a new way of knowing, a
redefinition of knowledge itself, and a new understanding of the
sort of authority knowledge could confer. Such education was
not superficial addition to the mind, but an inward revision of
the self. Marsh's method aimed to elicit from the student a latent inner light and to train the mind to make it capable of tak-

ing over its own continuing education. He hoped to make each student his own teacher in an unending process of education.

Marsh began to develop his educational ideas in the years just after he graduated from Andover, while he taught in Hampden-Sydney, Virginia. During this time he was reading Coleridge's earlier philosophical writings and discussing them in correspondence with his friend George Ticknor at Harvard.[64] He moved to Burlington to take over the presidency at Vermont in 1826, with his head full of educational schemes, and Vermont was the perfect place to put them to work since it had nothing to lose. The university was in moral, physical, and financial ruin. It was losing its contest with Middlebury for Vermont students; it had recently lost a major building by fire and had little prospect of raising money to replace it. Vermont was desperate for a change, for new life, and this desperation helps to explain its eagerness for educational reform at a time when similar efforts, initiated by George Ticknor, were failing at Harvard.

In the program he constructed at Vermont, Marsh turned educational tradition upside down, making capital out of the individual differences between students that prevailing methods overlooked or even tried to suppress. Conventional teachers worked to shape students in their own images and were naturally intolerant of troublesome straying from the canon of required knowledge. To prevent it they imposed discipline on students, asserted their authority, and scraped away at the free expression that seemed to Marsh one of the essential tools of education. "There are some," Marsh said, "who seem to know no way of managing young men, but by the terror of authority; but such a method tends to break down all independent spirit and love of study for its own sake, which I thought it of so much importance to cherish."[65]

Marsh translated these objections into educational practice by giving students greater control over the course of their education and extending college education to many who were excluded by the current practice of admitting only those who opted for the full course leading as a rule to a career in medicine, law, or the ministry. Prefiguring modern arguments for educational reform, Marsh gave students the right to choose some of their courses and made education more relevant to their everyday lives through courses designed to meet their practical needs. Just as Marsh believed that experimental rather than speculative religion generates true faith, he argued that practical rather than merely abstract education produces true knowledge. By converting the faculty from an absolute authority to an influence based on love, respect, and admiration, Marsh freed students to exercise their natural abilities.

The system Marsh developed at Vermont abandoned the idea that an external authority can impose discipline and knowledge and created an atmosphere in which the student could unfold his own native powers through dialogue, personal responsibility, exercise of choice, and appreciation of real achievement. He dispensed with regimentation, did away as far as possible with rigid distinctions between classes, and associated students in classrooms according to their abilities and attainments rather than according to their years in school.[66] Under the old system the teacher carried the passive students along at his pace. Marsh made the teacher just one of several instruments that helped the student to educate himself. Having largely freed the student from suppression by outside authority, Marsh left him to develop at his own speed. Instead of shaping him to fill out a preconceived form, Marsh encouraged him to discover a form that lay undeveloped within, to discover his true self, and to develop that self organically to its natural conclusion at its natural rate.[67]

Here we can see another significant shift in the location of universal authority as it moves toward the individual and away from social institutions or the general will. And Marsh responded to this shift by calling on nature and faith to control the possible wanderings of the self-educating mind. Puritans had used education to gain control over the wildness of nature and they had subordinated education to faith in Scriptural authority. With the displacement of Scripture, nature (now better understood, hence more orderly and less wild) became a candidate for the job of controlling education as did faith (now less bound to Scripture and more closely associated with the natural order). As controls on education, however, nature and faith proved unpredictable. Rather than imposing known and rigid forms on education, they lent their own import to the educational process and, by association, vastly expanded its implications.

MARSH's educational organicism—all growth, progress, and fulfillment, yet stable and unthreatening—captured American optimism in the first decades of the nineteenth century, an optimism that would wax cosmic in Concord. Marsh wanted
learning to reawaken the American religious spirit, and he
viewed the mind and the relationship between the individual
and society through the misty medium of his spiritual zeal. The
natural order provided Marsh with a most persuasive argument
for a systematic educational process. The validating principle
behind his educational reforms was his view of nature as a hierarchical and dynamic incarnation of the progressive rise of consciousness to God. He believed that true systems of knowledge
must reflect the unity and order of divine reason, and he opposed those which simply divide that unity into unrelated parts
to make it easier to examine. In such systems, Marsh lamented,
"departments of study which I regard as quite distinct and be-
longing to different stages of advancement are so confounded
together . . . that a pupil cannot be put upon the simplest without being at once involved in the most difficult."[68] At Vermont,
the student moved from lower and easier to higher and more
difficult courses, not merely from one autonomous subject to
another.

Marsh's system aimed to recapitulate the organic process of
consciousness from the lowest inanimate objects to the highest
principles of divine reason. It can be seen as part of a general
trend in American academic organization after 1820 to replace
the old divisions of natural and moral philosophy (itself a reflection of the theoretical division of matter and spirit after
Descartes that preserved religion from empiricism and deis-
tic incursions) with natural, moral, and mental or intellectual
philosophy.[69] While Ware and other adherents of the Scottish
school used the study of mental philosophy to bridge the gulf
between nature and morals, to guarantee ethical certainty,
Marsh arranged these categories hierarchically. They represented steps in the development of the spirit, from immersion
in mere nature to concern for worldly moral relations, culmi-
nating in knowledge of the mind itself, especially of that part of
the mind—reason—which was the highest earthly manifestation of divine spirit. In explaining this educational program,
Marsh said, "it is desirable as far as may be to carry students

along from the first elements by such steps that they may always have the necessary data and the requisite discipline for advancing the next step without unreasonable perplexity . . . yet again the different stages of progress in the knowledge of our own inward being are so connected from the inherent unity and interpenetration of its living powers that nothing can be adequately known till we are prepared to contemplate each in its relation to the whole." [70]

In order to use organicism as an antidote to the skepticism he saw lurking behind Norton's complacent denial of human spiritual insight, he depicted the mind as a growing plant, fulfilling its inherent potential, rather than as a mechanical receptor of external impressions. Education, like faith, must have a rational form, but the rational form of faith was closely associated with the form of the institutional church and the authority of its ministers, and these were designed to restrict individual freedom. Organic education, by contrast, imposed no final form on the process of growth. Instead, it revealed the form implicit in the process itself. The final form of organic education would always be an individual one. Such education, Marsh asserted, is self-expression rather than conformity, and it fulfills itself by discovering its own destiny. Experience elicits but does not determine the mind's inherent powers. It provides firsthand truths. The mind relates directly to nature, discovering powers that coincide with its needs as sunlight and water coincide with the needs of a growing plant. This sympathetic relationship between the individual mind and nature guarantees valid knowledge, promising a certainty superior to any authority—a certainty that calls the very possibility of authority into question.

THE most substantial effect of Marsh's desire to make a greater place for individualism in education was his revision of the Vermont curriculum and his introduction of a modified elective system into American colleges. Marsh's other educational innovations were essentially formal. They revised the mechanics of the educational process, altered the medium in which it would take place. They were, that is, reflections of Marsh's innovative notions of the process of learning. His curricular reforms, on the other hand, reflect an altered view of the significance of knowing itself. Marsh was not so intent on altering the content

153

of knowledge as he was on revising its method. The structure of the Vermont curriculum reflected his belief that educators provided the occasion for learning—stimulated learning in the student—rather than instilling it. The curriculum reflected his vision of the universal order as it developed the powers of the mind. Marsh portrayed education as both communal and dynamic, as the active engagement of the individual mind with the world and other minds rather than the solitary absorption of a fixed body of knowledge. Marsh had been subjected to too many mechanical classroom catechisms to impose similar tortures on his own students. Learning required active engagement in the subject, a principle that led Marsh to value group discussion far above formal presentation. He was convinced that the mind was no mere passive receptacle, and therefore he did not expect it to disgorge information by rote. Knowledge truly learned would be changed, individualized, as it was made one with the learner. Marsh's view of knowledge carries radical implications that undermine the most familiar features of the New England educational landscape. Attempts to impose or even to determine a cultural canon would be fruitless if that canon could be altered in the learning, and only influence of some new and unprecedented sort could be transformed by the student rather than transforming him.

The significant drift of Marsh's educational motives was to return the seat of educational authority to the direct spiritual relationship between man and God.[71] Thus, the greater flexibility of the Vermont curriculum distinguishes Marsh in more than mere educational preference from his peers at Harvard or Yale, where ultimate truths were represented as external and knowable and the curriculum embodied that truth and impressed its shape on the mind of the student. Ideally, after four years, a college would have shaped the minds of its students to conform with the established form of the curriculum. Marsh's Vermont curriculum dramatized his belief that, although age and experience confer some wisdom and teachers could and should therefore exert some authority, only the student himself could determine the particulars of his education. "The legitimate and immediate aim of education," Marsh said, "is, not . . . to shape and fit the powers of the mind to this or that outward condition . . . but, by means corresponding to their inherent nature, to excite, to encourage, and affectionately to aid *the free and perfect development of those powers themselves.* . . . The great question will be, not to what worldly purpose can the mind be made serviceable, but what are the inherent claims of the soul itself; to what does it tend in the essential principles of its own being."[72]

The curriculum did not embody useful knowledge as it did for Taylor or Norton or Wayland at Brown; instead it was the correlative object of the powers of the mind, the external objects or facts that would stimulate the awakening of latent mental energies. There was therefore no necessary resemblance between the shape of the mind and the shape of the curriculum. The curriculum was more like a set of directions intended to guide the mind along its way than a stamp that transfers its message to the awaiting sheet. In their antiauthoritarian and anticanonical drift, these ideas laid the groundwork for greater individualism in literature and politics and forecast the Transcendentalist principle of self-reliance and its assertion that truth is determined not by authority but by the individual heart. The particulars of education had become a route to the universal—reversing the Christian procedure of using the absolute universal truth of Scripture to determine the meaning of particular worldly facts. Particulars now led to universals, symbolism became the prescribed epistemological method. The universal would yield to discovery at the end of an individual adventure through nature and into the mind.

But Marsh was not ready in practice to sanction the uncontrolled authority of the mind over its own education that his own educational theory implied. The power of social forms was too great. He had too much respect for the *cultivated* reason to give free reign to an uncultivated one. He feared that too much freedom would invite the lazy to indulge their weakness and deprive even the serious student of desirable discipline. When, for instance, Marsh learned of the elective system briefly installed at Harvard, he disapproved since it seemed to him that it amounted to little more than the right to drop the classics for modern languages after the freshman year.[73] He valued the classics as teaching an essential sense of order and proportion, and while he was perfectly willing to let students exercise their individual tendencies by taking courses beyond requirements, he could not let them neglect studies that he felt were essential to mental development.[74] In Marsh's view, although God's truth was unknowable in all its details, its general principles could be known and taught, and these made up the bulk of the Vermont curriculum. The aim of this curriculum was to guide the mind's developing powers along recognized lines toward acknowledged spiritual truth while at the same time allowing scope through elective courses for individual inclination.

Marsh tried to defuse the anarchic potential of education by fitting it neatly into his essentially Christian vision of the universe; all of life appeared to him a growth of the spirit toward reunion with God. Education was a preparation for grace. The individual ascended toward heaven, Marsh believed, by discovering and cultivating his own spiritual powers. As the student studied first nature and then man, he both observed and participated in the ascent of the divine spirit through the material universe. He learned to recognize the divine mind in nature as it appeared in the simpler plants and animals and then in the more complex forms until he found the highest possible earthly expression of the divine mind in the human spirit. Throughout his education, the student would encounter in nature the objective form of divine spirit that spoke most directly to his own developing spirit.

"Show me . . . the youth," Marsh said, "whose soul has been wakened up and aroused from the thralldom and lethargy of sense, from the fascination of the present and the worldly, to the contemplation of spiritual truths . . . with the self-revealing ideas of responsibility and of God, and I will show you one who . . . has . . . the education of a man in the great essentials of his humanity, of a man in the image of his Maker. . . . Nor is it by a mere arbitrary agency, that [education] produces such an effect upon our minds. All our powers are actuated and unfolded by agencies corresponding to their character; and the natural light is not more perfectly correspondent to the power of vision and essential to its exercise, than the presence of divine light and truth, to the development and exercise of our rational and spiritual powers."[75]

Just as nature ascends toward God, so the student would ascend from an absorption in mere matter to communion with the highest spiritual truths. And during the ascent, the spirit in nature and in the mind would become one.

Although it offers an *orderly* progress, this theoretical view of education entailed other less reassuring consequences. It transcended the materialist gap between subjective consciousness and objective reality, between the spirit and matter. Subject and object, being and knowing, would become one as the mind created itself in response to the promptings of natural experience. Education removed the barrier between the knower and the thing known, between the self and the objective world, and fused subject and object in the divine spirit. It redeemed the student, returning him to the primal unity with the universe man lost through Adam's fall, a loss that had been confirmed for Marsh by the materialism of Locke and the skepticism of Hume. Educational growth would repair man's fragmented vision and restore him to his original place at the center of a universal order.

Marsh stopped just short of such post-Kantian romantic philosophers as Schelling or Hegel, who responded to the Cartesian split between nature and the mind by redefining redemption as a return to the primal unity which self-consciousness denied man. The artificial division between the two elements of the divided self had to be overcome in order to create a new and higher fusion.[76] This reunion could come about only through experience defined as a process of education. Redemption gradually and cumulatively would overcome the superficial differences that divided an essentially unified spirit. The goal was unity in diversity or, as Coleridge described it, a state in which the self and the other maintained their individual identities, distinct yet not divided.

Marsh, however, differed from both the German thinkers and Coleridge in his description of the process of redemption and in locating its final ends. While German and many English Romantics located the goal of redemption in time, Marsh clung to the Orthodox vision of a reunion with a transcendent and essentially atemporal deity. This fusion would occur not in this world but in the next, and the process of earthly education—in the largest sense just another term for life itself—simply prepares for that final spiritual reconciliation. Education alone can carry the student only so far. His highest possible study is the spiritual in man, leaving him far from his ultimate divine destination. Moreover, that final step is utterly beyond human capacities. Consequently, education is necessarily incomplete and imperfect in this world. Through education, men and society move toward, but not to, God, and this movement represents social progress.

Therefore, true education extends beyond college and is the most important purpose of life, the true end of man on earth. "As to perfection in attaining the end of education," Marsh said, "we all know that it is beyond the reach of human devices. In regard to that we are scholars not at College only but in the world. The Schoolboy is only a class below his instructor and the highest cultivation attained in this world but imperfectly reveals the mysteries of our moral being."[77] Education on earth heightens awareness of the spiritual powers of the self. It develops those powers to their fullest human potential. But it does not and cannot bring union with God. That comes, of course, only as a gift of God's grace, and it comes not with the conquest of self-consciousness but at the moment when the awareness of self-consciousness and of separation from God is sharpest, at the moment, that is, nearest despair.

Marsh's educational system depends entirely on a miracle and a mystery beyond human influence or understanding. The spirit of man is imperfect and changing. It is bound in time. God, on the other hand, is timeless and perfect. The two can be reconciled only by the miracle of God's free grace. Redemption itself is not gradual. It is radical, a sudden transformation of the self in its fusion with the holy spirit. Once achieved, this fusion mandates the complete eradication of the self that will occur in the next world. Diversity gives way to unity, the self is subsumed in the divine spirit. The true end of education lies in oneness with God, the highest possible development of the spiritual consciousness, and this perfection can come only through grace and will flower only in heaven. All activity on earth is only continual preparation. Without divine guidance and this final divine intervention, the growth of the spirit would be merely directionless change, and individual certainty would be fanciful delusion. At no time during the process of education can the student see the final end toward which he is moving, which is just another way of saying that he cannot be one with God in this world. But he is guided in the right direction at each step by a divinely preestablished harmony between the developing spirit of man and the perfect spirit of God. Individuals need not accept secondhand certainty from imperfect earthly authorities because they have access to the perfect truth of absolute authority. This faith in spiritual unity and God's transcendent guidance is the heart of Marsh's education theory.

Yet this emphasis on preparation marks just how far education led Marsh from his Puritan models toward a Romantic psychology. His conviction that all life is education and his association of education with the developing spirit put him only a short step away from Unitarians like Henry Ware, Jr. The line here between education and redemption is far thinner than it had been for John Cotton or Cotton Mather, who saw education as a medium rather than a means of Grace, helpful, almost—but not quite—necessary, and certainly not sufficient.[78] Marsh drew a thinner line and therefore defended it more stubbornly and stridently. Arminians such as Colman or Chauncey put redemption in human hands by defining it as the product of a sincere effort to conform to the divine will. In its educational application, this principle further reinforced the social conservatism that had been a motive of American education from the first, and, by shifting the measure of grace to social works, it foreshadowed the rise of Ware's Unitarian redefinition of redemption as a controllable process of moral improvement. Ware's *On the Formation of A Christian Character* lauded Christian virtue as a means of self-culture and promised heaven as the reward.

Perhaps because Marsh was uncommonly and uncomfortably close to this view himself, he perceived its dangers more clearly than most.

If we regard ourselves as not truly sinners, alienated in our personal being from God and our true end, not so

fallen and lost as to need a divine power to redeem and
save us from spiritual death, but only ignorant and im-
prudent, needing but instruction and warning to secure
the attainment of our true end, and capable of being educated into a life of holiness, then we shall of course regard Christ as but a teacher, sent to point out to us the
way of duty and happiness, and his gospel but a volume
of instructions, which we are of ourselves fully compe-
tent to observe. It could be for us, in that case, only a system or collection of truths and admonitions, not essentially differing in kind from the various systems of
ancient wisdom. . . . It might, indeed, be better than
these, but would still differ only in degree; and Christ, instead of being a manifestation of God and the divine humanity, a realization of the highest idea of reason under
the forms of sense, is but an individual man, and to be
classed as one of the ancient sages. With those superficial
views of the nature of sin, and of man as a sinner, . . .
Christ and the gospel of the grace of God can rationally
be understood in no higher sense.[79]

This statement is interesting not only for its insight into the religious implications of Ware's moral theories, but because in its
description of the logical consequences of Ware's morality it reveals the unwillingness of Unitarians to pursue those consequences themselves. But to Marsh these were the *only possible*
consequences of a heretical view of redemption. Though Ware,
like Marsh, urged self-culture, Ware interpreted the term in
light of faculty psychology and neoclassical standards that bred
vastly different implications. Education was to *serve* society in
a most practical way. He measured its success by its ability to
integrate individuals into existing social forms and to indoctri-
nate them, though subtly, in the values of the surrounding culture. Education was training for membership in an old and
well-established club. Marsh replied:

If, in providing for the instruction of the young, our guiding purpose be, as it too often is, to prepare them for attaining some worldly end, we make them, in fact, subser-

vient to that end. If their whole education be conducted with an ultimate reference to their success in the world as merchants, for example, or civil engineers, or as professional men, the results will be such a cultivation of their minds only as will shape them to the particular relations in which they are to act. The aim will be to make their powers *serviceable* for attaining the outward objects, rather than to provide for their harmonious and perfect development.[80]

The spiritual intent of Marsh's educational system was, however, also its greatest practical weakness. To many, Marsh's system imposed too few restraints on the individual, did too little of obvious social benefit, and provided insufficient guidance and direction. Although it was highly valued at the University of Vermont by most students and dramatically raised the reputation of the University in academic circles, it had a disastrous effect on college finances, and the policy of advancement by merit discouraged some of the less able students. As a result, Marsh was forced to concede, "several have left College who in a different system would probably have been retained."[81] Marsh had never been a particularly able administrator, and in 1833, with the University facing a new financial crisis, he resigned the presidency. Although he did stay on as Professor of Moral and Intellectual Philosophy and directed educational policy at Vermont until his death,[82] after that time Torrey and Wheeler revised the system there, abandoning some of Marsh's liberal practices for more conventional procedures designed to insure the social acceptability, and thus the financial stability, of the institution.[83]

Marsh's educational ideas were never designed or destined for social acceptance. They flourished at Vermont—and were adopted by the Transcendentalists in Boston—during a spiritual interlude in American thought *after* nature had been lifted from the grip of mere mechanism and reinvested with spiritual import and *before* scientific study stripped away nature's innocence and benevolence and revealed its uncompromising laws of competition. Marsh's spiritual communication between nature and the mind was as out of place in the world of Darwin as it had been in that of symmetrically balanced mental faculties prior to 1820. His principles were never widely implemented because they stubbornly refused to serve social purposes, and the school was, after all, a social institution. When Marsh's principles reappeared decades later in the hands of John Dewey,* they had taken on a new social direction that ran counter to their original drift.

In Marsh's thought on education, we see an institution trying awkwardly to disappear in favor of the individuals it serves. But institutions do not disappear, though their energies may be directed elsewhere. Even if they remain only as empty forms, those forms still shape action, imposing the past on the present. The ultimate goal of education for Marsh was the establishment of relationship with God, not with other men. His aims were internal and spiritual rather than external and practical, pointing not to the world, but *through* it to God. Marsh's educational theory concerned itself with the state of the soul rather than status in society. Education was to be, not simply a medium through which grace might pass, but a way of bringing oneself closer to God. Thus Marsh's theory was a step toward making the mind the final authority, toward giving a heightened human perception the role of determining truth. Although Marsh still restrained the awesome power of reason within the bounds of existing educational forms, we can see individual and institution scraping and jarring against each other in ways that suggest the artificiality of their union and predict the futility of formal restraints in aesthetics, where dogma offers less decisive guidance.

---

* The fascinating relationship between Marsh and Dewey says a great deal about the transition from a philosophy predicated on absolute grounds to one that gives them up for the relative instability of human social discourse. I have not been able to develop that subject here, nor did I do so in my earlier essay ("James Marsh to John Dewey: The Fate of Transcendentalist Philosophy in American Education," *ESQ* 24 (1978): 1–11), which had a more particular point to make. I am grateful to Richard Rorty's *Philosophy and the Mirror of Nature* for suggesting the full implications of their association and am only sorry that I discovered Rorty's work far too late for it to have had more than a retrospective influence on my view of the issues I have developed in this book.

## ART

THE educational method Marsh developed at Vermont juggled the world and heaven, training students as useful members of society only as a side-effect of the effort to bring them closer to God. It tried simultaneously to imitate two distinct and incompatible forms, one human and therefore knowable and the other divine and necessarily unknowable. By stressing the divine over the worldly goal, Marsh violated the sensibilities of a community that had less lofty aims. As a social institution, the college was bound to serve society. When it opposed or ignored social goals, it doomed itself to practical failure, whatever spiritual success it might claim.

Marsh had hoped to apply his vision of divine unity to repair the fragmentation of nineteenth-century American culture. Faith would unite the individual will with its appropriate expression. It would harmonize spirit and form just as the Holy Spirit joins the Father and the Son. Objective forms, however, whether in nature or society, had never been hospitable to spirit. Not even the Puritans expected nature to represent the divine completely, and even if it had, they knew that their fallen perceptions would likely misinterpret it. As we have seen, social forms proved stubbornly resistant to Marsh's tampering, and his efforts to reshape them according to his religious philosophy only confirmed the incompatibility of individual insight and social standards that he had hoped to overcome. The old Puritan conflict between antinomian and Arminian impulses surged forth once more, still stronger than it had been in the seventeenth century and still less susceptible to resolution, largely because scientific verification and objective accessibility had become essential prerequisites to belief. It was just this obstacle that Marsh's revised reason—partaking of both spirit and intellect—was intended to heal by closing the distance between the spirit in man and in the world.

In practice, however, reason was repeatedly frustrated by preconceived interpretations demanded by dogma and institutional conventions. In church and civil polity, Marsh overcame the continuing antagonism between spiritual substance and worldly form only by submitting spirit to clerical authority and insisting on the need for social integration, just as in his choice of vocation personal inclinations bowed to duty. In education, as we have seen, the mind was freed from the constraints of worldly form by an organic theory of intellectual growth in which the world's forms are the occasions for knowledge rather than its object, and by a godly rather than a worldly destination for that growth, a destination at once beyond human judgments and inherently compatible with (because the perfect model of) divine spirit. Perfect social relationships, like the perfect church or college, Marsh said, exist only in art or in heaven. They are produced symbolically by the imagination or divinely by God. When spirit refused to serve the world, social institutions returned the compliment, cramping spirit within their functional walls or ignoring it entirely. Marsh's spiritual method simply failed as a program of social reform. Its power was personal and could be put to work only to inspire a personal vision. It is not surprising, then, that Marsh's spiritual method found its fullest expression in art.

As it is freed of social restraints, Marsh's theory of the mind produces an aesthetic similar in important respects to that of the Transcendentalists, but one which raises questions about contemporary interpretations of that aesthetic. In art, as in religion or politics, the times were conservative. Most Unitarian commentators stopped short at classical standards or went beyond them only tentatively, approving the most morally unimpeachable of the Romantic writers and the less bawdy or vulgar scenes of Shakespeare. In opposition, and with a unanimity that is surprising in light of their differences on other issues, Marsh and the Transcendentalists adhered to an organic and intuitive view of art. Yet, despite William Hutchison's observation that the Transcendentalists came closer to agreement about aesthetic theory than they did about any other subject,[84] conflicting critical views of the Transcendentalist aesthetic continue to be troublesome and suggest that Transcendentalist aesthetics were less consistent than Hutchison's statement might suggest.

When Lawrence Buell says on one hand that the Transcendentalists were for the most part temperamentally aesthetes[85] and Sherman Paul says on the other that Transcendentalism included more social reformers than literary artists,[86] one is led to suspect that a crucial question about Transcendentalism may not be whether the Transcendentalists were "truly" aesthetes or reformers, but why this opposition—apparent even to the Transcendentalists themselves—seems so particularly irksome to students of the movement. The affinity between Marsh and the Transcendentalists in this field suggests that perhaps we need not excuse the Transcendentalists for their lack of abolitionist zeal by labeling them unredeemable aesthetes as Buell does, or defend their social consciences by stressing their reformist inclinations along with Paul. As an alternative, we might ask what in the motives behind Transcendentalism placed art at the center of its innovative energies? What about art made it the most productive vehicle for the development of Transcendentalist thought? What in Transcendentalism makes the conflict between art and social action so acute, and what attracted those who were aesthetes by temperament, yet not themselves literary artists?

Art assumed great importance for Marsh, as it did for the Transcendentalists, primarily because it plunged him directly and unavoidably into the clash between spirit and form, the heart and its objective representations, that he had managed to evade in religion, politics, and education. In education, we recall, there was no necessary connection between the form of the curriculum and the form of the spirit. The curriculum was a *correlative* of the mind, not its external form, and it did not claim to represent reason objectively. In education, therefore, Marsh managed to avoid the central Romantic labor of pinning the ineffable spirit down to an objective form. Art, however, differs from other forms of outward expression in that form *must* present objectively the spirit which produced it. The object of art embodies and expresses spirit. Its whole *raison d'etre* is to discover to open sight the principles that reside hidden in the soul and in nature, to bring otherwise inaccessible spirit into the world, to make the divine sensible so that it can be observed and known.

In Marsh's terms, art both gave form to and revealed reason, which is God. Art was a religious act that filled the world with spirit. It was, as Emerson said, "transubstantiation, the conversion of daily bread into holiest symbols."[87] Therefore, in Marsh's thought, as in that of many Romantic writers, art was the proving ground of Romantic philosophy. When art assumed the power to reveal the divine order in appearance, it replaced both

Scripture and tradition as the authority in spiritual and moral questions. But the nature of artistic inquiry into such issues raised a new set of questions different from those of dogmatic or moral epistemologies. It established a novel and more intimate relationship between the artist and his creation, endowing the latter with unforeseen and not altogether welcome authority and infusing the truths it revealed with an import less transferable or objectively verifiable, but not, therefore, less fatal.

BECAUSE eloquence could change minds and capture souls, the difficulties of artistic expression in language took a particularly urgent form, centering around the conflict language raised between spirit and idea. These terms vied with each other for preeminence in Marsh's mind, as they had been battling in American attitudes about language for two hundred years.[88] As Puritan ministers had clung resolutely to the plain style for fear that too much eloquence might carry the feelings away before the understanding could be persuaded, Marsh feared language and wanted to confine it within the neoclassical standards of balance, proportion, and logic that governed formal rhetoric in his time.

Though he never entirely forgot that language should manifest an organic relationship between spirit and idea, his judgments concealed a bias in favor of the idea, especially in the language of faith. This bias, which he associated with duty, enjoined that the languages in which we find our models ought to be the most refined, symmetrical and balanced ones, in other words the classical languages, rather than those which convey feeling with the greatest force. Like most educated nineteenth-century Americans, Marsh had been thoroughly trained in rhetoric and had learned the fundamentals of pulpit eloquence by studying classical rhetoricians and their modern imitators. Under this influence, Marsh encouraged imitation and insisted that the idea is prior to its expression, which provides only an artificial vehicle for the speaker's ideas.[89]

For Marsh, imitative literature modeled after the classics was formally correct and an appropriate vessel for Christian doctrine. Yet it was also cold and still, lacking the spiritual fire that enflames the soul and endows doctrine with conviction. In practice, Marsh was always disappointed in performances that carried out this conservative rhetorical program. Such utterances, he complained, drained the life out of faith and left its body empty. At such moments he rejected form for feeling. His readings in Puritan theology and in the Cambridge Platonists had made him sensitive to the discrepancy in both between the personal religious experience they tried to portray and the crabbed, legalistic style, the style of the Schoolmen, in which they tried to convey it.[90] Marsh was certain that the Puritan spirit could be reborn only in a language that combined symbolic power with scientific precision, a language that demolished the barrier between words and things, yet preserved its own internal integrity—symbolism without ambiguity.[91]

Ideally, such language should unite divine truth, individual aesthetic inspiration, and literary rules, just as the Trinity united the Father, the Holy Spirit, and the Son. But Marsh could never decide whether divine truth is best expressed by literary conventions, rhetoric derived from classical models, or by divine inspiration, of which the best example is Scripture, God's revelation through divinely inspired poets. Marsh's reading of Herder, who had associated eloquence with the spontaneous speech of the inspired prophet and had traced the origins of words to the emotional responses of primitive man, convinced him that preaching ought to communicate the divine spirit to laymen. The minister, he believed, must embody the Logos, or divine Word, in words, and this could only be done through inspired eloquence.[92] Such eloquence would speak authoritatively from the indwelling spirit and offer insight into divine truth, but it would violate conventional aesthetic form and often stray from the straight halls of doctrine.

FOR New England ministers from Cotton to Emerson, the power of language was above all a religious one, and the primer for the study of that power was the sermon.[93] New England's sermon styles reflected the same metaphysical assumptions that inspired its moribund theology. In the second quarter of the nineteenth century, Unitarian ministers appealed with a certain discomfort to feelings rather than to reason, speaking to that greater part of any congregation which was unregenerate. The sermon had to inject religious feeling into predominantly secular lives. Evangelism committed itself wholeheartedly to this principle and reaped rewards in larger and more enthusiastic gatherings than its more legitimate (and conventional) counterparts could muster. Unitarian sentiment was far more attuned to urban refinement than the more earthy appeals of Finney and his imitators. But despite stylistic differences, both Unitarians and evangelists employed the sermon as a converting ordinance working through the feelings.[94] Unitarians hoped to encourage moral action and improve character, evangelists to bring more apocalyptic change.

But both were essential consequences of the same movement away from a religion of the gathered elect and toward religion as a cry for piety in the spiritless landscape of daily life. Orthodoxy viewed both with the sternest disapproval, holding out for years against the extempore style of evangelism and Unitarianism since that style made precise doctrinal discussion difficult.[95] It found little more than empty formal elegance in its Unitarian opponents, who in turn condemned Orthodox preachers as narrow and dogmatic ranters.[96] Both objected in unison to evangelical preaching because it evoked feeling at the expense either of doctrine or of reason.

Marsh aimed to repair the discrepancies in preaching styles between New England sects as a first step toward the larger and more important goal of narrowing the deeper divisions between their metaphysical views. From the evidence of his earliest letters, Marsh was as dissatisfied with prevailing pulpit practice as he was with the principles that governed it, and he imagined a style that would at once elaborate a precise doctrine and fill it with life. Prompted by his aesthetic sense, Marsh preferred the animated sermons he heard during his stay in Virginia to the dry logic of Andover or Princeton pulpit oratory. Like Emerson,[97] Marsh admired sermons filled with the true spirit of Scripture. While in the South he wrote:

> Preachers have, I think, some decided advantages over our New England ministers. They have less discrimination and less critical accuracy in regard to speculative views and the analytical interpretation of the Sacred Scripture, but more of that moral power which is acquired by meditation upon the more important moral truths and the facts of revelation and upon the devo-

tional parts of the bible [sic]. I have heard extempore preaching in Virginia which made me ashamed to think of reading a sermon in our cold New England style.[98]

Marsh would have liked to incorporate the southern style into his own preaching, and he did recommend it to his colleagues in the North. "Let your sermons breathe and utter forth the solemn earnestness and the yearning love for the souls of men that characterize the gospel itself," he advised one; "the exhibition of such a spirit is, in my deliberate judgment, the only preaching."[99]

Yet, for all his advice to others, he could not free himself from the doctrinal biases of his Orthodox training, nor could he actually *produce* a language that would incorporate both fervor and dogma. His legalistic training demanded adherence to doctrinal truth, while his aesthetic sense argued for the fiery inspired language that warms the soul. His obligation to preserve spiritual truth to the letter forbade eloquent flights in his own sermons, which, he said, "are not such as I would approve for common use,"[100] and this inability to imitate Scriptural eloquence reveals Marsh as a true son of New England, whether he liked it or not. The spiritual fire and "moral power" of southern preaching was somehow inextricably linked to its lack of "discrimination" and "critical accuracy," and Marsh, who possessed these latter qualities in conspicuous abundance, could not scale the heights of eloquent inspiration if he had to leave speculative truth behind.

Perfect spiritual forms proved easier to conceive than to create. Marsh's own experience frustrated his stylistic ideals and impressed him with the incompatibility of eloquence and doctrinal accuracy in preaching. In his "Tract on Eloquence," Marsh explained that the mind of the eloquent artist has to be "synthetic" rather than "analytic," that it must "dissolve diffuse and dissipate" in order to create higher truth. The analytic mind, on the other hand, "begins with separating and intellectually classifying ideas," and the two cannot coexist. "The creative process of the imagination," Marsh said, "is in itself directly the reverse of the [analytic] and . . . they cannot have a coexistent exercise in the mind."[101] This notion suggests that, except in Scripture, which is God's eloquent revelation, doctrinal truth and eloquence are mutually exclusive, and language is an inadequate vehicle for religious feeling. Truth paralyzes eloquence and eloquence distorts truth. The two can be one only in the mind of God.

Behind these two literary styles, Marsh is disguising two opposed ways of understanding experience that correspond to distinct psychological models. The analytical model, founded on Locke, presupposes that understanding depends on the ability to make distinctions, to perceive differences, to recognize the integrity of separate forms. It then arranges these distinct forms into a larger order that depends for its coherence on the interrelationship of the parts. In contrast, the synthetic method discounts apparent forms, breaks down the barriers between things, and responds to the common spirit in them all. The former makes a mechanical order out of discrete objects which would otherwise dissolve into fragmentation and chaos. The latter dispenses with distinction entirely and substitutes oneness for order. While the analytic system may *appear* closer to particulars in its greater attention to individual forms, in fact the principles of arrangement—the ordering principles—are abstract and preconceived, while the synthetic method starts in an unmediated response to experience and concludes in a unity that exists only in the act of perception itself. Yet, since the synthetic mode denies forms, it also denies the possibility of a satisfactory artistic embodiment of divine truth.

Marsh was unable either to resolve these two views or to sacrifice one for the other, and in this he assumes as nowhere else the Transcendentalist posture. His movements, wavering between incompatible and individually unacceptable visions of the mind and of art, are the movements of Transcendentalist writing in *Nature*, *Walden*, and "Song of Myself." That and the impossible perfection he demanded of his artistic ideal illuminate both the pressures that twisted tender Transcendentalist impulses to artistic production and the internal fragmentation that characterizes Transcendentalist writing.

As long as art conveyed ideas, Marsh measured its value by the consistency of those ideas with Christian revelation. Marsh's response to the "eloquent artists" of his own day was tempered less by their failure to capture higher spiritual truth than by their imperfect adherence to Christian principles. He demanded a particular *form* for spirit. Despite his sensitivity to the aesthetic merits of Byron, Carlyle, or Wordsworth, he read them, finally, with analytic rather than synthetic eyes. The influential literature of his day, Marsh protested, too often confused inspirational language with doctrinal truth. Even the English Romantics suffered in his eyes because their poetic vitality—the very quality for which he prized them—seemed to obscure doctrinal principles. Marsh told R. H. Dana that Carlyle

> leaves the ultimate grounds for truth and the ultimate causes of events very much in the dark, and it would be difficult I think to determine from these works whether he was speculatively a believer in Christianity or a Pantheist, or in a state of philosophical indifference to all systems. Alas! how little of this literature that falls in the way of young people, and of that which is most fascinating, is what we could wish in this respect. With all the high aspirations of Wordsworth there is much in his writings that is more favorable to an undefined naturalism or Pantheism than to the truth of Gospel.[102]

Clearly, the poetic mission was to dress doctrinal truth in eloquent language. It should act as another educational medium, like the college or the church, but, unlike those more staid institutions, it could make "speculative" truth more palatable, entice readers into faith almost unaware, or embody Christian theory in dramatic action as an example to those who needed help in applying doctrine to their lives. This dramatic appeal actually made the Romantic poets dangerous, however, when they failed to use their power in the service of explicitly Christian doctrine.

When Marsh was forced to make judgments about specific works, he could not avoid comparing them with Scripture and was invariably dissatisfied with them insofar as they invariably deviated from the model and failed to walk the well-worn planks of doctrine. Marsh was disturbed by any suggestion that the truth of art might assume a form different from that of doctrine, and his discomfort marks the limitations that the principles of revealed religion place on literary expression. Marsh measured all literature against Scripture, the literary form in which God published his spiritual message to man. Revelation, as everyone knew, was at an end. There could be no new revelation, and though it was clear to Marsh that literature, like a sermon, must communicate the one truth of Christian dogma feelingly to its audience, enlivening feeling and the doctrinal form seemed always at odds.

The fact is that once literature had been turned into a sort of revelation, no form could be satisfactory without displacing the one true Scriptural revelation, a possibility Marsh could not accept. The Transcendentalists, who had already recognized numerous revelations, found the problem of form still more irksome since the form they sought would have had to express spirit perfectly and completely and such perfection understandably eluded them. Theodore Parker, for instance, complained that the *Dial* was too ethereal and precious; its symbols he said, should be "a baby, a pap-spoon, and a cradle." Yet he was no more satisfied with the more vigorous *Boston Quarterly Review*, which, he complained, lacked the *Dial*'s pure spirit.[103] Marsh opted for a more traditional view of art as a vehicle for discursive moral truths that can be learned, rather than as a medium for spirit that must be experienced. The former instructs the reader in established truths, the latter creates truth anew in each reader and with each reading. Marsh would see only doctrinal truth in literature; in his view, an artist who deviated from doctrine expressed not transcendent spirit, but fanciful delusion.

So hedged in by doctrine, Marsh could only hypothesize an imaginative literature in which art becomes the medium not for a new revelation, but for a new expression of the old one. In these speculations he was in the vanguard of American literary criticism in the early nineteenth century, urging that the mission of a reader or critic was not judgmental or evaluative but appreciative, and arguing that to comprehend a work of literature, the reader must be in sympathy with the author.[104] This notion of reading suggests that literature communicates the spirit of revelation rather than its discursive form which appears only in Scripture. It makes the work of a medium for the transference of that spirit from author to reader, just as Puritan education was a medium for grace rather than an actual instru-

172

ment of it. Such literature will not yield its fullest sense to eyes clouded by convention and enchanted by formal elegance. It calls for an antiformal mode of inquiry into a necessarily antiformal literature of inspiration—only spirit can receive spirit—whereas formal inquiry asks questions that are simply irrelevant to the answers inspired literature is prepared to give.

In that sense, Marsh was carrying out in literature the principles imbedded in his religious philosophy. Emerson and Whitman could later take up similar principles and make them more explicit because they did not share Marsh's burdensome conformity to a *particular* revelation. It derives for them from the Transcendentalist eagerness to establish an original relationship with the universe—an impulse that was itself an outcry against convention in literature and society. Though Emerson was as uncertain as Marsh about the ungainly products of this literary program and would have been more at home with his poetry had it assumed the graceful meters of English verse, he often accepted the truths he found in his writing as authoritative, even as a new revelation. But in casting off allegiance to any single revelation, he cast off as well any possible certainty that such inspiration reflected an authority more absolute than unaided imagination could supply, a truth more universal than the personal moment.

In his statements about fine art, Marsh found himself relieved of the need to reconcile literary inspiration with doctrine. Without such restraint, Marsh's radicalism suggests Emerson's, as he exercises the fullest implications of the intellectual method he could not apply in religion, politics, and education. In fine art, this method does not have to contend with formal expectations or dogmatic preconceptions. It can work out its own forms and powers, changing the relationship between the artist and his own creation and shifting the balance of authority between the artist and his audience. Marsh was free to be led by his belief in a vital, spirit-infused nature to a radical view of art as a moral and spiritual authority created by man, yet coequal with nature or revelation, one which redefines in the process the notion of authority itself, depriving it of its objectivity, universality, and consistency, but making its dictates incontestable where they apply.

The creative powers of the mind as Marsh describes them in art do not differ essentially from the impulses of the spirit in which Marsh discovered the life of the church, the substance of the ideal state, and the energy of educational growth. But in their repudiation of rigid form and their insistence that the world that exists is not the real world, these energies had been antagonistic to the preconceived assumptions that gave those institutions structure and made them effective agents of social influence. The predominance in fine art of impulses to free and unrestrained growth guided only by the unfolding creative act itself guaranteed not only that such art must exist outside of institutions where it can work according to assumptions it creates for itself, but that it will find its major subject in its alienation from institutional culture and spend its energies examining the conflict between them.

Though all of Marsh's thought reached out for reconciliation ultimately it revealed only the impossibility of the problem. In trying, for instance, to use fine art as the mediator between universal spirit and spiritless matter and to overcome the Cartesian split between mind and nature, he rejected the materialist notion that art should imitate physical nature and also disapproved the single-minded pursuit of higher, ideal truths at the expense of the concrete forms that express those truths in the natural world. He urged instead an artistic "living mean"[105] between extreme idealism and extreme realism, only to have this attempt at compromise launch him in a new direction and radically expand the spiritual powers of art, extending its influence to areas usually reserved for religion.

At this lofty level, however, Marsh minimized the differences between art and other disciplines, a move intended to make some of his statements about art seem less heretical since they were also statements about faith, but which also opened his discussion of art to all the issues that had troubled him in religion and politics and remained unresolved in those fields. In art, they take on new significance and bring consequences that were logically denied them before. Just as reason became in Marsh's hands a power of spiritual insight at once intuitive and intellectual, art is elevated in his spiritual vision into an expression of the highest powers of the soul. It is the ultimate human form

174

of reason, and as such it encompasses all areas of the mind's activity.

At this highest level, "philosophical science, religion, and art are identical in this that they involve the reception and conscious manifestation of the universal in the individual. In each the merely individual becomes self-abased and voluntarily yields itself up as the instrument and medium of the universal."[106] Here, as in education, Marsh tries to restrict the possible products of imagination by subsuming it in the universal. Presumably an artist who creates from the depths of his own spirit will not diverge from divine truth. But without the controlling mediation of dogma or convention as a check, a work of art assumes its own authority and finds its own form, following only the truths revealed by the processes and motives of its creation. Though Marsh insists that the particular "yields itself up" and works only as a medium for universal truth, in practice the particular work of art will claim to represent the universal, and there will be no authority to contradict it. By designating art as the representative of spirit, Marsh invested it quite literally with the power of revelation.

Invested with so much authority, art established new relationships between the artist and society, and even between the artist and his own soul. At the very top of the scale of life ascending from vegetative to perceptive to mechanical creativity for selfish ends, Marsh placed "the productive powers of the imagination as the guide of the self-seeking principle."[107] The goal of art is one with the goal of religion, the discovery of the divine principle at work in the soul, the revelation of God in the life of the individual. Thus, art, too, becomes a sort of education, but different both in its means and its effects. For while education proper was a means of improving the spiritual sight, art is the improved and self-improving sight itself. Education was a sort of training, art the power produced by that training. Taking on the qualities of reason, it becomes a way of knowing, a route to the universal truths that reside undetected by conventional sight in the individual facts of experience, a way of simultaneously knowing God and knowing the soul. But this is not conventional knowledge—mastery of certain facts. This knowledge is, as Marsh repeatedly said, a form of being, and that definition fundamentally alters our understanding of what knowing is, of how it is communicated, and of its power over the life of its possessor.

To know, according to Marsh's redefinition of reason, was to alter the self, to raise the spiritual powers of the mind to a level closer to that of divine reason. It was not either a way of filling the mind with facts or of refining the intellectual powers as the conventional wisdom of New England would have it. These latter views were designed to retain social controls on the shape of knowledge. If, for example, facts constitute knowledge, then any conclusion can be broken down into the facts which must have produced it, making its validity measurable against an objective body of material available to all. Special knowledge can come only from special access to private facts, and that sort of private experience was frowned upon in nineteenth-century New England. If, by the same token, knowledge is viewed as a balance of inherent intellectual and moral faculties, the very implications of balance and the necessity of a standard for refinement guarantee that knowledge would skirt antisocial or unconventional conclusions.

But when, in order to free knowing from dead empirical facts and open it to spirit, Marsh redefined it as a form of being and then associated it with artistic creativity, he freed art from external controls and strayed, all unaware, into a new and distinctly modern conception of a world in flux, a conception that was antagonistic to Christian faith in absolute values. Knowledge becomes not a thing or a collection of propositions, but a process, the creative activity of the individual's highest powers. Changes in knowledge are changes in the shape of the self, wrought not by God's grace nor by external experience, but by the individual artist in pursuit of spiritual self-revelation. Seeking himself in such art, the artist risks transforming what he seeks. In quest of his spiritual center, the artist may find that he is the creature of his art, as well as its creator, and that the center withdraws a step deeper into obscurity with each step he takes.

WHEN Marsh's notions of the mind ventured off from the religious context that spawned them, they left behind as well the unchanging instruction of Scripture, the anchor that secured human action to divine law. Without that protection, Marsh had to seek security elsewhere, and he responded to threats in social contexts such as politics, education, and art by retreating inward to the abode of the soul. This location seemed safe because it belonged to the spiritual world rather than to the real one, and therefore offered refuge from real-world problems. But the very boundaries between the real and the divine, the world and the soul, that he counted on for protection had been demolished partly by his own work. The soul—a spiritual entity temporarily inhabiting a gross physical form—had been transformed into the Romantic consciousness, which was a part of the world and subject to both time and change. One could no longer retire inward in order to ascend upward, as the Cambridge Platonists had promised. Inward lay the problem, not the solution, and the spiritual absolute that Marsh counted on to resolve the fragmentation around him had been displaced to some still more inaccessible realm.

"There is," Emerson said, "no pure Transcendentalist," hinting obliquely at the necessary irreconcilability of universal spirit and particular objective forms. Yet the cost of their continued alienation, Marsh knew, was a world cut off from order and meaning—all coherence gone. This bleak vision loomed, potent but unacknowledged, behind the insistent optimism of Emerson and Whitman and Thoreau as, following Marsh who followed Edwards, they exerted all their art to hold universal spirit and particular facts together. Yet, not despite but *because* of these efforts, the boundary between the two was more and more sharply drawn.

By making reason a divine authority in, but not of, the mind, Marsh made the journey to God a journey through the self and subverted his own conservative intent. While Marsh thought to reserve some special powers to grace and to social institutions by defining reason as God's emissary in the mind rather than as a natural part of the mind itself, he actually offered philosophical encouragement to those who wanted to assert that man did not need any help to reach God, that his own unaided powers were sufficient. By placing the appointed mediator in man himself rather than *between* man and God, Marsh implicitly reduced the spiritual space between them to near the vanishing point. Every man became his own Christ, not because he could

177

refine his habits, manners, and tastes to conform with a social ideal that would ensure his heavenly reward, but because he could produce apocalyptic spiritual change in himself. For the first time, access to divine truth was immediate, that is to say, unmediated. Men could know God first-hand as He appeared in divine reason rather than through a necessarily imperfect interpretation of Scripture or the still less authoritative pronouncements of social authorities.

Even more than education, art placed the power to bring man to God with the individual. It was the beginning of a new emphasis on psychology—a term Coleridge introduced into English—in American religion, a psychology in which the traditional boundaries between internal and external, subjective and objective, and hence antinomian and Arminian, had become blurred. In order to make spirit accessible, Marsh transformed the dualism between mind and matter into a psychologism—a distinction between reason and understanding—unifying them in the experience of the self, making nature a mediator between man and God. He converted an irreconcilable split between experience and reality into a relationship between two modes of experience and then argued that art must represent the higher spiritual experience in concrete form. It must capture not merely physical nature, but the spirit that creates and shapes matter.[108] In religion, he called his power "divine reason." But in art it lived in the creative mind and was called forth by experience in nature to produce the art work itself. Art, Marsh wrote, joins the divine power in nature with the soul of the artist so that "the simple power of things may flow together with the power of our mind, and both may be blended into one."[109] Thus art acquired the power to unite the individual reason with divine reason. Revelation had conferred only *knowledge* of the divine will, but such art as Marsh described also gives the *power* to *do* God's will. It makes knowing and doing one. In effect, Marsh made art a means of grace, capable of linking the soul and the will and healing the wounds of the Fall. Such art could close the divine circle, bring man out of the temporal world into a world of perfect mind and perfected nature.

Greater individuality does not, however, necessarily entail greater freedom. The individual truths created in the spirit by this imaginative art turn out to be *more* formative, more influential, and less avoidable than the truths offered by external sources. For in this case, authority cannot be distinguished from truth itself. It is an absolute (though decidedly *not* universal) authority resident with God-like power in the individual mind. Marsh provided a method for attaining truth that made that truth one with—the same as—the being or spirit of the truth-seeker. The conclusions attained by that method would bear an authority validated by their very residence in the self, one far more convincing than externals. The traditional notion of a preexisting empirical truth had sharply divided authority and truth. External authorities acted as a medium for transmitting truth to men, who could possess it, know it, without working any fundamental change in it or in themselves. But when the truth and the self become one and carry their own inseparable authority, the conditions for right action are altered. To know truth is to *be* it, and to be the truth is to do it. With the union of principle and being, knowledge brings right action as a natural form of self-expression, and, conversely, the failure to act rightly implies a defective spirit and a sort of lie.

While it was one of Marsh's cherished motives to return this profound responsibility to American moral life, he could not foresee the relativism latent in his intellectual method because he was too intent on reestablishing immediate access to a truly absolute spiritual authority and on returning stability to moral lives that had been attenuated by reliance on secondhand authorities. Enlightenment thought, in its eagerness to make the universe orderly and comprehensible, had oversimplified it by banishing questions of moral and spiritual responsibility that did not readily disclose their solutions to casual intellectual inquiry, a strategy which necessarily excluded essential elements of human experience. The universe was made comprehensible by ignoring what frustrated comprehension. It was this denial that troubled Marsh, who wanted to retain an enlightened optimism based on confidence in the mind's powers while once again embracing the subjective experiences that threatened the neat Enlightenment scheme.

Although the Congregationalist background from which Marsh developed his thought necessarily circumscribed the individual's power to shape his own life, art disentangled that power from dogmatic constraints. So unencumbered, it took on a form akin to that of the creative power the Transcendentalists wrought out of Unitarianism, which had already discarded human depravity and dependence. In effect, Marsh did for Congregationalist faith in the authority of indwelling spirit what the Transcendentalists did for Unitarian confidence in the mind's powers—he accommodated it to the new revelation of Kant and Romantic philosophy. For human frailty and salvation in the next world, Unitarianism permitted Emerson to substitute the mind's limitless power and a conviction that salvation was not too high an aspiration to be fulfilled in this life. Together, Unitarian optimism and the new mental philosophy derived from Marsh and others engendered in the Transcendentalists a tremendous confidence in the ability of the mind to comprehend the whole of human experience, both spiritual and material, and to unite them in harmony.

This confidence has led one scholar to identify Transcendentalism as the "flowering of the American enlightenment."[110] Yet it might more accurately be described as the last gasp of classical idealism. It unequivocally asserted that behind things as we normally perceive them lies a higher spiritual reality open to any who will look for it in the proper spirit. The background of Transcendentalism in Unitarianism made this belief more plausible than could Marsh's Orthodox vision of two worlds: false and true, material and spiritual, man's and God's. The Transcendentalists wanted to make the two worlds one without recourse to the divine intervention through grace that even Marsh thought necessary. Like Enlightenment thinkers—their own Unitarian fathers—though with different means, the Transcendentalists worked to establish in this world the changeless perfection lost to sight when spirit was relegated to the next.

Yet in trying to grasp perfect spirit, the Transcendentalists misplaced just that element of human experience that Marsh could not forget—sin. They insisted, despite their own doubts, that the world was perfect (if only we could see it clearly), or even (with Whitman) that the world was perfect and getting more perfect all the time. Such beliefs seemed almost undeniable where progress was so much a fact of life as in America, and it was perhaps inevitable that before long they would be coopted by the very social system they aimed to subvert—moral epigrams from Emerson drummed (by rote) into the heads of every school child and laced through the speeches of politicians. Such insistent perfectability seemed to Marsh to deny too many of the grim facts of life. In a time of apparently unlimited potential, Marsh tried to preserve a Calvinist sense of original sin—the paradigm of human imperfection—and a conviction that human life is, if not a tragedy, at best a tragi-comedy. This had been, after all, the shape of his own life: achievement purchased at the cost of personal desires frustrated, talents confined, inclinations thwarted, work distorted and blindly misapplied.

Marsh's Orthodox belief that this world is essentially and necessarily one of change, and pain, and sin, and his disenchantment with complacent optimism strike a pervasive countertone within the Transcendental harmony that is at once reminiscent of Puritan rigor and yet distinctly modern. The Puritan champions of rigorous reformation saw the mediatory resources of Catholicism as barriers that distanced man from God rather than as aids in bridging the gap. Dispensing with mediation cleared the way for an optimistic vision of an immediate personal relationship with God through His own Scriptural word. But when Scripture failed in the nineteenth century, this same promising vision turned bleak, leaving man still in search of God but now without guides and without help. And it became bleaker still when God became an unreachable part of the now modern self, living in the mind but unknowable in the absence of a grace that seemed no more than a comforting myth, leaving us alone in the void of ourselves that we have come to call, antiseptically, the modern condition.

It is this menacing but unspoken potential within Marsh's thought that locates his true heirs not in Andover or Princeton, as he would have willed, but in Cambridge and Concord, Pittsfield and Salem. Just as Columbus steadfastly denied the New World of map and mind that he had opened by mischance and educated error, Marsh retreated from the implications of his own discoveries into determinism and subjugation to Providence. But other explorers cleared the path Marsh had surveyed. Emerson, Hawthorne, Melville, and James practiced a kindred aesthetic and tried the consequences of making the mind responsible for its own shape as well as that of the world it perceives. For good or ill, they pursued their fictive inquiries into a question Marsh could ask only by implication: what might it mean to say that man is both the artist and the artwork and must account for his life, not to God or to society, but to himself?

# A Chronology of James Marsh's Life

| | |
|---|---|
| 1794 | Born on 19 July in Hartford, Vermont. |
| 1812 | Prepares for Dartmouth College at William Nutting's Academy, Randolph, Vermont. |
| 1813 | Enters Dartmouth College. |
| 1815 | Converted during religious revival at Dartmouth. |
| 1817 | Begins studies for ministry at Andover Theological Seminary. |
| 1818 | Called back to Dartmouth as a tutor, serving in that capacity for two years. |
| 1820 | Returns to Andover to complete studies for the ministry. |
| 1822 | Graduated from Andover. |
| | Publishes his essay "Ancient and Modern Poetry" in the *North American Review* (July 1822). |
| | Helps translate the geographical portions of J. J. Bellerman's *Handbuch der Biblischen Literatur* during a period of retreat at his father's farm. |
| 1823 | Goes to Hampden-Sydney, Virginia, to teach oriental languages at the invitation of John Rice. |

1824    Returns to New England to be ordained as a
        Congregationalist minister and to marry Lucia
        Wheelock, niece of an ex-president of Dartmouth,
        John Wheelock.
1826    Appointed to the presidency of the University of
        Vermont.
        Begins to publish serially in *The Biblical Repertory
        and Princeton Review* his translation of Johann
        Gottfried Herder's *Vom Geist der ebräischen Poesie.*
1828    First wife, Lucia, dies of tuberculosis.
1829    Reviews Moses Stuart's *Commentary on the Epistle to
        the Hebrews* in the *Christian Spectator.*
        Publishes a series of articles on public education in
        the *Vermont Chronicle* under the pen name
        "Philopolis."
        Publishes *Aids to Reflection* by Samuel Taylor
        Coleridge.
1830    Publishes *Select Practical Theology of the Seventeenth
        Century.*
        Marries Laura Wheelock, sister of his first wife.
1831    Publishes an edition of *The Friend* by Samuel Taylor
        Coleridge.
1833    Resigns as president of the University of Vermont to
        become Professor of Natural and Moral Philosophy.
1838    Second wife, Laura, dies of tuberculosis.
1840    Publishes second edition of *Aids to Reflection.*
1842    Dies on 3 July in Colchester, Vermont.

# Notes

Preface

1. This has been the general strategy in scholarly discussions of Marsh and his influence. See Marjorie Nicolson, "James Marsh and the Vermont Transcendentalists," *Philosophical Review* 34 (1925); 28–50; Ronald Wells, *Three Christian Transcendentalists* (New York: Columbia University Press, 1943), pp. 14–49; Henry A. Pochmann, *German Culture in America, Philosophical and Literary Influences, 1600–1900* (Madison: University of Wisconsin Press, 1961), 131–43; John Dewey, "James Marsh and American Philosophy," *Journal of the History of Ideas* 2 (1941): 131–50; and John J. Duffy in four articles, "From Hanover to Burlington: James Marsh's Search for Unity," *Vermont History* 38 (1972): 27–48; "Problems in Publishing Coleridge; James Marsh's First American Edition of *Aids to Reflection*," *New England Quarterly* 43 (1972): 193–208; "Transcendental Letters from Ripley to James Marsh," *Emerson Society Quarterly*, 50 (1970): 21–25; and "T. S. Eliot's Objective Correlative: A New England Commonplace," *New England Quarterly* 42 (1969): 108–115.

## Chapter 1: A Ground Unconditioned (*text pages* 1–33)

1. J. W. Alexander, Albert Dod, and Charles Hodge published "Transcendentalism of the Germans and of Cousin and Its Influence On Opinion in This Country" in *The Biblical Repertory and Princeton Review*, January, 1839. This passage is also quoted in Perry Miller, ed., *The Transcendentalists: An Anthology* (Cambridge, Mass.: Harvard University Press, 1950), p. 233.

2. Although, as I say below, American Orthodoxy had become so fragmented by the 1820s that no one term can encompass its variety, the word, as I use it here, refers to a theological heritage shared by all of the various descendants of Congregationalism in New Haven, Andover, and Princeton. They were united most fundamentally, perhaps, not by any common opinions about doctrine but by their view of themselves (if not of each other) as Orthodox.

3. William Hutchison, *The Transcendentalist Ministers: Church Reform in the New England Renaissance* (New Haven: Yale University Press, 1959), p. 18.

4. For the best discussions of distinctions among the factions that collectively comprised Orthodoxy, see Sidney E. Ahlstrom, *A Religious History of the American People* (New Haven: Yale University Press, 1972); idem, "Theology in America: An Historical Survey," *Religion in American Life*, 3 vols. James W. Smith and A. Leland Jamison, eds. (Princeton: Princeton University Press, 1961), 1: 232–322; and Frank H. Foster, *A Genetic History of the New England Theology* (New York: Russel and Russel, 1907).

5. Marsh to Lucia Wheelock, 1 July 1821, in Joseph Torrey, "Memoir," *The Remains of the Rev. James Marsh D.D.* (Burlington, Vt.: Chauncey Goodrich, 1843) pp. 45–46.

6. See Joseph Haroutunian, *Piety Versus Moralism: The Passing of the New England Theology* (New York: Holt, Rinehart and Winston, 1932), Chapter 1.

7. Ibid., p. 44.

8. Ahlstrom, "Theology," p. 244.

9. Rufus Choate to James Marsh, 11 August 1821. Quoted in Samuel G. Brown, *The Life of Rufus Choate* (Boston: Little, Brown & Co., 1870), pp. 24–25.

10. Quoted in Hutchison, *Transcendentalist Ministers*, p. 115.

11. Leon Howard, "The Eighteenth Century: An Age of Contradic-

tions," in *Transitions in American Literary History*, ed. H. H. Clark (Durham, N.C.: Duke University Press, 1953), p. 61.

12. Henry Adams, *The Education of Henry Adams* (Boston: Houghton Mifflin Co., 1918, rep. 1961), p. 34.
13. Daniel Howe, *The Unitarian Conscience* (Cambridge: Harvard University Press, 1970), p. 37.
14. Ahlstrom, "Theology," p. 254.
15. Lawrence Buell, *Literary Transcendentalism: Style and Vision in the American Renaissance* (Ithaca: Cornell University Press, 1973), p. 34.
16. Howard, *Transitions*, p. 70. See also, Herbert Schneider, *A History of American Philosophy* (New York: Columbia University Press, 1946), p. 219.
17. Alexander Kern, "The Rise of Transcendentalism," in Clark, ed., *Transitions*, p. 285.
18. Larzer Ziff, *Puritanism in America* (New York: Viking Press, 1973), pp. 106–107.
19. Quoted in Miller, ed., *The Transcendentalists*, pp. 211, 213.
20. Howe, *Unitarian Conscience*, pp. 34–35.
21. Buell, *Literary Transcendentalism*, p. 33. See also, Perry Miller, *The New England Mind: From Colony to Province* (Cambridge: Harvard University Press, 1953), pp. 448–449.
22. Quoted in Hutchison, *Transcendentalist Ministers*, p. 89.
23. Marsh to Samuel Taylor Coleridge, 23 March 1829, Marsh Papers, Guy W. Bailey Library, University of Vermont, Burlington, Vermont (hereafter cited as UVM).
24. Whether or not one accepts Haroutunian's portrayal of the decay of Puritanism into a watered-down nineteenth-century moralism, the crucial fact for our purposes is that this was Marsh's own view of his time, a view he shared with countless Orthodox contemporaries, including most of those I discuss here. See, for example, the essay by Hodge, Alexander, and Dod, cited above.
25. After he left Dartmouth in 1817, Marsh set an ambitious academic course for himself far beyond the regular requirements of the seminary. It encompassed all available works in ancient history and literature; the study of Spanish, German, and Hebrew to aid in critical studies of both the Old and New Testaments; and at least one hour a day in the study of modern literature (when he could contrive to fit it into his schedule). This independent study was

prompted by his impatience with the formal instruction at Andover.

26. Quoted in Henry Pochmann, *German Culture in America: Philosophical and Literary Influences, 1600–1900* (Madison: University of Wisconsin Press, 1961), p. 129. The faculty subjected Stuart to a heresy trial for introducing subjects which, they feared, "tended to chill the ardor of piety . . . and even to induce for the time, an approach to universal skepticism." For these crimes the Andover Trustees censured Stuart and burdened Marsh, who had supported Stuart, with a lasting reputation for radicalism. Pochmann's work includes the best discussion to date of Marsh's thought *from a philosophical perspective*. Like Frederic Henry Hedge, however, Pochmann's overriding interest in the technical aspects of German philosophy leads him to miss the implications of Marsh's work because, from his perspective, it imperfectly represents Kant.

27. Foster, *A Genetic History*, p. 9. See also, William Charvat, *Origins of American Critical Thought, 1810–1835* (Philadelphia: University of Pennsylvania Press, 1936), p. 61.

28. Quoted in Clarence H. Faust, "The Background of the Unitarian Opposition to Transcendentalism," *Modern Philosophy* 35 (1938): 304.

29. Haroutunian, *Piety*, p. 202.

30. Ahlstrom, "Theology," pp. 264–66.

31. Quoted in Foster, *Genetic History*, p. 13.

32. I am grateful to Professor Bruce Kuklick for adjusting my view of Taylor.

33. For the details of Marsh's biography, the best single source is still Joseph Torrey, "Memoir," *The Remains of the Rev. James Marsh D.D.*

34. Ibid., p. 19.

35. Ibid., p. 20.

36. See Howe, *Unitarian Conscience*, p. 120.

37. James Marsh to Leonard Marsh, 15 November 1829, James Marsh Collection, Guy W. Bailey Library, University of Vermont, Burlington, Vermont (hereafter cited as JMC).

38. James Marsh to Leonard Marsh, 15 November 1829, JMC.

39. Quoted in Ziff, *Puritanism*, p. 117.

40. Ibid.

41. Miller, *Colony*, p. 323.

42. Marsh to George Bush, 6 January 1816 and 29 January 1818, James

Marsh Family File, University of Vermont, Burlington, Vermont (hereafter cited as FF).

43. The search for the perfect life, one that fully expressed the spirit, is one that frustrated the Transcendentalists as well as Marsh, and it offers the most personal example of the difficulties inherent in the Romantic attempt to objectify spirit. Thoreau chose the life of nature and of art, Alcott that of solitary study and writing, Parker the pulpit, but these lives were all partial and seen to be so by those who lived them.

44. Miller, *Colony*, pp. 69–70.

45. Ziff, *Puritanism*, p. 18. See also, Larzer Ziff, "The Literary Consequences of Puritanism," in *The American Puritan Imagination: Essays in Revaluation*, ed. Sacvan Bercovitch (New York: Cambridge University Press, 1974), pp. 41–43.

46. Marsh, fragmentary letter, 14 April 1822, in Torrey, *Remains*, pp. 49–50.

47. Marsh to Leonard Marsh, 27 April 1822, JMC.

48. Torrey, *Remains*, pp. 53–54.

49. Ibid., p. 56.

50. Marsh, fragmentary letter, March 1823, ibid., pp. 61–62.

51. Quoted in Torrey, *Remains*, p. 27.

52. Marsh, fragmentary letter, November 1820, ibid., pp. 31–32.

53. Marsh to Leonard Marsh, 6 October 1831, JMC.

54. Marsh to B. B. Newton, 9 March 1837, in Torrey, *Remains*, pp. 139–40.

55. Sacvan Bercovitch, *The Puritan Origins of the American Self* (New Haven: Yale University Press, 1975), pp. 6–7.

56. Marsh to the Corporation of the University of Vermont, 5 June 1833, JMC. See also, Marsh to Leonard Marsh, 1835, JMC.

57. Quoted by B. B. Newton in a letter to Marsh, 28 February 1835, JMC.

58. Marsh, fragmentary letter, March 1823, in Torrey, *Remains*, pp. 61–62.

59. Marsh, fragmentary letter, December, 1823, *Remains*, pp. 68–69.

60. Hawthorne, too, liked to believe that his art would provide a means of communication with the outside world. In the preface to *Twice-Told Tales* he writes, "it is, in fact, the style of a man of society. Every sentence, so far as it embodies thought or sensibility, may be understood and felt by anybody who will give himself the trouble to read it, and will take up the book in the proper mood.

. . . They are not the talk of a secluded man with his own mind and heart, but his attempts to open an intercourse with the world." (Nathaniel Hawthorne, *The Centenary Edition of the Works of Nathaniel Hawthorne*, 14 vols., ed. Claude Simpson [Columbus, Ohio: Ohio State University Press, 1972], 9:6).

61. Torrey, *Remains*, p. 42.
62. Ibid., p. 48.
63. Ibid., p. 43.
64. Marsh to Lucia Wheelock, 1 July 1821, ibid., p. 47.
65. Perry Miller, *The New England Mind: The Seventeenth Century* (Cambridge: Harvard University Press, 1954), p. 45.
66. Hawthorne allegorized his own search for redemption through the pains of art as a journey into a cavern. In his notebook he wrote, "the human Heart to be allegorized as a cavern; at the entrance there is sunshine, and flowers growing in it. You step within, but a short distance, and begin to find yourself surrounded with a terrible gloom, and monsters of diverse kinds; it seems like Hell itself. You are bewildered, and wander long without hope. At last a light strikes upon you. You peep towards it, and find yourself in a region that seems, in some sort, to reproduce the flowers and sunny beauty of the entrance, but all perfect. These are the depths of the heart, or of human nature, bright and peaceful, the gloom and terror may lie deep; but deeper still is the eternal beauty" (Nathaniel Hawthorne, *The Centenary Edition of the Works of Nathaniel Hawthorne*, 8:237). Meyer Abrams describes a similar motif in English Romantic poetry in *Natural-Supernaturalism* (New York: Norton, 1971).
67. Marsh, "Religious Inquiry," FF.
68. Ahlstrom, "Theology," pp. 259–60. See also Sidney E. Ahlstrom, "The Scots and American Theology," *Church History* 24 (1955): 257–72. Marsh was remarkably well suited, by both experience and association, for the mediatory mission he conjured up for himself. He was known and respected equally among the conservatives at Andover and Princeton and among the arbiters of Unitarian taste in Boston and Cambridge. In the early 1820s, Marsh corresponded and visited with Charles Hodge at Princeton, who in turn regularly consulted Marsh about readings in German philosophy. Ironically, it was the arch-conservative Hodge who first suggested that Marsh translate Herder's *The Spirit of Hebrew Po-*

*etry*, a work with radical implications for both theology and literature, rather than the more conservative theological tract that Marsh had originally suggested.

For all his ties to Orthodoxy however, Marsh maintained even more active relationships with several prominent members of the Unitarian community, relationships that proved most fruitful. He became acquainted with George Ticknor, the Channings, Edward Everett, and Ripley, among others. His association with Ticknor resulted in an article entitled "Ancient and Modern Poetry," published in the *North American Review* in 1822, which brought together all the learning and meditation of Marsh's years at Andover in an attempt to resolve his own conflicts between his conservative theology and his Romantic inclinations. For years after the publication of this essay, Jared Sparks, editor of the *Review*, regularly solicited more articles from Marsh, but heavy teaching duties, administrative chores at Vermont, and finally ill health prevented him from meeting Sparks's requests.

## Chapter 2: Avatars of Coleridge (*text pages* 34–56)

1. Joseph Torrey, "Memoir," *The Remains of the Rev. James Marsh, D.D.* (Burlington, Vt.: Chauncey Goodrich, 1843), p. 86.
2. Meyer Abrams, *Natural-Supernaturalism* (New York: Norton, 1971), p. 91.
3. Perry Miller, *The New England Mind: From Colony to Province* (Cambridge: Harvard University Press, 1953), p. 424.
4. James Marsh to R. H. Dana, 14 March 1838, in Ronald V. Wells, *Three Christian Transcendentalists: James Marsh, Caleb Sprague Henry, Frederic Henry Hedge* (New York: Columbia University Press, 1943), p. 164.
5. Oskar Walzel, *German Romanticism* (New York: Putnam, 1932), p. 7. See also, Meyer Abrams, *The Mirror and the Lamp* (New York: Norton, 1958), p. 78. Marsh's kinship with the Germans lies at least partly in their common debt to English Neo-Platonism. As Walzel points out, Hamaan and Herder, the principal German influences on Marsh's thought before he read Kant, found support for their primitivist linguistics and their pietist philosophy in such eighteenth-century English Platonists as Shaftesbury and Bishop Lowth, who had in turn been influenced by the Cambridge Platonists.

6. Building on his early study at Andover, Marsh himself soon became the foremost student of German literature in America. He produced influential translations of Bellerman (1822) and Herder (1826), and was regularly consulted by German students throughout the country for advice and guidance in their own Germanic inquiries.
7. Walzel, *Romanticism*, p. 7.
8. Abrams, *Natural-Supernaturalism*, p. 401.
9. Torrey, *Remains*, p. 110.
10. See Floyd Stovall, ed., *The Development of American Literary Criticism* (Chapel Hill, N.C.: University of North Carolina Press, 1955), p. 22.
11. Quoted in Torrey, *Remains*, pp. 90–91.
12. Ibid., p. 24. In his discussion of Cambridge Platonist influence on the English Romantics, Meyer Abrams notes similarities between Platonic and Romantic imagery and then asserts that "the Copernican revolution in epistemology—if we . . . apply it to the general concept that the perceiving mind discovers what it has itself partly made—was effected in England by poets and critics before it manifested itself in academic philosophy. . . . In their early poetic expositions of the mind fashioning its own experience, for example, Coleridge and Wordsworth do not employ Kant's abstract formulae. They revert, instead, to metaphors of mind which had largely fallen into disuse in the eighteenth century, but had earlier been current in seventeenth-century philosophers outside of, or specifically opposed to, the sensational tradition of Hobbes and Locke" (Abrams, *Mirror*, p. 58). Abrams then goes on to note that both Wordsworth and Coleridge had studied the writings of the Cambridge Platonists extensively.
13. Marsh, fragmentary letter, 1819, in Torrey, *Remains*, p. 24.
14. Marsh, fragmentary letter, 1819, ibid., p. 24.
15. For a discussion of this trend, see William Charvat, *Origins of American Critical Thought, 1810–1835* (Philadelphia: University of Pennsylvania Press, 1936), pp. 16–17.
16. Torrey, *Remains*, p. 25.
17. Charvat, *Critical Thought*, p. 75.
18. Marsh, fragmentary letter, February 1821, in Torrey, *Remains*, pp. 41–42.
19. "The charm of the system, in Puritan eyes was that it annihilated the distance from the object to the brain, or made possible an epis-

temological leap across the gap in the twinkling of an eye, with an assurance of footing beyond a metaphysical slip" (Perry Miller, *The New England Mind: The Seventeenth Century* [Cambridge: Harvard University Press, 1954], p. 147).

20. For the most insightful discussion of Cambridge Platonism, see Ernst Cassirer, *The Platonic Renaissance in England*, trans. James P. Pettegrove (Austin: University of Texas Press, 1953).

21. Ibid., p. 28.

22. Marsh to Archibald Alexander, 7 March 1829, in John J. Duffy, ed., *Coleridge's American Disciples: The Selected Correspondence of James Marsh*, (Amherst: University of Massachusetts Press, 1973), p. 76. Marsh wrote to those ministers who, he felt, would welcome his edition of seventeenth-century writers. The distance between Alexander's approval of *this* project and his later objections to "foreign influences" measures Marsh's own divergence from Orthodoxy as he moved from the Cambridge Platonists to *Aids to Reflection*.

23. The Cambridge Platonists rebelled against Calvinist doctrines that confined human freedom and power. Henry More, for example, testified to his inability to "swallow down that hard Doctrine concerning *Fate . . . or Calvinistick Predestination.*" Quoted in C. A. Patrides, ed., *The Cambridge Platonists* (Cambridge, Mass.: Harvard University Press, 1970), p. 22.

24. Quoted in Wells, *Christian Transcendentalists*, p. 20.

25. Abrams, *Mirror*, p. 68.

26. Quoted in Patrides, ed., *Cambridge Platonists*, p. 10.

27. Basil Willey, *The Seventeenth Century Background* (New York: Doubleday, 1953), p. 141.

28. Marjorie Nicolson, "James Marsh and the Vermont Transcendentalists," *Philosophical Review* 34 (1925): 33.

29. John Dewey, "James Marsh and American Philosophy," *Journal of the History of Ideas* 2 (1941): 134.

30. Torrey, *Remains*, p. 92.

31. S. T. Coleridge, *The Complete Works of Samuel Taylor Coleridge*, ed. G. T. Shedd, 7 vols. (New York: Harper, 1853), 5: 290–91.

32. For a remarkably learned and insightful discussion of the combat between material and spiritual philosophies, see Thomas McFarland, *Coleridge and the Pantheist Tradition* (London: Oxford University Press, 1969).

33. See, for example, Rene Wellek, *Kant in England* (Princeton: Prince-

ton University Press, 1931); Gordon McKenzie, *Organic Unity in Coleridge* (Berkeley: University of California Press, 1939); and especially Claud Howard, *Coleridge's Idealism* (Boston: Gorham Press, 1924).

34. Quoted in Richard Haven, *Patterns of Consciousness* (Amherst: University of Massachusetts Press, 1969), p. 14.
35. Coleridge, *Works*, vol. 1, p. 171.
36. Quoted in Stephen Prickett, *Romanticism and Religion* (Cambridge: Cambridge University Press, 1976), p. 29.

## Chapter 3: Understanding Reason (*text pages* 57–84)

1. On the evidence of quotations and citations in Marsh's essay on "Ancient and Modern Poetry" in the *North American Review* (1822), we can say that Marsh had by that time familiarized himself with Coleridge's letters in *Blackwood's Magazine* and with *Lyrical Ballads*.
2. Marsh to Samuel Taylor Coleridge, 23 March 1829, Guy W. Bailey Library, University of Vermont, Burlington, Vermont (hereafter cited as UVM).
3. Samuel Taylor Coleridge, *Aids to Reflection*, ed. James Marsh (Burlington, Vt.: Chauncey Goodrich, 1829), p. lviii. This work and Marsh's other major publications are reprinted in my *Selected Works of James Marsh* (Delmar, N.Y.: Scholars' Facsimiles and Reprints, 1976).
4. Charles R. Sanders, *Coleridge and the Broad Church Movement* (Durham, N.C.: Duke University Press, 1942), p. 33.
5. Ronald V. Wells, *Three Christian Transcendentalists: James Marsh, Caleb Sprague Henry, Frederic Henry Hedge* (New York: Columbia University Press, 1943), pp. 22–23.
6. James Marsh, *The Remains of the Rev. James Marsh, D.D.* (Burlington, Vt.: Chauncey Goodrich, 1843), pp. 211–12. Marsh argues that the true object of science is the "power of living energy" from which phenomena come. "What power," he asks, "do the phenomena require us to *assume*, as the abiding ground of phenomena, and in order to account for them?" Marsh then goes on to describe the ascent of these powers through the forms of nature toward God.
7. Marsh, "Notes on Religion," James Marsh Family File, University of Vermont, Burlington, Vermont (hereafter cited as FF).

8. Ibid.
9. Ibid.
10. Ibid.
11. Ibid.
12. Ibid.
13. Larzer Ziff, *Puritanism in America* (New York: Viking Press, 1973), p. 98.
14. See Cameron Thompson, "John Locke and New England Transcendentalism," *New England Quarterly*, 35 (1962): 435–57.
15. Joseph Torrey, "Memoir," *The Remains of the Rev. James Marsh D.D.* (Burlington, Vt.: Chauncey Goodrich, 1843), p. 580.
16. Ibid., p. 583.
17. Ibid., p. 581.
18. James Marsh, "Ancient and Modern Poetry," *North American Review* 15 (1822): 108. Reprinted in Carafiol, ed., *Selected Works*.
19. Torrey, *Remains*, pp. 252–53.
20. Wells, *Christian Transcendentalists*, pp. 39–40.
21. Torrey, *Remains*, p. 253.
22. Marsh to Richard Henry Dana, 14 March 1838. Quoted in Wells, pp. 162–65.
23. Ibid., pp. 258–59.
24. Marsh himself feared that he too often engaged in speculation rather than action. While still at Andover, he said, "I confess, too, I have some wish to remove an impression, which, I fear, has been too correct, that I was a mere scholar, and had little regard for any thing but merely speculative inquiries" (Ibid., p. 34).
25. Marsh to George S. Wilson, 2 February 1838, in Torrey, *Remains*, pp. 140–41.
26. John Dewey, "James Marsh and American Philosophy," *Journal of the History of Ideas* 2 (1941): 131–50.
27. Marsh to John H. Bates, 12 February 1840, John Marsh Collection, Guy W. Bailey Library, University of Vermont, Burlington, Vermont (hereafter cited as JMC).
28. Marsh to George S. Wilson, 2 February 1838, in Torrey, *Remains*, pp. 140–41.
29. Marsh to George S. Wilson, 2 February 1838, ibid.
30. Ibid., p. 382.
31. Ibid., p. 383.
32. Ibid., p. 384.
33. Quoted in R. W. B. Lewis, *The American Adam: Innocence, Tragedy,*

*and Tradition in the Nineteenth Century* (Chicago: University of Chicago Press, 1955), p. 62.

34. Torrey, p. 398.
35. Ibid., p. 386.
36. Ibid., p. 387.
37. Ibid., p. 411.
38. Ibid., p. 414; see also p. 413.
39. Ibid., p. 404.
40. In early 1829, while Marsh was planning his edition of English Platonists, he urged Torrey to visit Coleridge, "the true philosopher," in England. "His Aids to Reflection," Marsh maintained, "is better than any other of his works. I have studied it much of late, have used it much in reviewing Stuart, and have spoken of him in a note in terms which will seem extravagant to those who are not well acquainted with his worth. I shall probably review his Aids in the same work soon and shall I think venture to write him before you will see him" (Marsh to Joseph Torrey, 14 February 1829, UVM). Marsh's intentions in the Stuart review were much the same as those behind the edition of seventeenth-century divines, and as he absorbed more of Coleridge's philosophy, the *Aids* replaced English Platonism in his mind as the best corrective for America's spiritual confusion.
41. Marsh to Samuel Taylor Coleridge, 23 March 1829, UVM.
42. It was not uncommon for even highly respected scholars to be utterly ignorant of Coleridge's writings. Francis Wayland, one of the most influential teachers of moral philosophy in America and president of Brown University, replied to Marsh's request that he review the *Aids* by confessing that he knew almost nothing about Coleridge and that what little he did know he had picked up in casual conversation rather than from firsthand study. (Francis Wayland to Marsh, 20 October 1829, UVM). The few who were not entirely ignorant of Coleridge's works had read them only superficially and, in their ignorance, held an even worse opinion of them than men like Wayland did.
43. Marsh to Joseph Torrey, 16 July 1829, UVM.
44. Charvat, *Critical Thought*, p. 80.
45. Marsh, ed., *Aids*, p. xvi.
46. Ibid., pp. xiii–xiv.
47. Ibid., p. xiv.
48. Ibid. p. xvi.

49. Ibid.
50. Ibid.
51. Ibid.
52. Ibid., p. xvii.
53. Ibid.
54. Ibid.
55. Ibid., p. xxxix.
56. Ibid., p. xi.
57. Ibid., pp. xviii–xix.
58. Ibid., p. xx.
59. Ibid., p. xxiv.
60. Henry May, *The End of American Innocence: A Study of the First Years of Our Time, 1912–1917* (New York: Knopf, 1959), p. 146.
61. Marsh, ed., *Aids*, p. xlviii.

## Chapter 4: WITH TYRANNOUS EYE (*text pages* 85–114)

1. Marsh's *Aids* precipitated something of a boom in Coleridge studies in America during the 1830s. Joseph Torrey felt that the time was ripe for Marsh's edition, that its potential audience "might be said to comprise every earnest and reflecting mind not already committed to some system" (Joseph Torrey, "Memoir," *The Remains of the Rev. James Marsh, D.D.* [Burlington, Vt.: Chauncey Goodrich, 1843], p. 95). Younger Orthodox ministers were increasingly repudiating such concessions as Taylor's to Lockean rational religion, and their counterparts in Boston were looking for alternatives to Unitarianism, which no longer had the vitality of its original conception. This new generation wanted change, and among its members Coleridge created a sensation by offering a rational justification for their spiritual sentiments. Only three months after the American publication of *Aids*, Marsh wrote proudly to Coleridge that "the edition of 1500 published in November is so far sold and the work is engaging so much attention as to make it probable another edition may be called for in the course of the year" (Marsh to S. T. Coleridge, 24 February 1830, Marsh Papers. Guy W. Bailey Library, University of Vermont, Burlington, Vermont (hereafter cited as UVM). Despite the popularity of the 1829 edition, Marsh delayed publication of the second American edition until 1840 so he could incorporate Coleridge's last corrections and emendations from the fourth London edition of 1839.

2. William Charvat, *Origins of American Critical Thought, 1810–1835* (Philadelphia: University of Pennsylvania Press, 1936), p. 77.
3. Quoted in Charvat, ibid., p. 76.
4. Quoted in Charles R. Sanders, *Coleridge and the Broad Church Movement* (Durham: Duke University Press, 1942), p. 267. Coleridge and his English associates realized that he owed his increasing American popularity largely to Marsh's work, and they perceived Marsh as Coleridge's foremost disciple in America. (See Stanley M. Vogel, *German Literary Influences on the American Transcendentalists* [New Haven: Yale Univ. Press, 1955], p. 26n). H. N. Coleridge viewed Marsh's "Preliminary Essay" so favorably that he included it in the final English edition of *Aids* (1839), confirming once again the tendency of the essay to fit itself to the views of its audience.
5. There have been several attempts to account for the peculiar reception *Aids* met in America. Henry Pochmann feels that many modern scholars have been led astray by Marsh's spiritual rhetoric. "Dr. Wellek," Pochmann observes, "offers the opinion that 'on the whole the *Aids to Reflection* seems . . . like an attempt at a reconstruction of Kant for the purposes of a philosophy of faith.' The point is important, for if Dr. Wellek can so interpret Coleridge, it is all the more likely that Emerson and his American disciples might have thus interpreted him" (Henry Pochmann, *German Culture in America: Philosophical and Literary Influences, 1600–1900* [Madison: University of Wisconsin Press, 1961], p. 91). While Pochmann blames this ambiguity on Marsh's oversimplification of Kant for a popular audience, in my view it is Pochmann who misreads Marsh by looking for philosophical precision. Wellek seems far closer to a sympathetic understanding of Marsh's motives and methods, while Pochmann, like most of Marsh's contemporaries, misreads *Aids* in ways that reflect his own predisposition to a technical reading of German philosophy. Marsh himself knowingly contributed to this difficulty by camouflaging Coleridge's Romantic philosophy in the traditional terms of American theological debate, in part to avoid criticism. Just before he published *Aids*, he wrote, "I am convinced of its truth and have not considered much the consequences to myself of advancing it. I have, however, so guarded it that I think no exceptions can be taken by the theologians" (Marsh to Torrey, 14 February 1829, UVM).
6. Charles Hodge to Marsh, 22 November 1830, UVM.

7. Alonzo Potter to Marsh, 18 August 1831, UVM.
8. T. P. Smith to Chauncey Goodrich, 27 January 1832. James Marsh Collection, Guy W. Bailey Library, University of Vermont, Burlington, Vt., Hereafter cited as JMC.
9. Marsh to S. T. Coleridge, 24 February 1830, UVM.
10. C. S. Henry to Marsh, 14 March 1832, UVM. Of Stuart's limitations as a pioneer in metaphysics, R. H. Dana said, "We owe a great deal to Professor Stuart. He certainly waked up our clergy to the importance of learning. But he is far from being a safe leader. He frequently advances particulars in exegesis in opposition to his main principle, and which, if carried out, would go nearly the length of the Rationalists. He is led into this by his vanity, which affects novelty and independence. He has an ardent, but dry mind, and turns with a most self-complacent contempt from that which is too deep for his sensuous philosophy" (R. H. Dana to Marsh, 14 July 1832, JMC).
11. C. S. Henry to Marsh, 14 July 1832, UVM.
12. Ibid.
13. B. B. Newton to Marsh, 28 February 1835, JMC.
14. Leonard Woods to Marsh, 11 January 1830, UVM.
15. Ibid.
16. Ibid.
17. For insight into the power and purpose of language and especially of the sermon for the Puritans, see Larzer Ziff, *Puritanism in America* (New York: Viking Press, 1973), Chapters 1 and 2; Emory Elliott, *Power and the Pulpit in Puritan New England* (Princeton: Princeton University Press, 1975), especially the Introduction and Chapter 2; David D. Hall, *The Faithful Shepherd: A History of the New England Ministry in the Seventeenth Century* (Chapel Hill: University of North Carolina Press, 1972); and Sacvan Bercovitch, *The American Jeremiad* (Madison: University of Wisconsin Press, 1978).
18. B. B. Newton to Marsh, 19 January 1833, JMC.
19. Ibid.
20. B. B. Newton to Marsh, 27 December 1834, JMC.
21. B. B. Newton to Marsh, 28 February 1835, JMC.
22. Ibid.
23. After Marsh's death in 1842, his philosophy was left in the hands of his colleagues and his close friends, and, sadly, his thought fared no better there than it had with Marsh's other readers. In life, Marsh's personal humility and intellectual honesty had compelled

respect for his ideas and had softened their radical implications. But those who tried to carry on Marsh's work after his death lacked his ability to fuse radical philosophy and conservative intent. In their eagerness to portray Marsh as an exemplary Orthodox churchman, his "admirers" generally took the edge off of his ideas, sacrificing his philosophy to his reputation. When John Wheeler linked Marsh to Jonathan Edwards and failed even to mention Coleridge, or when Torrey gently chided Marsh for practicing excessively liberal educational methods as a tutor at Dartmouth and praised him for his more strenuous virtues, these men demonstrated that they were far less liberal than Marsh and far less willing or able to follow up the principles of his philosophy. (John Wheeler, *A Discourse at the Funeral of James Marsh* [Burlington, Vt.: Chauncey Goodrich, 1843], p. 13; and Torrey, *Remains*, p. 26.) G. B. Cheever, in his discourse on Marsh, virtually parodied Marsh's ideas on the fundamentally spiritual character of Christianity, pushing the conservative, antiintellectual implications of Marsh's ideas in particular to absurd extremes. The result is a paper delivered in eulogy of a man who would have been as horrified to hear himself so caricatured as he would have been to see what Emerson did with his ideas. (G. B. Cheever, "The Characteristics of the Christian Philosopher," *The Hill of Difficulty* [New York, 1849], pp. 203–50.) Marsh's colleagues were unable to build a practical life on the principles that appealed so strongly to them in the form of speculative theology. Like all readers of *Aids*, they emphasized those elements of the work that catered to their preconceptions and suppressed or ignored the rest.

24. Marsh to R. H. Dana, 21 August 1832, in Wells, *Christian Transcendentalists*, p. 161. William Ellery Channing stands out as an important exception to the otherwise nearly universal antipathy for Coleridge among the older generation in Boston. According to Dana, Channing had long been an enthusiastic student of Coleridge, though not, in Dana's view, a profound one. Channing himself claimed to "owe more to Coleridge than to any other philosophic thinker" (Quoted in Elizabeth P. Peabody, *Reminiscences of W. E. Channing* [Boston: Crosby, Nicols, Lee, 1880], p. 75). His interest in Coleridge and the French expositors of spiritual religion, Jouffroy and Cousin, confirms his allegiance to the original Unitarian principle of free inquiry rather than to its later dogmatic sectarianism. These latitudinarian inclinations made him work to

moderate the Unitarian attack on Transcendentalism led by Andrews Norton. Many critics have gone so far as to place Channing on the outskirts of the Transcendentalist movement itself, a position in which he would have been ill at ease, despite the distinctly Transcendental tone of his opinions about man's divine nature. Channing had a remarkable capacity to accommodate these views to Unitarian theology, and he never approved the more extreme approach of the Transcendentalists. He severed himself from them when it became clear that they would not stay within Unitarianism. (Peabody, *Reminiscences*, p. 430.) On the other hand, Channing's liberal literary tastes had their influence. Odell Shepard, the biographer of Bronson Alcott, conjectures that it was Channing who introduced Alcott to Coleridge, thereby assisting at the intellectual birth of at least one Transcendentalist.

25. Charles Follen to Marsh, 14 April 1832, UVM.
26. R. H. Dana to Marsh, 31 December 1834, UVM.
27. Charvat, *Critical Thought*, p. 77.
28. Sacvan Bercovitch, *The Puritan Origins of the American Self* (New Haven: Yale University Press, 1975).
29. For a partial list of these influences, see Alexander Kern, "The Rise of Transcendentalism," *Transitions in American Literary History*, ed. H. H. Clark (Durham: Duke University Press, 1953), pp. 273–74.
30. Ibid., p. 275.
31. Kenneth W. Cameron, *Emerson the Essayist*, 2 vols. (Raleigh, N.C.: The Thistle Press, 1945), 1:125.
32. Quoted in F. O. Matthiessen, *The American Renaissance: Art and Expression in the Age of Emerson and Whitman* (New York: Oxford University Press, 1941), p. 65.
33. Ralph Waldo Emerson, *Nature*, in *The Collected Works of Ralph Waldo Emerson*, 2 vols. ed. R. E. Spiller and Alfred R. Ferguson (Cambridge: Harvard University Press, 1971–), 1:8.
34. James E. Cabot, *A Memoir of Ralph Waldo Emerson*, 2 vols. (Boston: Houghton Mifflin Co., 1887), 1:244–245.
35. Quoted in Perry Miller, ed., *The Transcendentalists: An Anthology* (Cambridge, Mass.: Harvard University Press, 1950), p. 67.
36. Ronald V. Wells, *Three Christian Transcendentalists: James Marsh, Caleb Sprague Henry, Frederic Henry Hedge* (New York: Columbia University Press, 1943), p. 130.
37. See Miller, ed., *The Transcendentalists*, pp. 66–72.

38. Wells, *Christian Transcendentalists*, p. 118.
39. Ibid., pp. 123–26.
40. R. H. Dana to Marsh, 15 July 1831, JMC.
41. James Freeman Clarke, *James Freeman Clarke: Autobiography, Diary, and Correspondence*, ed. Edward Everett Hale (Boston: Houghton Mifflin Co., 1891), p. 38.
42. Quoted in William Hutchison, *The Transcendentalist Ministers: Church Reform in the New England Renaissance* (New Haven: Yale University Press, 1959), pp. 170–71.
43. Kern, *Transitions*, pp. 273–74.
44. Orestes Brownson, "Two Articles From the Princeton Review," *Boston Quarterly Review*, 3 (1840): 265–323. Excerpts from this essay appear in Miller, ed., *The Transcendentalists*, pp. 240–46. This passage is quoted in Miller, p. 241.
45. Quoted in Miller, ed., *The Transcendentalists*, p. 298.
46. Ibid., p. 298.
47. George Ripley to Marsh, 23 February 1837, UVM.
48. George Ripley to Marsh, 17 October 1840, UVM.
49. George Ripley to Marsh, 23 February 1838, UVM.
50. Ibid.
51. Quoted in Kern, *Transitions*, p. 260.
52. Quoted in Hutchison, *Transcendentalist Ministers*, p. 81.
53. Bronson Alcott, *The Journals of Bronson Alcott*, ed. Odell Shepard (Boston: Little, Brown & Co., 1938), p. 31.
54. Ibid.
55. Ibid., p. 32.
56. Ibid., p. 32n.
57. Odell Shepard, *Pedlar's Progress: The Life of Bronson Alcott* (Boston: Little, Brown & Co., 1937), p. 159.
58. Alcott, *Journals*, p. 471.
59. Ibid., p. 66.
60. Ibid., p. 471.
61. In a letter to Henry J. Ware, Jr., Emerson said, "I shall read what you and other good men write as I have always done, glad when you speak my thought and skipping the page that has nothing for me" (Ralph Waldo Emerson, *The Letters of Ralph Waldo Emerson* ed. Ralph L. Rusk [New York: Columbia University Press, 1939], 1:167).
62. Rene Wellek, "The Minor Transcendentalists and German Philoso-

phy," *Confrontations* (Princeton: Princeton University Press, 1965), pp. 153–87.

63. Cameron, *Emerson the Essayist*, 1:162n. See also pp. 95n and 162.
64. Cameron, *Emerson the Essayist*, 1:166.
65. Emerson, *Letters*, 1:291.
66. Ralph Waldo Emerson, *The Journals of Ralph Waldo Emerson*, ed. Edward Waldo Emerson and Waldo Emerson Forbes (Boston: Houghton Mifflin Co., 1909), 2:278–79. See also, Cabot, *Memoir*, 101–2.
67. Quoted in Vivian Hopkins, *Spires of Form* (Cambridge: Harvard University Press, 1951), p. 8.
68. Rusk, *Letters*, pp. 412–13.
69. Bliss Perry, ed., *The Heart of Emerson's Journals* (Boston: Houghton Mifflin & Co., 1939), p. 89.
70. Ralph Waldo Emerson, *The Early Lectures of Ralph Waldo Emerson*, eds. Stephen Whicher and Robert Spiller (Cambridge: Harvard University Press, 1966), 1:379.
71. Cabot, *Memoir*, pp. 357–58.
72. Emerson, "Divinity School Address," *Works*, 1:150.


Chapter 5: FROM EDWARDS TO EMERSON (*text pages* 115–82)

1. Henry Steele Commager, *Theodore Parker: Yankee Crusader* (New York: Little, Brown & Co., 1936), p. 50.
2. Marsh to H. J. Raymond, 1 March 1841, in Ronald V. Wells, *Three Christian Transcendentalists: James Marsh, Caleb Sprague Henry, Frederic Henry Hedge* (New York: Columbia University Press, 1943), pp. 166–68.
3. Marsh to Nathan Lord, December 1835, James Marsh Collection, Guy W. Bailey Library, University of Vermont, Burlington, Vermont (hereafter cited as JMC).
4. Marsh, "Burchard," James Marsh Family File, University of Vermont, Burlington, Vermont (hereafter cited as FF).
5. John Richards to Marsh, 13 January 1836, JMC.
6. W. Child to Marsh, 22 January 1836, JMC.
7. Marsh to George Wilson, 15 February 1836, JMC.
8. Marsh to Nathan Lord, December 1835, JMC.
9. Ibid. As Henry Steele Commager notes, Transcendentalists op-

posed evangelists in terms very similar to those Marsh used against Burchard. See Commager, *Parker*, p. 37.

10. Frank H. Foster, *A Genetic History of the New England Theology* (New York: Russel and Russel, 1907), p. 38; and Perry Miller, *The New England Mind: From Colony to Province* (Cambridge: Harvard University Press, 1953), p. 84.
11. Conrad Wright, *The Beginnings of Unitarianism in America* (Boston: Starr King Press, 1955), p. 126.
12. See Miller, *Colony*, p. 99.
13. Marsh to Nathan Lord, December 1835, JMC.
14. Ibid.
15. Ibid.
16. The other side of this tendency is exemplified in Coleridge's involvement in the English "Broad Church" movement, a liberalizing effort (not unlike Transcendentalism) to substitute spirit for form and creed. See O. B. Frothingham, *Transcendentalism in New England: A History* (New York: Harper, 1876), p. 89; and Charles P. Sanders, *Coleridge and the Broad Church Movement* (Durham: Duke University Press, 1942).
17. Orestes Brownson, *The Works of Orestes A. Brownson*, 20 vols., ed., Henry F. Brownson (Detroit: A. Nourse, 1882–1907), 6:113.
18. Marsh to Nathan Lord, December 1835, JMC.
19. Marsh to George Wilson, 15 February 1836, JMC.
20. James Marsh, *The Remains of the Rev. James Marsh, D.D.* (Burlington, Vt.: Chauncey Goodrich, 1843), p. 634.
21. Ibid., p. 636.
22. Ibid.
23. Marsh, "Burchard," FF.
24. Ibid.
25. Ibid.
26. Marsh to Lucia Wheelock, 1 July 1821, in Torrey, *Remains*, p. 45.
27. Marsh, *Remains*, p. 631.
28. L. L. Tilden to Marsh, 25 April 1836, FF.
29. Marsh, "Burchard," FF.
30. Alan Heimert, *Religion and the American Mind from the Great Awakening to the Revolution* (Cambridge: Harvard University Press, 1966), pp. 354–59 and 452–53. Although, as Sydney Ahlstrom argues, Heimert overstates evangelical *influence* on the Revolution, the similarities between evangelical and revolutionary *rhetoric*

are undeniable. See Sidney E. Ahlstrom, *A Religious History of the American People* (New Haven: Yale University Press, 1972), p. 426n; Larzer Ziff, *Puritanism in America* (New York: Viking Press, 1973), p. 283.

31. This abortive attempt to secure independence from the British Crown was prolonged during 1837 and 1838 by the aid and refuge given to the rebels by sympathetic Vermonters. After an initial victory for the rebels, the British troops forced the dissidents across the border and into Vermont in late 1837. Despite an official American neutrality, the rebels lauched raids on Canada from bases in Vermont using American weapons and often reinforced by American volunteers. A final raid in 1838 ended the rebellion, when 3,000 men were routed by the British and several of the rebel leaders were captured and executed.

32. Marsh to David Read, 21 December 1837, JMC.

33. Marsh to David Read, 21 December 1837, JMC, and 6 January 1838, JMC.

34. James Marsh Family File.

35. James Marsh Family File.

36. Citizens' judgment was not to be trusted; they suffered from "the a priori principle of action . . . which impels them to hurra for the very *name* of liberty before they know whether it be anything more than a name or not" (Marsh to David Read, 22 December 1837, JMC).

37. Marsh to David Read, 6 January 1838, JMC.

38. Marsh to David Read, 11 January 1838, JMC.

39. James Marsh Family File.

40. Marsh to David Read, 11 January 1838, JMC.

41. Sacvan Bercovitch, "Introduction," *The American Puritan Imagination: Essays in Revaluation* (New York: Cambridge University Press, 1974), p. 13.

42. Alexander Kern, "The Rise of Transcendentalism," in *Transitions in American Literary History*, ed. H. H. Clark (Durham: Duke University Press, 1953), p. 295.

43. Ibid., p. 285. See also, Stow Persons, *Free Religion: An American Faith* (New Haven: Yale University Press, 1947), pp. 64–66; and Mildred Silver, "Emerson and the Idea of Progress," *American Literature* 12 (1940): 1–19.

44. Marsh to H. J. Raymond, 1 March 1841, in Wells, 166–68.

45. See Wells, *Christian Transcendentalists*, p. 111.
46. Marsh to H. J. Raymond, 1 March 1841, in Wells, *Christian Transcendentalists*, pp. 166–68.
47. Marsh, "Slavery," FF.
48. Ibid.
49. Ibid.
50. Ibid.
51. See Washington's tolerance for the transgressions of his mother and his unknown white father on the grounds of their helpless submission to the evils of slavery, Booker T. Washington, *Up From Slavery: An Autobiography* (New York: Doubleday, rep. 1942), pp. 2–4.
52. James Marsh Family File.
53. Torrey, *Remains*, pp. 68–69.
54. See Sacvan Bercovitch, *The Puritan Origins of the American Self* (New Haven: Yale University Press, 1975).
55. Marsh, *Remains*, p. 607.
56. Ibid., p. 608.
57. H. H. Clark, "Conservative and Mediatory Emphases in Emerson's Thought," *Transcendentalism and Its Legacy*, eds. Myron Simon and Thornton H. Parsons (Ann Arbor: University of Michigan Press, 1966), p. 37.
58. Ziff, *Puritanism*, p. 68.
59. Quoted in Daniel Howe, *The Unitarian Conscience* (Cambridge: Harvard University Press, 1970), p. 258.
60. Howe, *Unitarian Conscience*, p. 256.
61. Quoted in Wells, *Christian Transcendentalists*, p. 141.
62. Marsh, fragmentary letter, December 1820, in Torrey, *Remains*, pp. 33–35.
63. Marsh to George Ticknor, 3 February 1826, in John J. Duffy, ed., *Coleridge's American Disciples: The Selected Correspondence of James Marsh* (Amherst: University of Massachusetts Press, 1973), p. 76.
64. Ticknor's efforts to reform the Harvard curriculum ran aground on political conflict within the College Board. See Howe, *Unitarian Conscience*, pp. 265–68. But Ticknor's reforms were not nearly so comprehensive as Marsh's. In fact, Marsh disapproved of Ticknor's plans. During a trip to Boston, Marsh sat in on a discussion of "what they call the voluntary course at Cambridge. The argument, I confess, did not meet my objections, but seemed to me to

rest upon a quite superficial view of the whole subject of education. It was, however, adopted, and henceforth students at the end
of the freshman year, may pursue the classics farther or not at
their option, 'with a full knowledge' . . . on the part of the boy and
his parents of the course left, and of the one taken as a substitute.
How they are to get the knowledge, we are left to our Yankee privi-
lege of guessing." (Marsh to H. J. Raymond, 1 March 1841, in
Wells, *Christian Transcendentalists*, pp. 166–68).

65. Marsh, fragmentary letter, September 1820, in Torrey, *Remains*,
pp. 25–27.
66. *An Exposition of the System of Instruction*, by the faculty of the
University of Vermont (Burlington, Vt.: Chauncey Goodrich, 1831).
Reprinted in Carafiol, *Selected Works of James Marsh*, 3 vols. (New
York: Scholars' Facsimiles and Reprints, 1976), vol. 1. Despite the
general attribution, this pamphlet came from Marsh's pen.
67. Information about Marsh's educational system at the University of
Vermont comes principally from *Exposition*.
68. Marsh to Nancy Swift, 17 March 1841, Guy W. Bailey, Library, University of Vermont, Burlington, Vermont (hereafter cited as UVM).
69. Herbert Schneider, *A History of American Philosophy* (New York:
Columbia University Press, 1946), p. 208.
70. Marsh to Nancy Swift, 17 March 1841, UVM.
71. Ticknor and Marsh were not alone in their efforts to redirect
America's educational aims. Educational tradition, represented
most stalwartly by Yale and Princeton and codified in the "Yale
Report on the Classics," which appeared only a year after Marsh
became president of the University of Vermont, had come under
attack from those who believed, as the defenders said, that collegiate education should be "accommodated to the business character of the nation." The "Yale Report" defended the genteel tradition against the pragmatic interests holding sway at such places
as the University of Pennsylvania and the University of Virginia in
addition to Harvard, where the conviction that education should
meet the needs of life rather than conform to conventional ideals
was gaining adherents.

For the most part, such reforms meant, as they did at Harvard
and Union, merely the substitution of modern languages for the
Classics. Occasionally, as at Pennsylvania or Virginia, they offered
the opportunity to specialize in one area or "school" of knowledge.
Generally, however, they met with only limited success, falling to

the demands of conservative faculty or to financial distress. The only reformer to go so far as Marsh toward dismantling the long-standing educational structure was Francis Wayland, the president of Brown. Wayland instituted a complete elective system, graduated students upon the completion of a specified body of work rather than in a specified amount of time, and added a wide variety of new courses to the curriculum. His was the most influential of the reforms aimed at making higher education meet the needs of modern life. Marsh's reforms, which began several years before those at Brown, were less influential precisely because they were prompted primarily by spiritual interests, not by the pragmatism that ruled at Brown, Union, Pennsylvania, and the rest. Wayland's reforms were founded on the principles of Scottish "Common Sense" and treated the mind as an organ that would be improved by a variety of experiences. Their purpose was practical, to prepare the mind for the varied tasks of modern life.

Although Marsh, too, thought education should fit students for the nineteenth century, he felt it could best do so by developing their powers of insight into themselves, powers that at the same time could provide insight into spiritual truth. His system was more formal and more coherent than Wayland's, but it was also less pragmatic and therefore less popular, lacking even the authority of tradition that bolstered gentility at Yale. It was the most radical departure from that genteel tradition, and, in its unworldliness, the educational embodiment of the Transcendental view of the mind. For a readable history of American collegiate education, see George P. Schmidt, *The Liberal Arts College* (New Brunswick: Rutgers University Press, 1957), especially pp. 50–70.

72. Marsh, *Remains*, pp. 589–91.
73. Marsh to H. J. Raymond, 4 March 1841, in Wells, *Christian Transcendentalists*, pp. 166–68.
74. Torrey, *Remains*, p. 75.
75. Marsh, *Remains*, p. 595. Marsh is not only adopting the notions of correspondence between the mind and nature that appealed to Emerson but formulating a spiritual version of T. S. Eliot's aesthetic "objective correlative." Marsh would extend to the whole universe the coherence that Eliot's notion gives to the world of art.
76. Meyer Abrams, *Natural-Supernaturalism* (New York: Norton, 1971), pp. 188–89.

77. Marsh to the Corporation of the University of Vermont, 25 March 1827, UVM.
78. Edmund Morgan, *The Puritan Family: Religion and Domestic Relations in Seventeenth-Century New England* (New York: Harper and Row, 1966), p. 95.
79. Marsh, *Remains*, p. 496.
80. Marsh, *Remains*, p. 590.
81. Marsh to James M. Mathews, 5 November 1830, in Duffy, *Coleridge's American Disciples*, p. 114.
82. Henry Pochmann, *German Culture in America: Philosophical and Literary Influences 1600–1900* (Madison: University of Wisconsin Press, 1961), p. 132.
83. Julian I. Lindsay, *Tradition Looks Forward, The University of Vermont: A History, 1791–1904* (Burlington, Vermont: University of Vermont Press, 1954), pp. 150–65.
84. Hutchison, p. 29.
85. Lawrence Buell, *Literary Transcendentalism: Style and Vision in the American Renaissance* (Ithaca: Cornell University Press, 1973), p. 45.
86. Sherman Paul, *Shores of America: Thoreau's Inward Exploration* (Urbana: University of Illinois Press, 1958), p. 12.
87. Quoted in Vivian Hopkins, *Spires of Form* (Cambridge: Harvard University Press, 1951), p. 8.
88. Miller, *Colony*, p. 12, and Ziff, *Puritanism*, Chapters 1 and 2.
89. Marsh, *Remains*, pp. 615, 628. See also "Fine Arts," FF.
90. Ernst Cassirer, *The Platonic Renaissance in England*, trans. James P. Pettegrove (Austin: University of Texas Press, 1953), p. 2.
91. James Marsh Family File.
92. Marsh, *Remains*, pp. 622 and 628.
93. For further studies of the sermon and its language, see Kenneth Murdock, *Literature and Theology in Colonial New England* (Cambridge: Harvard University Press, 1949); Josephine K. Piercy, *Studies in Literary Types in Seventeenth-Century America* (New Haven: Yale University Press, 1939), Babette Levy, *Preaching in the First Half-Century of New England History* (Hartford, Conn., 1945, rep. New York: Russell Reprints, 1967); David D. Hall, *The Faithful Shepherd: A History of the New England Ministry in the Seventeenth Century* (Chapel Hill: University of North Carolina Press, 1972); and Ziff, *Puritanism*.

94. See Howe, *Unitarian Conscience*, p. 163; Ziff, *Puritanism*, pp. 122–23, 277, and 309; and Miller, *Colony*, p. 214.
95. Howe, *Unitarian Conscience*, p. 170.
96. Buell, *Literary Transcendentalists*, p. 25.
97. Perry Miller, "From Edwards to Emerson," *Errand Into the Wilderness* (New York: Harper and Row, 1956), p. 194.
98. Marsh to R. C. Morse, 28 February 1823, Yale University Archives.
99. Marsh to J. H. Meyers, 2 October 1840, in Torrey, *Remains*, pp. 146–48.
100. Ibid.
101. Marsh, *Remains*, p. 614.
102. Marsh to R. H. Dana, 14 March 1838, in Wells, *Christian Transcendentalists*, pp. 162–65.
103. Quoted in Commager, *Parker*, pp. 44 and 134.
104. William Charvat, *Origins of American Critical Thought, 1810–1835* (Philadelphia: University of Pennsylvania Press, 1936), pp. 60–66.
105. Wells, *Christian Transcendentalists*, p. 171.
106. Marsh, "Religion," FF.
107. Marsh, "Fine Arts," FF.
108. Wells, *Christian Transcendentalists*, p. 170.
109. Ibid., p. 173.
110. Schneider, *American Philosophy*, p. 223.

# SELECTED BIBLIOGRAPHY

Abrams, Meyer. *The Mirror and the Lamp*. New York: Norton, 1958.
———. *Natural-Supernaturalism*. New York: Norton, 1971.
Adams, Henry. *The Education of Henry Adams*. Boston: Houghton Mifflin, 1961.
Ahlstrom, Sidney E. *A Religious History of the American People*. New Haven: Yale University Press, 1972.
———. "Theology in America: An Historical Survey." In *Religion in American Life*, vol. 1:232–322. Eds. James W. Smith and A. Leland Jamison. Princeton: Princeton University Press, 1961.
Alcott, Bronson. *The Journals of Bronson Alcott*. Ed., Odell Shepard. Boston: Little, Brown & Co., 1937.
Barfield, Owen. *What Coleridge Thought*. Middletown, Ct.: Wesleyan University Press, 1971.
Barth, J. Robert, S.J. *Coleridge and Christian Doctrine*. Cambridge: Harvard University Press, 1969.
Becker, Carl. *The Heavenly City of the Eighteenth-Century Philosophers*. New Haven: Yale University Press, 1932.
Bercovitch, Sacvan. *The Puritan Origins of the American Self*. New Haven: Yale University Press, 1975.

————. *The American Jeremiad*. Madison: University of Wisconsin Press, 1978.

————, ed. *The American Puritan Imagination: Essays in Revaluation*. New York: Cambridge University Press, 1974.

Boulger, James D. *Coleridge as Religious Thinker*. New Haven: Yale University Press, 1961.

Brooks, Van Wyck. *The Flowering of New England*. New York: E. P. Dutton, 1936.

Brownson, Orestes. "Two Articles From the Princeton Review." *Boston Quarterly Review* 3 (1840): 265–323.

Brown, Samuel G. *The Life of Rufus Choate*. Boston: Little, Brown, 1870.

Buell, Lawrence. *Literary Transcendentalism: Style and Vision in the American Renaissance*. Ithaca: Cornell University Press, 1973.

Cabot, James E. *A Memoir of Ralph Waldo Emerson*. 2 vols. Boston: Houghton Mifflin, 1887.

Cameron, Kenneth W. *Emerson the Essayist*. 2 vols. Raleigh, N.C.: The Thistle Press, 1945.

Cassirer, Ernst. *The Platonic Renaissance in England*. Trans. James P. Pettegrove. Austin: University of Texas Press, 1953.

Charvat, William. *Origins of American Critical Thought, 1810–1935*. Philadelphia: University of Pennsylvania Press, 1936.

Clark, H. H. "Changing Attitudes in Early American Literary Criticism, 1800–1840." In *The Development of American Literary Criticism*, pp. 15–74. Ed. Floyd Stovall. New Haven: Yale University Press, 1964.

————. "Conservative and Mediatory Emphases in Emerson's Thought." In *Transcendentalism and Its Legacy*, pp. 25–62. Eds. Myron Simon and Thornton H. Parsons. Ann Arbor: University of Michigan Press, 1966.

Clarke, James Freeman. *James Freeman Clarke: Autobiography, Diary, and Correspondence*. Ed. Edward Everett Hale. Boston: Houghton Mifflin, 1891.

Curti, Merle. "The Great Mr. Locke: America's Philosopher, 1783–1861." *Huntington Library Bulletin* 11 (1937): 107–155.

Dewey, John. "James Marsh and American Philosophy." *Journal of the History of Ideas* 2 (1941), 131–50.

Duffy, John J. "From Hanover to Burlington: James Marsh's Search for Unity." *Vermont History* 38 (1972): 27–48.

————. "Problems in Publishing Coleridge: James Marsh's First

American Edition of *Aids to Reflection.*" *New England Quarterly* 43 (1972): 193–208.

———. "Transcendental Letters from Ripley to James Marsh." *Emerson Society Quarterly* 50 (1970): 21–25.

———. "T. S. Eliot's Objective Correlative: A New England Commonplace." *New England Quarterly* 42 (1969): 108–15.

Elliott, Emory. *Power and the Pulpit in Puritan New England.* Princeton: Princeton University Press, 1975.

Emerson, Ralph Waldo. *The Early Lectures of Ralph Waldo Emerson.* Eds. Stephen Whicher and Robert Spiller. 3 vols. Cambridge: Harvard University Press, 1966.

———. *The Journals of Ralph Waldo Emerson.* Eds. Edward Waldo Emerson and Waldo Emerson Forbes. Boston: Houghton Mifflin, 1909.

———. *The Letters of Ralph Waldo Emerson.* Ed. Ralph L. Rusk. New York: Columbia University Press, 1939.

Faust, Clarence H. "The Background of the Unitarian Opposition to Transcendentalism." *Modern Philology* 35 (1938): 297–324.

Feidelson, Charles. *Symbolism and American Literature.* Chicago: University of Chicago Press, 1953.

Feuer, L. S. "James Marsh and the Conservative Transcendentalist Philosophy: A Political Interpretation." *New England Quarterly* 31 (1958): 3–31.

Foster, Frank Hugh. *A Genetic History of the New England Theology.* New York: Russel and Russel, 1907.

Frothingham, O. B. *Transcendentalism in New England: A History.* New York: Harper, 1876.

———. *George Ripley.* Boston: Houghton Mifflin, 1882.

Greenwood, Douglas. "James Marsh and the Transcendental Temper." Diss., University of North Carolina, 1977.

Goddard, Harold C. *Studies in New England Transcendentalism.* New York: Columbia University Press, 1908.

Griswold, Rufus W. *Prose Writers in America.* Philadelphia: A. Hart, 1849.

Hall, David D. *The Faithful Shepherd: A History of the New England Ministry in the Seventeenth Century.* Chapel Hill: University of North Carolina Press, 1972.

Haller, William, Jr. *The Puritan Frontier: Town Planning in New England Colonial Development, 1630–1660.* New York: Columbia University Press, 1951.

————. *The Rise of Puritanism*. New York: Columbia University Press, 1938.

Haroutunian, Joseph. *Piety Versus Moralism: The Passing of the New England Theology*. New York: Holt, 1932.

Haven, Richard. *Patterns of Consciousness*. Amherst: University of Massachusetts Press, 1969.

Heimert, Alan. *Religion and the American Mind*. Cambridge: Harvard University Press, 1966.

Hofstadter, Richard. *Anti-Intellectualism in America*. New York: Knopf, 1963.

Howard, Claud. *Coleridge's Idealism*. Boston: Gorham Press, 1924.

Howard, Leon. "The Late Eighteenth Century." In *Transitions in American Literary History*, pp. 49–90. Ed. H. H. Clark. Durham, N.C.: Duke University Press, 1953.

Howe, Daniel. *The Unitarian Conscience*. Cambridge: Harvard University Press, 1970.

Hutchison, William R. *The Transcendental Ministers: Church Reform in the New England Renaissance*. New Haven: Yale University Press, 1959.

Jones, H. M. *Ideas in America*. Cambridge: Harvard University Press, 1944.

Kern, Alexander. "The Rise of Transcendentalism." in *Transitions in American Literary History*, pp. 245–314. Ed. H. H. Clark. Durham, N.C.: Duke University Press, 1953.

Levy, Babette. *Preaching in the First Half-Century of New England History*. New York: Russell Reprints, 1967.

Lewis, R. W. B. *The American Adam: Innocence, Tragedy and Tradition in the Nineteenth Century*. Chicago: University of Chicago Press, 1955.

Lindsay, Julian I. *Tradition Looks Forward: The University of Vermont: A History, 1791–1904*. Burlington: University of Vermont Press, 1954.

McFarland, Thomas. *Coleridge and the Pantheist Tradition*. Oxford: Oxford University Press, 1969.

McKenzie, Gordon. *Organic Unity in Coleridge*. Berkeley: University of California Press, 1939.

Martin, Terrence. *The Instructed Vision*. Bloomington: Indiana University Press, 1961.

May, Henry. *The End of American Innocence: A Study of the First Years of Our Time, 1912–1917*. New York: Knopf, 1959.

Miller, Perry. "New England Transcendentalism: Native or Imported?" in *Literary Views*, pp. 115–30. Ed. Camden Carrol. Chicago: University of Chicago Press, 1963.

————. *Errand Into the Wilderness*. New York: Harper and Row, 1956.

————. *The New England Mind: The Seventeenth Century*. New York: Macmillan, 1939; Cambridge: Harvard University Press, 1954.

————. *The New England Mind: From Colony to Province*. Cambridge: Harvard University Press, 1953.

————, ed. *The Transcendentalists: An Anthology*. Cambridge: Harvard University Press, 1950.

Morgan, Edmund. *Visible Saints: The History of a Puritan Idea*. Ithaca: Cornell University Press, 1963.

————. *The Puritan Family: Religion and Domestic Relations in Seventeenth-Century New England*. New York: Harper and Row, 1966.

Morison, Samuel Eliot. *Harvard College in the Seventeenth Century*. Cambridge: Harvard University Press, 1936.

Muirhead, John. *Coleridge as Philosopher*. New York: Macmillan, 1930.

Nicolson, Marjorie. "James Marsh and the Vermont Transcendentalists." *Philosophical Review* 34 (1925): 28–50.

Orians, H. "The Rise of Romanticism." In *Transitions in American Literary History*, pp. 161–244. Ed. H. H. Clark. Durham, N.C.: Duke University Press, 1953.

Patrides, C. A., ed. *The Cambridge Platonists*. Cambridge: Harvard University Press, 1970.

Paul, Sherman. *The Shores of America: Thoreau's Inward Exploration*. Urbana: University of Illinois Press, 1958.

Peabody, Elizabeth P. *Reminiscences of William E. Channing*. Boston: Crosby, Nicols, Lee, 1880.

Perry, Bliss, ed. *The Heart of Emerson's Journals*. Boston: Houghton Mifflin, 1939.

Persons, Stow. *Free Religion: An American Faith*. New Haven: Yale University Press, 1947.

Piercy, Josephine K. *Studies in Literary Types in Seventeenth-Century America*. New Haven: Yale University Press, 1939.

Pochmann, Henry. *German Culture in America: Philosophical and Literary Influences, 1600–1900*. Madison: University of Wisconsin Press, 1961.

Porter, H. C. *Reformation and Reaction in Tudor Cambridge*. Cambridge, England: Cambridge University Press, 1958.

Porter, Noah. "Coleridge and His American Disciples." *Bibliotecha Sacra* 4 (1847).

Prickett, Stephen. *Romanticism and Religion*. Cambridge, England: Cambridge University Press, 1976.

Riley, I. W. *American Thought from Puritanism to Pragmatism and Beyond*. New York: Holt, 1923.

Rusk, Ralph L. *The Life of Ralph Waldo Emerson*. New York: Scribners, 1949.

Sanders, Charles R. *Coleridge and the Broad Church Movement*. Durham, N.C.: Duke University Press, 1942.

Schmidt, George P. *The Liberal Arts College*. New Brunswick: Rutgers University Press, 1957.

Schneider, Herbert. *A History of American Philosophy*. New York: Columbia University Press, 1946.

Shepard, Odell. *Pedlar's Progress: The Life of Bronson Alcott*. Boston: Little, Brown, 1936.

Silver, Mildred. "Emerson and the Idea of Progress." *American Literature* 12 (1940): 1–19.

Spiller, R. E. "Critical Standards in the American Romantic Movement." In *The Third Dimension*. New York: Macmillan, 1965. pp. 89–102.

Thompson, Cameron. "John Locke and New England Transcendentalism." *New England Quarterly* 35 (1962): 435–57.

Thompson, Frank T. "Emerson's Indebtedness to Coleridge." *Studies in Philology* 23 (1926): 55–76.

Todd, E. W. "Philosophical Ideas in Harvard College, 1817–1837." *New England Quarterly* 16 (1943): 63–90.

Tuveson, Ernest C. *The Imagination as a Means of Grace*. Berkeley: University of California Press, 1960.

Vogel, Stanley M. *German Literary Influences on the American Transcendentalists*. New Haven: Yale University Press, 1955.

Walzel, Oskar. *German Romanticism*. New York: Putnam, 1932.

Wellek, Rene. *Confrontations*. Princeton: Princeton University Press, 1965.

———. *Kant in England*. Princeton: Princeton University Press, 1931.

Wells, Ronald V. *Three Christian Transcendentalists: James Marsh, Caleb Sprague Henry, Frederic Henry Hedge*. New York: Columbia University Press, 1943.

Whicher, Stephen. *Freedom and Fate*. Philadelphia: University of Pennsylvania Press, 1943.

Winters, Yvor. *In Defense of Reason*. Denver: Alan Swallow Press, 1947.

Ziff, Larzer. *Puritanism in America*. New York: Viking Press, 1973.

# INDEX